Domestic violence
Action for change

Gill Hague and Ellen Malos
with cartoons by Tamsin Wilton

New Clarion Press

First published 1993
Reprinted 1994

New Clarion Press
8 Evesham Road
Cheltenham
Glos GL52 2AB

New Clarion Press is a workers' co-operative.

A catalogue record for this book is available from the British Library.

ISBN   paperback   1 873797 06 0
        hardback   1 873797 07 9

New Clarion Press acknowledges the financial assistance of the Department of Social Policy and Social Planning, University of Bristol.

Typeset in 10/12 Times by Jean Wilson – Typesetting

Printed in Great Britain by T. J. Press (Padstow) Ltd

Contents

Is it too much to ask?

A man can come and go and walk out of the door
If a woman sleeps around she's classed as a whore
A man is known to be a stud
A woman is treated like mud
If a woman leaves her child, she's an unfit mother
If a man leaves his child, nobody bother

Society made it this way
We want to see a change today
Now we have equal rights
But men won't accept it out of spite
When a man beats his wife, he gets away
All the woman can do is run away
The law should lock these men away
Instead these women have to pay
If the law is to take the decision
Put the men and not the women in prison!

No responsibilities and no ties
These men get away with wicked lies
The law is hard on police violence
When it comes to women they turn off their sirens
A woman has to be in her grave before action is taken
If they think they know their law, they're very well mistaken!

by two women living in a refuge

Acknowledgements

This book was made possible through the contributions of many women over many years. We would first of all like to thank all the women who have suffered domestic violence and their children who have freely given us their time and help throughout our work with Women's Aid and the movement against domestic violence in general, and our writing of this book in particular.

We are particularly indebted to Nicola Harwin of the Women's Aid Federation (England) for her dedicated assistance with this project which went beyond the bounds of duty, and for the many hours which she spent working with us on the manuscript.

Jacky Barron of the WAFE Legal and Research Group and the Hammersmith Domestic Violence Intervention Project has also helped us extensively with the writing of this book and made detailed comments on the various drafts. We are very grateful to her.

The book was only made possible by the assistance of our colleague, Wendy Dear, who prepared and edited the manuscript, and assisted with the research for it.

Thanks are also due to many organizations and individuals for commenting on drafts of sections of the book and/or for helpful input and assistance about both specific points and general issues. These include: Andrea Tara-Chand, Olwen Edwards, Robyn Holder, Alison Assiter, Lorraine Radford, Maria Smith, Rachel Bentham, Bernadette Frayne, Mary Ann Hushlak, Margaret Boushell, Elaine Farmer, and workers from Northern Ireland Women's Aid, the Women's Aid Federation (England) including, most especially, Thangam Singh and Caroline McKinlay to whom particular thanks are due, Scottish Women's Aid, Welsh Women's Aid, Southall Black Sisters, the CHANGE project, and various local refuge groups, including past and present members of Bristol Women's

Aid. We would also like to thank Evanna Romain and her co-author for their poem.

On a personal level, we would sincerely like to thank the following:

For Ellen: John Malos, for all his support especially over the last few months, my son and daughter, Robert and Anna Malos, whose childhoods were so closely intertwined with the birth of Bristol Women's Aid, twenty years ago this year, and all the women whose courage has been the reason for it existing and from whom I have learned so much.

For Gill: the women from many women's groups, and from Women's Aid, who have nurtured me over the years, and Dorothy Williamson, Dave Merrick, Maureen Wright and my children, Cassie and Keiran Hague, for help with the writing of this book and for their enduring love, patience and co-operation.

Ellen Malos and Gill Hague

This book is dedicated to the memory of Pam Cooke (Khalil), whom we knew and who recovered from domestic violence to build a strong, new life. Pam was an inspiration to other women attempting to escape violence in the home.

On 22 August 1986, Pam was killed by her former husband.

1
Domestic violence: what is it?

Domestic violence is one of the commonest crimes. It is present throughout society, usually hidden, but there nonetheless. In any house, on any average street, avenue or road, women regularly experience abuse and violence. Most frequently, it happens behind firmly closed doors. It is worth standing on such an average street – your street perhaps – and trying to imagine the reality of it behind those closed doors. You may not be aware that it is happening, but it is.

Many of us know someone in our close family or among our friends whom it has happened to, or we have experienced it ourselves, but we tend to think that we are different or alone, not realizing perhaps just how widespread and enduring domestic abuse is. It seems that it occurs in almost all cultures and countries, across all known divisions of wealth, race, caste and social class. There may never have been a time when it did not exist, and it certainly stretches back deep into history. Centuries, indeed millenniums, are filled with millions of assaults, attacks, rapes, violations, psychological abuses, maimings, killings – of women in their own homes by men.

It is a profoundly disturbing and distressing picture, if we care to be aware of it. Some people choose to turn away. Some say it is inevitable, that it is just human nature and you will never change it. This book is written from an opposite conviction, a conviction that nothing is inevitable, that it is we, both men and women, who shape and build human societies and are also shaped by them. The devastating legacy of violence and abuse against women need not stay with us for ever. We can try to imagine a world in which masculinity is free of violence, a world in which women's lives can be free of fear, and women and children can be safe in their own homes. The task, of course, is the making of such a world.

It seems that, throughout history, women have attempted to resist domestic violence by all sorts of means, wherever they have been able to. In Britain, there has been a social movement of women against domestic violence for many years. It was particularly evident in the nineteenth and early twentieth centuries, and became active again in the early 1970s. In the last twenty years, this movement has campaigned vigorously, its activists sustained by the vision of an end to male violence and of women growing more powerful together. Mainly as a result of its activities, we now hear about domestic violence frequently. It is talked about on radio and television, there is meant to be legal protection against it, and there are services available. This is in marked contrast to the situation before the 1970s, when there was silence about the issue, and women experiencing violence in the home had virtually no one to turn to for help.

The main co-ordinating organizations which deal with domestic violence in Britain and which represent the interests of abused women and children are the Women's Aid federations. They have established a network of refuges and other related services and provide information, advice and support. While this is good news, the reality is that there are not nearly enough of these services to meet the need. Domestic violence is still condoned by much of society and many of the improvements are small and rather piecemeal. None of them, however, would have been achieved without the determined and persistent efforts of organizations like Women's Aid and other committed activists. It has been a hard struggle and it continues to be so.

Even so, in the last five or six years, domestic violence has been in the public eye as it has never been before. Various governments now tell us that violence in the home is a crime and that it is not to be tolerated. Statutory and voluntary agencies say that it is unacceptable. International proclamations are made. Some of the women who have been active in the struggle against domestic violence for many years might be forgiven for asking what has really changed, but at least the beginnings are there. We have yet to see whether the public attention will last, and whether the political will is there to implement the changes needed in comprehensive ways.

At the international level, the United Nations Decade for Women led to publicity and research in many countries of the world on the issue of violence against women. The 1985 Nairobi World Conference on Women highlighted domestic violence in the forward-looking strategies adopted, to which member countries have since contributed.

In consequence, the United Nations established an Expert Group on Violence in the Family, and has recently prepared a *Manual for Practitioners on Domestic Violence*. The UN is currently drafting a declaration on violence against women which states that it is a violation of human rights and results from the historically unequal power relationships between men and women. Domestic violence will undoubtedly be a topic at the 1995 World Conference of Women.

In Britain, the Home Office issued a circular in 1990 about how the police respond to violent incidents in the home. The point of the circular was to get the police to take domestic violence more seriously, to instigate more pro-arrest policies and to establish supportive domestic violence units for abused women. Police forces up and down the country are now trying, with varying degrees of commitment and success, to act on the circular. In 1992 the Law Commission made various proposals for changing the civil law on legal remedies to make them more comprehensive, to give them more teeth. Also in 1992, amid a wealth of publicity, Princess Anne launched a major report, *Domestic Violence*. This report, published by Victim Support, was produced by a National Inter-Agency Working Party of which the Women's Aid Federation (England), the leading agency in England dealing with domestic violence, was an active and influential member. The House of Commons All Party Home Affairs Committee conducted an inquiry into domestic violence in 1992/3, and in March 1993 made wide-ranging recommendations for improving both the legislation and the provision of refuges. After years of campaigning, domestic violence is firmly on the public agenda. Finally we can talk about it. It is no longer a secret.

In this book, domestic violence is mainly discussed in the British context with some illustrations from Australia, Canada and the United States. However, positive developments are taking place in many countries throughout the world, and the struggle to put a stop to the abuse of women in the home is an international one.

Definitions: what do we mean by domestic violence?

In the British context, domestic violence is usually regarded as violence between adults who are in an intimate or family relationship with each other, most often a sexual relationship between a woman and a man. The evidence and the lived experience of most of us point to the fact that, overwhelmingly, the recipients of the violence are women and the perpetrators are men. Various research studies have estimated that between 90 and 97 per cent of domestic violence is perpetrated against women by men. Over the years, there has been some publicity about the plight of battered husbands, and it is clear that women do sometimes abuse men and that violence can also occur in lesbian and gay relationships. But the overriding majority of domestic violence incidents consist of men abusing, intimidating and violating women whom they know intimately and often profess to love.

The depth of the imbalance in power between men and women is revealed in a stark way by the reality of domestic violence. However, the term itself – and the use of the word 'domestic' in particular – can hide who is actually the abuser and who is being abused. It sounds general, as though it means any violence which happens in the domestic environment. In consequence, many women have questioned its usefulness. The terms 'wife abuse' or 'wife-beating' are sometimes used instead, especially in North America, even for women who are not married. This is because they go some way towards indicating the power dynamic involved, since wives are still widely regarded as having an inferior status to husbands. In Britain, however, these terms are heard less often, partly because so many women who are abused are not married. Some activists prefer terms like 'male violence against women in the home' or 'criminal assault and abuse' either 'of women in the home by men' or 'of women in their intimate relations with men'. Such phrases locate the violence much more precisely. However, they hardly slip easily from the tongue or pen. And of course domestic violence does not only occur in the home or between current sexual partners. Women can be abused by ex-partners or ex-husbands, by men with whom they have sexual relationships but no joint living arrangements, by men whom they are dating more casually, by male acquaintances and friends, by close male family members or by relatives.

The term 'battered women' is widely used in the United States, where the movement against domestic violence tends to be referred to as the 'battered women's movement'. In Britain, however, women who have experienced domestic violence have felt unhappy with the term. They have pointed out that it can make women feel that they are being judged and labelled as though they have done something wrong. The use of the adjective 'battered' can give the impression that women are somehow diminished or made inferior or pathetic by becoming 'battered', which of course is not the case. As a result, the term is no longer in general usage in Britain. It does seem that some groups of people still refer in conversation to refuges as 'battered wives' homes', but the feminist movement and all the agencies providing services to women use more dignified terms such as 'women experiencing domestic violence', 'abused women' or 'women survivors of domestic violence'.

In Britain, terms like this are used to differentiate domestic violence from other sorts of violence in the family, such as violence against elders and child abuse. The children of women experiencing domestic violence are very often negatively affected by witnessing such violence and may be abused themselves. It is important to distinguish the various forms of abuse which can occur, in order to think about them clearly.

They are often lumped together, however, under the general term 'family violence'. There have been objections to the use of this term. Usually in violent incidents, the abuser is more powerful in various ways than the abused – which is why the violence and abuse goes in one direction and not the other. An expression like 'family violence' clouds this issue. It makes it sound as though everyone in the family is equally violent. Nevertheless, there is a large school of thought which uses the term 'family violence', especially in the United States. Teachers, researchers, psychologists and social workers who are part of it tend to distance themselves from the social movement against domestic violence, and from feminist attempts to explain male abuse of women in the home.

Neither the term 'family violence' nor the term 'domestic violence' makes it clear that violence in the home is directed primarily against women and children. Feminists in some countries have objected to 'domestic violence' just as they have objected to 'family violence'. However, in Britain, 'domestic violence' is generally understood as shorthand for male violence against women in the home. The term is probably worth preserving, even though it is ambiguous about gender. In any case, there are no particular moves to change it at the moment. Rather it is used in conjunction with terms like 'woman abuse' and 'women survivors' which help to explain its meaning.

Domestic violence is now understood to extend beyond physical violence and beyond the home. The Women's Aid federations define domestic violence as comprising a range of types of abuse. These include physical, sexual, mental, and emotional or psychological violence. Threats of violence are also included. The perpetrator may be a woman's husband, boyfriend, partner, lover, cohabitee, ex-partner or ex-husband, friend, son, father, brother, uncle or other close family member.

The violence may be life-threatening, systematic and long-term. It can, and does, occur anywhere – although the home is still the main place where it happens. The home is after all behind closed doors, away from the public eye, protected by spoken and unspoken rules about privacy, about not interfering in other people's business and about 'an Englishman's home is his castle'. And it is also the place where feelings between intimates run highest. For women and children, the home – that safe haven, that place of comfort and security cushioned from the difficulties of the outside world – is not, and never has been, a safe place. For many women, it is a place of danger, terror and injury, and for some, a place of death.

On 14 April 1990, *The Times* reported that a half of all women murdered in Britain were killed by their husbands or lovers, by far the largest single category of women victims. Homicide statistics consistently reveal that between 40 and 45 per cent of women victims and only about 7 per cent of male victims are murdered by their partners. If all killings are included, figures over several years have indicated that about 18 per cent or more have been committed by men killing their female partners, whereas women have killed their male partners in only about 2 per cent of cases. Contrary to sentiments often expressed in the popular media and to much recent publicity about women who kill their husbands, the vast majority of domestic murders are by men – killing women. Between one and two women are murdered by their male partners every week.

If women are not safe in their own homes, then where are they safe? It is a disturbing question. The range of physical injuries which women suffer, or are threatened with, is enormous. These injuries are often accompanied by emotional, psychological and sexual abuse. Physical violence is just one part of domestic abuse, not necessarily even the main part. In fact some women say that other types of violence which they have experienced have been worse than the physical assaults. Women often experience several different kinds of violence in combination. All the evidence is that there is often a pattern to abusive behaviour by men and that the pattern may be complex.

Physical abuse

The physical violence which women experience comprises many types of physical attack and injury. Commonly, it starts with a single slap or blow, followed by disbelief and shock on both sides and by commitments from the man that it will never be repeated. But sadly, once it has happened a single time, it is rare for it not to happen again. There may be long gaps with no violence but, eventually, men who have acted violently once tend to do so again, and then again. Researchers from all schools of thought about domestic violence agree that it is rarely a one-off event. Incidents often start occurring more frequently as time goes on, and becoming gradually more severe. It is not unusual for women to endure many years of attacks without requesting or receiving any help whatsoever from anybody.

Physical violence by men against women may involve anything from threatening behaviour, slaps and being pushed about, to black eyes, bruises and broken bones, to extremely serious incidents of multiple assault. It can be life-threatening, resulting in internal injuries, permanent handicaps, and disabilities or death. Attempted stranglings seem to be particularly common. Women in refuges have described being burned or being set fire to, being hit against walls or with pieces of furniture, being repeatedly kicked and punched, and being stabbed or systematically cut with knives. Some women bear the marks and scars of attack after attack. In many cases, the violence is less severe than this, but it is almost always terrifying and deeply distressing. Women often feel violated to the core. They describe, for example, the humiliation and degradation of being slapped and kicked, or being grabbed hold of and pushed around, by someone who claims to love them. Quite small acts of violence might be repeated again and again and again, sometimes in an almost arbitrary way, until women begin to feel they are going mad. Such acts might be accompanied by frightening threats of further violence so that women live in distress and fear, often alone except for their partners, or with children, isolated in the home.

Some women who come to refuges manage to escape as soon as the violence begins, realizing that it may be the start of a repetitive pattern. Others may have been in relationships for years and may return to their violent partners several times to give it another try, always hoping it will be better in the future, or believing their partner's protestations of remorse and that it will not happen again. Some women experience violence which results in hospitalization and the need for medical care. For others, the injuries may not show. Certain men, in fact, are particularly skilled at inflicting violence on their partners so that it is not visible to the outside world. Violence may happen particularly frequently during pregnancy.

Sexual abuse

Women who are physically abused are very often also subjected to a range of sexual humiliations and assaults, or men may use threats of violence in order to make women submit to coercive sex. An American research study found that a third of the women in the study who had been attacked physically had also been raped by their partners. Many women in Women's Aid have used the idea of a continuum of male violence against women which includes sexual violence and which links day-to-day harassment to severe assault as part and parcel of the same phenomenon.

Liz Kelly, a British researcher and feminist activist, has developed this idea further in terms of sexual abuse. In her book *Surviving Sexual Violence*, published in 1988, she discusses the idea of a continuum of sexual violence, as a result of research in which she talked at length with women about their sexual experiences. The continuum includes the whole distressing sweep of women's experiences of sexual violence, from everyday examples of dominating sexual behaviour by men towards women, to sexual assault and rape. The ultimate form of sexual violence is the murder and sexual mutilation of girls and women by men. Short of this horrific extreme, however, Kelly suggests that, in general, it is not useful to think of the continuum as being graded in severity. Only women themselves can define the seriousness of a particular action as it affects them personally. Feminist ideas of a continuum are more about the links which connect forms of sexual violence which many women experience in their lives, and which men may see as acceptable behaviour, with forms of sexual violence which are classified by society as crimes. It encompasses a whole spectrum of types of harassment, degradation and coerced sexual activity including the use of pornography – for example, in the acting out of pornographic and violent male sexual fantasies.

The idea of the sexual continuum – that it is focused on women's own experience of sexual violence and on their feelings about what has happened to them – is almost a revolutionary one. Many feminists have pointed out that society does not always want to hear what women have to say about this subject, and men have a vested interest in keeping definitions of sexual violence as narrow as possible. It is vital that women continue to speak out, to tell their stories. Naming and renaming experience of sexual violence is not a simple or easy process, however. There may be no words for the pain and the shame. Some women may block such traumatic events out of their conscious memories for many years, especially if the experiences were in childhood. We all know also that women and girls are frequently not believed when they speak. All too often they are blamed in some way for the sexual violence which they have experienced. Once men get to hear that a girl or a woman has been sexually assaulted, she is often viewed immediately as 'easy', as a slut, or as the justifiable butt of sexually titillating or voyeuristic joking. There is a distressing pornographic trade in prisons involving the circulation of details of sexual assaults on girls and women for which men have been convicted.

There is no simple division between physical violence and sexual violence for women being abused by their male intimates. The two are entwined. Women in refuges fleeing domestic violence describe a multitude of experiences in which they are combined inseparably. For example, men often force women to have sex with them after violent episodes. Rape may be an integral part of a physical attack. Pornography may be acted out in sadistic, violent ways. Domestic violence activists and refuge workers sometimes feel that there is no end to the inventiveness of men when it comes to physical abuse and sexual degradation. Almost every day, they hear the unhearable, think about the unthinkable, as they attempt to comfort distraught women trying to escape from such experiences.

Psychological and emotional abuse

In all abuse, emotional and psychological issues are involved. It is very rare for women to experience physical violence which is not accompanied by emotional abuse and threats. In fact, the use of intimidating threats is one of the commonest forms of violence, often used by men to exert control and dominance over their wives or lovers. What is threatened can vary. It can be injury, like a beating-up or a broken arm. Very often it is murder. While both men and women have a tendency to shout, when angered, that they will kill the other, such threats are usually in no way serious. Women with a history of suffering domestic violence know, however, with fearful clarity when threats of murder are being made seriously and are real in intent. They must be listened to and their words acted on when they make such claims. Men may also make threats of harm to children, sexual violence (most commonly rape), financial deprivation and all manner of other degrading possibilities.

Emotional abuse takes other forms apart from verbal threats, and very often involves degradation and humiliation. Examples include being persistently belittled, criticized and insulted, or being subjected continually to intimidation or aggressive verbal abuse. All of these contribute to the rather old-fashioned but useful term 'mental cruelty'. Women can suffer mental and psychological abuse in many different ways. Often it can be financial – being denied money for children's food, for example. It can also be related to extreme possessiveness by the male partner and his fears of allowing his wife or lover to associate with other adults, most particularly other men. Many women describe repeated interrogations about imagined infidelities, frequently concerning routine male visitors to the home, such as the milkman. Women tell of being shut in the house all day, not being allowed to go out, having every action monitored, being stopped from having any friends.

In our time working in refuges, women have described being kept actually locked in cupboards, rooms and garden sheds. While the last examples are extreme, analyses by refuge groups and by researchers of types of violence which women experience have confirmed that all of these forms of psychological abuse are common. For example, women interviewed during a piece of research for the London Borough of Hammersmith and Fulham conducted by the Polytechnic of North London (now the University of North London) in 1989 described emotional abuse which included specific examples of being made to act in degrading ways; being repeatedly criticized; being stopped from working, studying or seeing friends and families; being denied money; being threatened with sexual and physical violence; and being repeatedly and aggressively questioned about other men.

The extent of the violence and how to measure it

It is notoriously difficult to estimate the full extent of domestic violence. In a useful 1989 Home Office Research Study (No. 107), Lorna Smith, a senior Home Office researcher, conducted a thorough overview of the literature on domestic violence and reviewed the problems involved in attempting to estimate its incidence. She points out that:

> the extent of domestic violence is unknown and that whatever conclusions are reached from the studies which have been undertaken must remain tentative and must be treated with caution. Edwards (1986) has described domestic violence as the biggest blind spot in official statistics. By its intrinsic nature, domestic violence is an elusive research topic: it takes place behind closed doors; is concealed from the public eye; and is often unknown to anyone outside the immediate family.

The problem of underreporting is compounded by women's fears and shame about having experienced domestic violence, and by widely held beliefs about privacy and the myth of the happy nuclear family. Betsy Stanko is a feminist academic who has written widely about violence in women's lives. In her 1985 book *Intimate Intrusions: Women's Experience of Male Violence*, she explains how, in a world in which sexism and discrimination against women are endemic, women themselves come to understand that their own views and experiences are regarded as having less import, being of less value than men's. This can be particularly true of domestic violence which happens in the family, in the home, traditionally regarded as spheres of female influence and responsibility. It can be very shaming to admit to violence within them. Women often try hard to hide, to minimize, or even to belittle the violence they have suffered. In the United States the FBI believes that domestic violence is the most underreported crime and estimates that it is probably ten times more underreported than rape.

In addition, statistics on domestic violence, where they exist at all, tend not to distinguish types of abuse and to give no definition whatsoever about how severe the violence is, how often it happens or for how long it has been going on. As a result, the usefulness of such statistics is severely limited. To complicate the matter still further, it is very difficult, in fact almost impossible, to extrapolate from small-scale research studies to the general population. Nevertheless many attempts to estimate the extent of domestic violence have been made.

In a ground-breaking book, *Violence Against Wives*, published in 1980, the domestic violence researchers Rebecca and Russell Dobash found that more than 25 per cent of all violent crime reported to the police was domestic violence by men against women, making it the second most common violent crime. But in the same study, the Dobashes found that only about 2 per cent of domestic violence incidents were reported to the police in the first place. Some other studies have found a higher reporting rate, although they all agree that underreporting to the police is significant. A 1989 BBC1 programme, *Punching Judy*, found that 100,000 women per year seek treatment in London for violent injuries received in the home. In 1983 Margaret Borkowski and her colleagues at the University of Bristol suggested that incidents of physical violence are experienced in at least one in five marriages. A study published in 1993 by Middlesex University found that one in ten of the women they interviewed had experienced violence from their partners in the previous twelve months; and in a 1992 report, the Women's Aid Federation (England), frequently known as WAFE, estimated in support of other studies that up to one in four women may on occasion experience violence in their sexual relationships with men. Severe, repeated and systematic violence is clearly less common, but it has been estimated to occur in at least five in a hundred marriages in Britain. In a 1985 survey by *Woman* magazine, one in four women who anonymously reported such violence had told no one else about it.

Very large-scale random studies of domestic violence are few and far between. The two principal surveys, ten years apart, have been conducted by the well-known family violence researcher Murray Straus and his colleagues in the United States. Their work has dealt a comprehensive blow to any lingering idea that domestic violence is an unusual occurrence which happens only in disturbed or 'pathological' families. One in every six couples in the initial 1975 study had 'engaged in violence' in the previous year, and one in four had done so at some time in the past. Straus' findings are contentious, however, due to his use of the Conflict Tactics Scale or CTS, which his team developed as a way of measuring incidents of violence. The scale has come in for extreme criticism from other researchers and has been the subject of heated controversy for many years. It is described in some detail here because of its importance in domestic violence work and the large influence which it continues to have.

What the CTS does is to make it easy for research respondents to categorize the violence they have experienced or perpetrated. It lists different categories of violent acts which can be ticked off, much as in a standard American multiple-choice questionnaire. Unfortunately, however, the scale failed in its original form, and indeed in most of its revised forms, to recognize differences in power between men and women or in degrees of male and female physical strength. Importantly, it did not differentiate between aggressive violence and violence used in self-defence. Nor did it distinguish between degrees of violence which could be classified similarly – say, as a 'kick'. Clearly the amount of force behind the kick and the part of the body kicked would dictate the damage and injury caused, but such factors were overlooked. Many types of violence and abuse which women experience – for example, sexual violence – were left out. A further problem with the scale is the difficulty of obtaining truthful self-reporting. Many researchers and workers in the domestic violence field have demonstrated that, in general, men very often minimize and underreport the violence they have perpetrated, whereas women, who often feel guilty and apologetic if they have engaged in violent acts, may exaggerate or overreport their actions.

Most significantly perhaps, the original CTS did not place the violence within the social situation in which it occurred. In other words, it took it out of context. The sequence of events, the process of what happened and in what order, was ignored. For example, if each partner reported a slap – which would come out equally on the scale – who was the aggressor? Was one partner defending themselves? The CTS did not give any weight to the social consequences or the effects of the violence, to how the recipient felt afterwards and what then happened. It ignored the traumatic life events which could follow and the way in which these differentially affect women and men. It is women not men, for example, who are forced to abandon their homes and belongings, and become homeless, as a result of domestic violence.

Using the scale, Straus and his colleagues, most notably Richard Gelles and Suzanne Steinmetz, found that husbands were only slightly more likely to use violence against their wives than vice versa. This finding has been widely disputed by women's advocates and by researchers throughout the field, including some who used the CTS and followed it up with in-depth interviews with the same people. But it was more or less replicated in a follow-up study by Straus' team, still using the CTS, ten years later in 1985, and by some other researchers in the family violence school of thought making use of the scale. An American feminist, Kersti Yllo, who in 1988 co-edited a useful book, *Feminist Perspectives on Wife Abuse*, and who has worked extensively with Straus, explains that Straus and his team were surprised by their results and have stated many times that they did not consider the violence in context, or the implications of the use of violence by women in self-defence. However, wide-ranging claims about domestic violence are still made on the strength of the results that the scale gives. A recent study at the University of Leicester, for example, used a version of the CTS and found that male and female students used approximately equal amounts of violence in their relationships with each other. The study ignored the controversy about the use of the scale.

In a book published in 1990, *Physical Violence in American Families*, edited by Richard Gelles and Murray Straus himself, the drawbacks and limitations of the scale are discussed and acknowledged by Straus and his colleagues in detail. However, as the Dobashes and many other researchers have firmly pointed out, the damage has been done and cannot be undone. The arguments over the CTS continue to reverberate almost twenty years after the original research. Mainly they are between social scientists, with the family violence researchers on one side and researchers who could broadly be described as feminist on the other. The arguments are not just about the CTS but tend to expand to cover how research into social issues should be done in general, and they can be fierce. The divisions are not always quite that clear-cut though, and some feminist sociologists work hard to bridge the gap, to say there is value on both sides.

It is beyond the scope of this book to analyse these academic arguments in detail. Nonetheless it is important to understand how such academic research methods can have a far-reaching effect. The influence of the CTS remains with us, not only within research circles but among social workers and service providers, and in the popular sphere as well. The world of social science, and of American social science in particular, tends to be keen on surveys and on trying to make scientific-style measurements. And the surveys done by Straus and his team using the CTS were uniquely large, and were designed to be extrapolated to cover the whole of the United States. Their work is extensively used as a major and supposedly accurate source of data on family violence, despite all the problems inherent in trying to impose a survey-style method of research on something like domestic violence. Although they have a role, abstract scales and surveys are not very useful when it comes to explaining complex social problems, especially if they are faultily constructed anyway.

The 'battered husband syndrome'

In 1978 Suzanne Steinmetz published an article in the academic law journal *Victimology*, claiming the existence of a 'battered husband syndrome' on the strength of results gained using the CTS. The media throughout North America were quick to pick up this idea and to broadcast it widely. In February 1978, it was claimed on the well-known and popular American TV programme previously hosted by Johnny Carson, the *Today Show*, that 12 million American husbands were beaten by their wives. While this claim was retracted two weeks later as a faulty extrapolation of Steinmetz's figures, the idea of a battered husband syndrome still gets quoted today. The subject refuses to go away. The scholarly and academic book *Women, Violence and Social Change*, written by the Dobashes in 1992, uses a broad brush stroke approach to chart the social movement of women against domestic violence both in Britain and the USA. They analyse the dynamic relationship between this movement and the law, the criminal justice system and the state itself. They look at ideas about domestic violence used in therapy, and they place everything they have talked about in a theoretical context of knowledge, research and social change. All of this – and yet, on the back cover, two major questions are headlined to catch attention and sell the book. One of them is: 'Are there really as many abused husbands as abused wives?'

In Britain, the subject of battered husbands seems to get raised at almost all public meetings on domestic violence. Domestic violence activists and refuge staff are used to it. In 1992 a television documentary looked at the plight of three husbands who had been abused by their wives. The programme appeared to be claiming, as Steinmetz did in the 1970s, that the problem is as common as domestic violence against women. While no one would want to minimize the plight of men in this situation or deny them assistance and support, workers and activists throughout the domestic violence field know from everyday experience that it is simply not true that as many men are abused by women as vice versa. There are no refuges for abused men, and no widespread demand from anyone to establish one. One phone line exists in the country which men who have suffered violence can use as well as women, and one small house for such men existed for a matter of weeks at the end of 1992.

In their original study done in Scotland, the Dobashes found that three-quarters of violent crime involving family members, which was reported to the police, was the assault of wives by husbands. In over 3,000 cases of violence of all types, including 1,044 cases of violence between family members, women assaulted their husbands in only twelve cases. In the same sample, 791 men assaulted their wives. There is a lot of documentation around about domestic violence against women, although almost all of it is about physical abuse only. From national crime surveys, from police records, from refuges, from social services departments, from hospitals, from historical studies, from the world of literature – all the evidence points to the widespread abuse of women by men. Every refuge for women fleeing domestic violence in the country is full almost as soon as it opens.

It is worth dwelling on this fact for a minute. Where do the women come from? Where were they before? How many more women are there waiting to come? There are now hundreds of refuges in Britain. Those run by Women's Aid temporarily house over 30,000 women and children every year in England alone. Even so, many refuges are unable to accommodate up to a half or more of the women and children contacting them, desperate for emergency accommodation due to domestic violence.

Research suggests and the testimonies of women in refuges confirm that, although there are a few cases where men are systematically abused by women, most violence by women is conducted in self-defence and is limited in its nature. Such retaliation may come only after years and years of intimidation and abuse. Domestic violence research in both Britain and elsewhere has found that women only rarely respond to men's attacks on them by counter-violence. In the Dobashes' original study, fewer than 4 per cent of the women interviewed responded to violence by using any significant degree of physical force themselves. Staff working in many refuges, listening to story after story from women homeless due to violence by their male partners, only occasionally meet women who have engaged in counter-violence themselves.

Some studies in the United States have shown, on the other hand, that between 23 and 71 per cent of women enduring domestic violence have used violence in retaliation at least once. For example, studies by Daniel Saunders, an American researcher and male activist against woman abuse, found that a high proportion of women experiencing violence used some types of non-severe violent response such as throwing something or 'pushing, shoving and grabbing'. The most frequent motive for this behaviour, however, was self-defence. It was usually intended not so much to cause injury as to stop the violence. Saunders suggests that to claim any sort of equality in rates of domestic violence between men and women is literally to add insult to injury for women who are often in fear of their lives, who would never initiate an attack, but who may strike back in self-defence. One has to ask what this fuss about women's supposed violence towards men is all about. Is it because in a society still controlled by men there is an almost automatic collusion to minimize the violence and damage and injury that men do to women? Is it about blaming and victimizing still further women who are already on the receiving end of violent abuse and degradation?

The effects on women and children

While there is no evidence of systematic patterns of violence against men by women, there is a large body of human knowledge and experience which testifies to the systematic and persistent use of force by men against women. Many, possibly most, women are afraid of men on one level or another. On the street, women are very often afraid of violence from men they do not know, especially at night. And it is indeed true that men 'control' the streets. Walk around any city centre late in the evening to find out. In some places and at some times, the streets are literally not safe for women. Researchers have shown, however, that by far the most likely place for violence against women to occur is in their intimate relationships. In the Dobashes' Scottish study, for example, only 13 per cent of violence which did not involve family members was committed by men against women. The same is true for rape and sexual assault. For all types of violence, women are far more at risk from men in their family or with whom they have a close relationship than from male strangers. They are scarcely at risk at all from other women. In *Women, Violence and Social Change*, the Dobashes point out graphically that

> The onset of systematic and severe violence against women is almost exclusively associated with entering a permanent relationship with a man.

Violence against women in the home is a unique phenomenon in the world of violence. Only in a prison or similar total institution would an individual be likely to encounter such persistent abuse, violence and terror.

This sort of treatment can of course have devastating effects on women. Most commonly, women describe how being exposed to violence in all its various forms can result in a loss of self-confidence and self-esteem. In this culture, women still tend to be regarded as being responsible for family life, for doing the emotional 'housework' within the family. So if things go wrong, it is often assumed that it is their fault. As a result, women very often blame themselves or feel guilty if they experience violence from their partners. They might feel the classic 'if only'. If only I had been a better wife to him; if only I had been more sexually receptive; if only I had done more of what he wanted. Women often experience a painful mixture of guilt, blame and shame.

For women, domestic violence may result in physical injury and permanent physical damage, in homelessness, in loss of employment, in loss of family, friends and even children, and importantly, in depression, attempted suicide and mental illness. Women may experience high levels of anxiety and panic attacks, or may develop disturbed patterns of eating and sleeping, problems in concentrating and a feeling of hopelessness. Refuge workers testify, however, to the amazing resilience and spirit of women in this situation. After only a short stay in a refuge, many women are able to start all over again – often literally. Women in refuges often have no home, no money, no family or friends close by, and no possessions or belongings whatsoever.

For other women, the process is longer and harder. Some women end up seeking long-term help from the caring and mental health professions. There have been many books and articles written by psychiatric and social work professionals and academics, particularly in North America, about the psychological and behavioural problems of women who have suffered violence. Many feminists, however, tend to feel that, while some women do develop such problems as a result of violence, psychological studies which come up with general conclusions about how women in this situation are and what they feel can result in 'labelling' and stereotyping. No woman who has suffered domestic violence responds the same as another woman. This means that, although services are needed to meet many different needs, there is no one set of psychological characteristics which women who have suffered violence share. To suggest that there is can seem like making out that a woman who has suffered violence is sick or ill, and can result in 'pathologizing' the victim.

While many feminists have resisted attempts by psychologists and psychiatrists to ascribe particular behavioural and emotional symptoms to abused women, they do not pretend that no damage has been done. Increasingly, refuges in Britain offer or try to offer formal and informal counselling services to women coming to them. Refuges are called shelters or transition houses in North America, where the whole culture is more geared towards therapy, counselling and individual psychological explanations of people's problems. And this has always been reflected in the way shelters work. Some shelters run quite complicated psychiatric intervention programmes for women.

An American feminist, Lenore Walker, has developed what she calls the 'battered woman syndrome' to explain what happens when women consistently suffer violence. Her ideas have some usefulness, although they have been disputed by other feminists. She suggests that women often learn over time that they can do nothing to prevent the violence, and therefore adopt a coping strategy of 'learned helplessness'. This can lead to a response of passivity and powerlessness – an extreme example of the way most women are conditioned to behave anyway. Women are beaten down emotionally and physically, the theory goes, although they may eventually snap. Using the 'straw that breaks the camel's back' idea, feminist lawyers in the States now widely use the battered woman syndrome as a defence for women who have murdered their husbands after enduring years of degradation and abuse. 'Expert witnesses' are then called in to testify that the woman has been suffering from the syndrome. Serving as an expert witness is a highly lucrative business in the States. So far it has happened rarely in Britain in relation to domestic violence, although there have been a few cases where such expert witnesses have been called.

Some feminists, however, feel that the use of the battered woman syndrome analysis can buy into non-feminist and judgemental ways of thinking which blame the victim by suggesting that women themselves contribute by their behaviour to the violence they experience. While Walker places her own work in a broader feminist understanding of women's position in society, it has unfortunately been picked up by some social workers and caring professionals who tend to explain their clients' behaviour in terms of individual failure or inadequacy – but add a supposedly feminist gloss. A few women we know who have escaped from violent relationships confirm that they did indeed learn to be passive, although not necessarily helpless, to deal with the violence. But they suggest that it was only when they felt strong enough to leave the helplessness behind and to take action that they were able to get away and build new lives. Most importantly, what they needed to know was that there was somewhere to escape to and some way of financially supporting themselves and their children.

Many Women's Aid refuges say that they have found little evidence of learned helplessness in all their years of operation. In 1991 an American psychological study at the University of Cincinatti confirmed, as previously suggested by various feminists in the USA, that the battered woman syndrome may be a sign, not of helplessness, but of a struggle for survival very similar to that of international hostages imprisoned by political organizations. Hostages often develop what is called the 'Stockholm syndrome' in which they may be friendly and intimate with their captors, and the suggestion is that abused women do too. When hostages do it, however, it is widely viewed as an understandable strategy for self-preservation, not as a sign of weakness.

Starting to recognize domestic violence as a crime, and to do something about it in terms of providing assistance and services, has taken long enough. Recognizing the damage done to child witnesses of domestic violence and their need for assistance and services has only just begun. Children have few rights; they have very little power over what happens to them. Not many people listen to what they say and feel, or grant them any semblance of equality and respect. Women's Aid tries hard to do just that, by recognizing that children are often treated unfairly by adults and are powerless in traumatic situations. It attempts to provide specialist children's workers in all refuges in order to start to meet the needs of the children living there, and to provide support and services especially for them.

The Women's Aid Federation (England) has produced general information on the effects of domestic violence on children, some of which we include in some detail here.

> Approximately two in every three women who come into Women's Aid refuges, or who contact us for advice and support, have young children who will almost certainly have been affected by the abuse their mother has suffered. Some of them will have witnessed the abuse. All of them will sense that their mother is unhappy and will feel insecure and fearful without necessarily knowing why this is. A proportion of these children

will themselves have been abused, physically or sexually, by their fathers, stepfathers or other adults ...

From our work in refuges we have identified a number of difficulties which children who have survived domestic violence may experience ... Effects may include: stress related illnesses, confused and torn loyalties (i.e. to both mother and father), lack of trust, unnaturally good behaviour, taking on the mother role, an acceptance of abuse as 'normal', guilt, isolation, shame, anger, lack of confidence, fear of a repeat or a return of violence ...

Women who have suffered violence find that their children sometimes become quiet and nervous while still at home or after leaving. Others become very active or develop disturbed or aggressive behaviour patterns. Boys in particular may respond in this way, but girls can become aggressive too, although they can sometimes be withdrawn, timid and suspicious.

Boys and girls, of course, learn different things from domestic violence and behave in different ways as a result. However, Liz Kelly and others have pointed out that, while the experience of domestic violence will affect how children develop their gender identity as either women or men, the differences between how girls and boys react are not as clear-cut as we might think. Both boys and girls express their distress in ways which turn inward and also in ways which turn outward. Kelly and women in Women's Aid suggest that we need to develop a way of understanding the impact of domestic violence on children which takes gender into account, but which allows for differences within as well as between the responses of girls and of boys. At the moment, however, our knowledge about the effects on children is limited. Mainly it relies on observations in refuges and elsewhere. There has been very little systematic research on the effects on children of witnessing domestic violence. The English federation (WAFE) is anxious to remedy this situation and to conduct some research projects centring on the experience of children.

What work has been done has been mainly in North America. The contributions of Peter Jaffe in Canada have been particularly outstanding in this respect. While his work is couched in professional, psychological language and theories perhaps more often used in a North American context, it has relevance in Britain. In one of his books, *Children of Battered Women*, he explains some of the harsh and distressing consequences experienced by children. His aim is that, as a result of his work, effective service programmes will be designed to meet the needs of children who have seen and been part of domestic violence and of adults who had such experiences in childhood. He describes how children of both sexes tend to blame themselves for the violence between the adults. They often try to protect and defend their mothers, and may get caught up in a conspiracy of silence about the violence which can force them to become manipulative and ashamed. They may get depressed or hate themselves as a result. They may lose their trust and faith in adults – or even in life.

Jaffe outlines how some child survivors of domestic violence may develop at some point in their later lives symptoms very similar to those experienced by people who have gone through a major trauma – for example, a train disaster or a bombing. These symptoms have now been lumped together by doctors into something they call post-traumatic stress disorder. It is this disorder which some children and adults who have suffered domestic violence in childhood clearly manifest. Like women who have experienced domestic violence, however, child witnesses respond in a wide variety of ways. It can be dangerous to elaborate specific syndromes. It can also be dangerous to suggest that propensities to receive or to perpetrate domestic violence are passed on between the generations. Such ideas are often expressed in 'cycle of violence' theories which we will discuss more fully later. Nevertheless, older children in this situation and adults who are still being damaged by childhood experiences of domestic violence are pleased that their life experiences are finally being acknowledged, and are coming out into the open.

As suggested by WAFE, the children of women who have experienced violence have frequently been involved in violent incidents experienced by their mothers, and may have been hurt themselves. They may also have been either physically abused or sexually abused on separate occasions (as we discuss further in Chapter 7). Children's workers and general support staff in refuges work with many children who have been sexually abused. Unfortunately, however, there is very little research or public knowledge about this troubling issue. Much more public attention needs to be paid to the children of abused women in terms of research, of education and prevention work, and of the provision of specialist services to meet their needs. A start has been made by the Women's Aid federations and at a couple of conferences held in London in 1992 which specifically considered the issue.

Which women and which men?

Perhaps the next question is to ask: which women experience domestic violence? The answer seems to be, potentially, all women. There have been various unsuccessful attempts to classify the sort of women who would be likely victims. Some of these are contradictory in a way which would be almost laughable if the issue were not such a serious one. For example, women are too passive and behave like victims, and are therefore subject to violence. Women are too aggressive and self-confident, and are therefore subject to violence. Women are too indecisive, too forceful, too masculine, too submissive. They do not stand up for themselves enough; they stand up for themselves too much. They are too independent and do not look after their menfolk properly. They are too dependent, coddling men and not giving them a chance to breathe. Many of these explanations – especially in the past, it must be said – have fallen into the woman-hating or 'blame the victim' schools of thought. One of the first studies in Britain of women who have experienced domestic violence was conducted by a consultant psychiatrist, J. J. Gayford, in 1974. While some of his write-ups of this study have some usefulness, one includes horrifying classifications of 'types' of women who experience violence – for example, 'Fanny the Flirt' and 'Go-Go Gloria'.

Social class has been, and continues to be, an issue for researchers and activists working against domestic violence. Some work has been done, especially in the United States, which shows a concentration of domestic violence in low-income, blue-collar families. Other researchers, such as Mildred Daley Pagelow, who has done a lot of work on domestic violence in the USA, contend that such ideas are a myth. As Lorna Smith points out in her Home Office review, suggestions that domestic violence is concentrated among working-class men and women should be treated with caution and scepticism. Middle-class women are less likely to report it, and more likely to pursue private solutions than to approach public agencies like social services. Research has shown that middle-class men are less likely to come to the attention of the police, and that social and public agencies in general are less likely to intervene in middle-class lives. Most importantly, perhaps, as far as such research is concerned, both middle-class men and women are far less likely than working-class men and women to get 'researched' by researchers!

Working-class men beat their wives -- I, on the other hand, have come to believe, after a rational process of thought, that physical chastisement is a positive element in an equal marriage!

A lot of what we have all learned in recent years about domestic violence comes from refuges, which have always attracted more working-class than middle-class women. Due to social and political inequalities, it is working-class women who are more likely to have nowhere else to go, and to lack the money to buy themselves some other way out. This is quite clearly a simplistic explanation, but it has some validity. Nevertheless, some middle-class women do use the accommodation provided by Women's Aid. Other services for women experiencing domestic violence run by Women's Aid – for example, advice and information services – are quite commonly used by middle-class women.

In recent years, there have been various public accounts of violence in affluent families or involving public figures. As a result, images of domestic violence as the preserve of the working class and the poor have been thoroughly dented. However, there is still a commonly held view in British society that violence against women occurs only in the homes of working-class people, mainly in the inner cities, and is associated with poverty and alcoholism. This sort of view has a long history. It harks back to attitudes towards the Victorian poor, forced to live in miserable and overcrowded conditions, crammed into the rapidly growing cities after the Industrial Revolution. In Britain in the 1990s, dominated by recession, unemployment and cutbacks in public services, it is of course true that there can be harmful effects within some working-class families. Poor housing, high unemployment, bad working conditions and lack of facilities take their toll. And in some subcultures, social conditioning of young men to be 'macho' and violent can combine with poor opportunities for life fulfilment to cause violence, some of which can be expressed in taking it out on women. But domestic violence occurs very widely outside low-income communities and run-down council estates.

Some studies have shown large amounts of violence in affluent areas. In a study in Yorkshire carried out by Jalna Hanmer and Sheila Saunders, social class and housing type made no difference to the levels of violence experienced by women in their sample. Pagelow's work in the United States leads her to believe that middle-class men may be more, not less, likely to beat their wives than working-class men, although she suggests that the violence which they use may have different characteristics. Some research studies have indicated, for example, that it may be more covert, less easily visible, and more psychological in nature. However, these provisos have a scent about them of class stereotyping. Put simply, what they are saying is that middle-class men know how not to leave bruises and injuries which are easily visible to outsiders. This sort of idea was evident in the 'designer violence' of the recent Hollywood film, *Sleeping with the Enemy*, starring Julia Roberts. In this film, a rich and fabulously beautiful young woman, whose life as far as anyone could tell was perfect, was in fact experiencing frequent and severe violence from her menacing husband. But nobody would have guessed.

Activists in the movement against domestic violence in several countries over the last twenty years have consistently made it clear that domestic violence occurs across all classes and communities. Many books, documents and reports make this point time and time again. The result is that we all have to face up to the reality of domestic violence, whatever our class, cultural or racial background. Some middle-class people, and perhaps middle-class professionals in particular, like to pretend, however, that it only happens 'out there' to other people.

A tragic case of child abuse and murder in New York in 1987, brought to court in 1988–9, grabbed the attention of the media on an international scale. It involved a woman, Hedda Nussbaum, who, after years of horrifying abuse and control by her violent, crazed partner, Joel Steinberg, could not prevent him from murdering their adopted daughter, Lisa. Steinberg had abused Lisa for some years prior to her murder. Acres of newsprint and thousands and thousands of words have been produced about this case. The murder trial was watched live on television by millions of Americans.

While the case was widely discussed, women in particular argued among themselves about it. Some castigated Nussbaum for failing to protect her daughter, and for using drugs as commanded by Steinberg. Others excused her, due to the debilitating effects of the enormous amount of abuse and violence (including psychological abuse) which she had endured. Famous feminists in the States lined up on both sides. But, as many of them pointed out, there are other tragic and horrifying cases of child murder in New York City. The reason why this one hit the headlines, not only in New York, not only in the United States, but in many countries world-wide, was simple. Nussbaum and Steinberg were well-off, respectable and middle-class. She was a book editor. He was a lawyer.

In Britain, there is a set of ideas about what a family should be which approximates to a sort of middle-class ideal, and which is usually supported by government policies, whichever party is in power. Since 1979, however, the British Conservative governments of Margaret Thatcher and John Major have taken a particularly strong pro-family line, similar to, although not as extreme as, the pro-family stance of the US Republican administrations of Ronald Reagan and George Bush before Bill Clinton's presidency. Dominant ideas about the family in western countries give credence only to one particular family form, namely the small, white nuclear family consisting of a man, a woman and two or three children, usually living a fairly affluent lifestyle. A look at the advertisements on TV will reveal many examples of this sort of family. Very few people actually live in such families, of course, and there are all sorts of other ways of organizing families and sexual relationships. It fails to reflect real life and it is prejudiced and discriminatory for white people, for heterosexuals and for national governments to attempt to impose this 'norm' of family life on people of other races, cultures and sexualities. Unfortunately, that is exactly what they have always done, and go on doing today.

Lesbians, for example, tend to be made invisible by this society. They are underrepresented or not represented at all in almost all research, including much which is conducted by feminists. Some lesbians experience violence in personal relationships. Refuges are open to all women, but specialist services for lesbians fleeing abuse are virtually non-existent. Women in this situation may face discrimination and sometimes outright hostility if they openly seek help following violence from either a male or female partner. Lesbians who have been abused by a male ex-partner or partner may get little sympathy. Instead they are likely to face voyeuristic or punitive attitudes, along the lines of 'she asked for that' or 'she deserves all she gets'. Young lesbians suffering abuse and living at home may experience particular difficulties, and may not know where on earth to turn for help. And a woman with children who is a lesbian faces an agonizingly charged situation. Seeking help to stop the violence may bring unwanted attention from the authorities which could lead to her children being removed from her care on the grounds of sexuality. Violence between women partners is uncommon, but it does occur. However, it is a different issue from domestic violence by men against women, and needs to be thought about and understood in different ways. Women are currently discussing and evolving new understandings about this painful matter.

In different cultures and countries, and among the many diverse ethnic peoples of the world, relationships, communities and styles of living vary vastly. Domestic violence by men against women may take different forms and mean different things in these various communities. While we know that such violence occurs among people of almost all racial, ethnic and cultural heritages, there is no evidence that it occurs to a greater extent among some groups than others. Nevertheless certain racist myths persist. For example, some people believe that Asian women are more likely than white women to be badly treated and subjected to violence due to cultural patterns of family life. Others argue that African-Caribbean men are more violent than white men, particularly in relationships with white women. These racist ideas are not supported by research, but they have been around for a long time, going back deep into Britain's colonial and imperial history.

Discrimination against black people and discrimination against women can intersect in specific ways as people play out their personal lives, and this can have complex implications in some cases of domestic violence. Cultural traditions may also play a part. Black researchers and commentators assert that there is a need for committedly anti-racist research into such issues, as they affect the different ways in which domestic violence is manifested. Amina Mama in *The Hidden Struggle*, a pioneering book on black women and domestic violence, suggests that for black women domestic violence needs to be redefined. She points out that existing research has been contradictory and often tainted with racist sentiments, concentrating almost exclusively on the non-issue of whether black and minority families are more or less violent than white.

Despite some positive changes over recent years, racism imbues British society from top to bottom. It expresses itself in the attitudes and behaviour of white people and white communities, but it is more than that. Sometimes called structural or institutional racism, it is embedded, like discrimination against women, in the basic structure of British society, in the very way in which society goes about organizing itself. One example is the racist nature of the immigration laws and the way that they are applied in different ways to white and to black immigrants. Another is discriminatory employment practices, which can occur in an institutional way even in organizations in which all the individuals involved claim that they are anti-racist.

For black women fleeing violence, the existence of such pervasive racism complicates all the options. They may find that their accounts are not believed. If they are abused by a black man, they may wish to protect both him and their community from potentially racist police intervention or surveillance – and so be reluctant to seek help. Women whose immigration status is dependent on their husbands' position may face particular difficulties, including eligibility for state benefits and the risk of deportation if they leave their husbands. Women who do not speak English or who are unfamiliar with the country may feel condemned to remain with their abusive husbands, due to the lack of supportive services or of language interpretation. The issues are many and complicated, and will be returned to throughout this book.

In a society dominated by the young, older women fleeing violence may also face difficulties. They may experience problems in being acknowledged, in having their needs taken seriously, and in contacting services which respond sympathetically and show some knowledge and understanding of their situation. Women with disabilities who experience violence are often in a particularly traumatic and tragic position. If their disabilities are quite severe, they may be particularly isolated, confined to the home and unable to gain access to information, support and help. This situation is magnified greatly if their abuser is also their carer. It may then be almost impossible for them to escape the violence. In addition, it is rarely acknowledged that domestic violence is a problem which women with disabilities are likely to experience, so they may have additional barriers of disbelief and unhelpful attitudes to surmount.

Women can also be disabled by the violence which they have experienced. Women we have met have been blinded or deafened, or have lost the use of limbs. We recently conducted a study into housing options for women and their children who are homeless due to domestic violence. Among the women we talked to in this study, one woman had lost an eye and another could no longer stand up, except for a few minutes, due to extensive damage to her legs. Physical violence was often combined with mental or sexual violence or both, and with threats towards both the woman and her children. Some women described repeated injuries, the same bone smashed and re-smashed, brain haemorrhages, hospitalizations, attempted murder. Other women told of distressing mental cruelty verging on torture, such as being made to stand on a chair facing the wall for hours or being forced to eat continuously. A few women gave accounts of children killed as babies or sustaining distressing mental handicaps as a result of violence experienced during pregnancy or after birth.

Such deeply disturbing accounts occur again and again throughout the domestic violence literature. They are heard often by workers in refuges, by social workers and by the police. Everyone who works with women who have suffered domestic violence and their children hope that the dreadful stories will stop, that women will stop needing to come forward for help, that the atrocities will come to an end; but they never do.

2

Refuges and the movement against domestic violence

The great mobilization of women began with a vision, supported by action. The vision was of a world transformed ...

Rebecca and Russell Dobash,
Women, Violence and Social Change

What are refuges and how do they work?

Ever since the 'mobilization of women' in the late 1960s and early 1970s of which Rebecca and Russell Dobash speak, Women's Aid has been the key agency in Britain for women who have experienced physical, emotional and sexual violence, and for their children. Women's Aid groups provide emergency and temporary accommodation, advice, information, support and a range of other services for abused women and children. Most run refuges and some also run separate advice centres, support groups and related projects. The refuges they provide form a nationwide network, and include both general refuges for all women and some specialist projects for Asian, African, African-Caribbean and other black women, for women from some other ethnic minority communities, and for certain women with special needs. However, there are not nearly enough refuges of the latter types. In general, the refuge network and the associated services for women who have experienced violence and their children remain inadequately funded and resourced, a problem which we shall return to throughout this book.

Women's Aid refuges are co-ordinated by four autonomous but closely associated federations: Welsh Women's Aid, Scottish Women's

Aid, Northern Ireland Women's Aid and the Women's Aid Federation (England), usually known as WAFE. There are now more than 275 Women's Aid groups throughout the British Isles, many of which run more than one refuge, and which together give shelter to more than 40,000 women and children annually. Over 100,000 further women contact the Women's Aid federations and their member refuge groups annually for advice and help.

Most of the refuges are in England due to its large size and population, and include several specialist refuges for black and ethnic minority women. Welsh Women's Aid co-ordinates 35 refuges and 13 advice centres. Three new groups are just forming, including the first refuge for black women in Wales. There are no refuges in Wales which are not affiliated to Welsh Women's Aid. Scottish Women's Aid is a network of 37 local groups, of which 35 have refuges. More refuges are currently being developed. Two refuge groups in Scotland provide refuge services specifically for black and ethnic minority women. Northern Ireland Women's Aid has nine refuges providing over 200 bedspaces and including a specialized refuge for women who have suffered sexual abuse or have special needs. These refuges include advice centres. The 1993 strategy for Northern Ireland Women's Aid includes setting up a regional helpline, as well other objectives broadly shared by the other federations, such as extending the refuge network and its after-care services, and further developing domestic violence training initiatives and public awareness campaigns.

There are also some refuges which work closely with Women's Aid but which are not affiliated to the federations. These include some of the specialist refuges for black women, including Asian women. While there are some other refuges run by church groups and by charitable and statutory organizations which are not associated with the Women's Aid movement at all, the federations remain the only national co-ordinating bodies representing the interests of women who have experienced domestic violence and their children. The majority of refuge groups are affiliated to them or work closely alongside them.

The refuges provided by Women's Aid and associated organizations aim to be safe houses for women and children escaping domestic violence. They exist in most towns and cities throughout the British Isles and in some country areas as well. Their addresses and telephone numbers are kept confidential in order to protect the women and children living in them. However, social workers and the police know where they are, and many have special public contact numbers.

Social services, the police and other agencies refer women to refuges – although, for most of them, women can also refer themselves. No refuge will turn a woman away without help, and without assisting her and any children she has with her to find somewhere safe to go. Women are also referred from one refuge to another, since they very often have to move around the country in order to find a place of safety. Staying in their home area is often unsafe for abused women and children. They may also have to move on to another refuge if the woman's violent partner discovers where they are, and starts to harass them. Violent men often try hard to find their wives or partners, and may be extremely abusive if they do. There are various disturbing examples of women being attacked and even murdered in refuges on discovery by their partners. Thus the refuge network works together to facilitate women and children being able to move on rapidly if they need to, and provides 24-hour contact between refuges when required. WAFE runs a national telephone helpline for selected hours. This helpline plays a vital role as a contact and referral point for women who cannot easily gain access to a local refuge, or for women wishing to talk or seek advice or help while remaining anonymous. In London, there is a centralized London-wide referral and advice service run by London Women's Aid.

In a refuge, a woman will normally have to share a room with her children. The houses are usually full and crowded, but not dangerously overcrowded. They are self-catering and the women and children are responsible for keeping them clean. Women and children can stay for anything from one night to several months. Some refuges have a time limit, although in the last few years, women and children attempting to get rehoused by local councils have had to wait for gradually lengthening periods for housing offers in many areas. In consequence, their stays in refuges are also getting longer and longer. To cater for this need, some refuge groups operate move-on or second-stage accommodation where it is possible to live somewhat more independently and privately than may be possible in the first-stage refuge. Women and children may use such accommodation while they wait for rehousing.

Refuge groups are managed by voluntary management committees which are sometimes called support groups. Women volunteer managers often put in many hours of unpaid work and commitment to manage the project, and to assist it to function smoothly and effectively. Many groups also employ volunteer workers. In most projects, however, funding has been obtained to employ at least some workers on a proper, paid basis. Most groups employ staff who offer support to women living in the refuge. These workers assist women in claiming welfare benefits, applying for housing and pursuing legal remedies. They engage in advocacy work on behalf of women and children with other agencies, and accompany women when required to the Department of Social Security, solicitors, housing offices and so on. They provide advice and information, and often operate a telephone helpline as well. Refuge staff will also on occasion return with a woman and police escorts to a woman's former home to collect belongings. In addition, they offer emotional support. Women in refuges have frequently left behind not only their male partners but also their communities, families, friends and possessions. They are often in the most severe crisis of their lives and may be extremely distressed. Refuge workers and other women in the refuge usually offer as much support as they can.

Many refuges also employ specialist children's workers to offer children support and assistance, to provide childcare activities and facilities for creative play, and to represent children's interests. Children's workers do advocacy work on behalf of children with social services, schools and other agencies. For children, the move to a refuge can be particularly confusing and distressing. They will have lost not only their fathers and relatives but also their schools and all their friends, whom they may never see again. They are faced with starting at a new school or preschool project and making new friends. The children's workers can help to give them a sense of security and can provide emotional support. WAFE has produced an information pack for women working with children in refuges called *A Women's Aid Approach to Working with Children.*

Where possible, refuge groups employ outreach workers to work with women who have suffered violence but who do not wish to come into the refuge, or who are living in other types of temporary accommodation; and outreach workers also do community development work. Some refuge groups, for example, employ outreach or development workers specifically to work with African-Caribbean or Asian women. Where possible, refuge groups employ follow-up workers to offer support to women and children who have left the refuge and found their own accommodation, or have been rehoused by the council. Leaving the communal environment of the refuge to live in a flat or house in an unknown community can be very difficult for a woman and her children. They may be facing life as a single-parent family for the first time, and may be lonely and isolated, trying to make friends and establish themselves. They are often in a completely different and unfamiliar part of the country from their home area, where they know no one apart from the women and workers from the refuge. Children have to start new schools or playgroups, possibly for the third or fourth time if they have had to move from one refuge to another. Follow-up workers can assist women and children with these difficult adjustments, and can provide information and act as advocates on their behalf. In some areas, they have been able to help with setting up supportive groups of women who have left the refuge and ended up living quite close together.

All the Women's Aid federations offer information, resources, advice, training and support to refuges, to statutory and voluntary agencies, and to the public. They provide an extensive range of publications and leaflets on domestic violence, resource material for refuge groups, national publicity for domestic violence issues, and training manuals and training courses for Women's Aid staff. The national federations also give priority to advocacy, lobbying and campaigning. Women's Aid has had a vital role over the last twenty years in trying to ensure that the interests of abused women and children are effectively represented, and in working to change the inadequacies of legal, welfare and housing provision. The federations monitor legislation and social, economic, legal and political developments which affect Women's Aid services and women and children experiencing domestic violence. Recently, for example, they have submitted evidence to the government Home Affairs Committee Inquiry on Domestic Violence and have participated in the Department of the Environment Working Party on Relationship Breakdown.

The history of refuges

Services and refuges for women and children escaping violence have existed in Britain for only a relatively short time. However, women have attempted to put an end to domestic violence in different places at different times, and it seems that women in various countries throughout the world have sometimes established safe houses for each other in different historical periods. A very small number of safe houses for abused women and children to use as places of hiding were set up in the nineteenth century in Britain and North America, and both liberal and feminist campaigners worked on the issue.

In Britain, as in most societies, women had few rights and freedoms in the past. There has been a long tradition of men chastising and punishing their wives and daughters in order to control their behaviour. In fact, chastisement of a wife has been seen historically not only as a husband's right and privilege, but as his duty. Many people know and use the common expression 'rule of thumb' in their everyday conversation. What they may not realize is that one origin of the expression derives from the right of a man to beat his wife with a stick, providing it was no thicker than his thumb. Over the last two centuries, this right and duty has been slowly eroded due to the efforts of campaigners, both feminist and philanthropist, and through a slow turning of moral and public opinion. In Britain, the law allowing the chastisement of wives was repealed in 1829. But it is doubtful how much difference this change made at the time.

The history of wife-beating has been well documented by Rebecca and Russell Dobash in *Violence Against Wives*. They point out that it has always been difficult to carry out the letter of the law where domestic matters are concerned. There has been a long-standing principle of law enforcement, dating from as long ago as Roman times, which says that law-enforcers should not interfere in domestic disputes. The effectiveness of legal sanctions against wife assault has always been eroded, or indeed sabotaged, by the power and control that men had – and still have – over their wives or partners.

The twentieth century brought considerable improvements in women's rights and in public attitudes. However, women continued to be beaten, abused, sexually violated and subjected to a seemingly unending range of maltreatment and violence. With the evolution of a moral climate less accepting of wife-beating (although reflecting a social system reluctant to do much about it), the abuse gradually became more hidden. People did not talk openly about it. And it was often the woman rather than the man who was gossiped about behind hands and disgraced if the truth came out. Those who remember the 1940s and 1950s can recall the moral censure, the embarrassment, the shame and the almost total silence about domestic violence – perhaps more marked among the middle class, but firmly there across classes and social boundaries.

Until the most recent wave of the women's movement in the late 1960s and early 1970s, women suffering domestic violence had no one to turn to. They had nowhere to escape to, no one to talk to, no one to help them, except perhaps each other. Women have always found support and drawn strength from other women. But there were no refuges, no support and advice services, no housing alternatives, no counselling centres, no publicity outlets or media coverage, not much in the way of legal remedies, and very little help from the police, who have traditionally regarded a man's home as indisputably his castle. Divorce was uncommon and frowned upon; women in violent marriages had no way out.

Public attitudes began to change in the 1960s, and towards the end of the decade the Women's Liberation movement started. From it stemmed the movement against domestic violence in general, and Women's Aid in particular. The connection is a quite straightforward one, though it is sometimes overlooked or forgotten today. Services, projects and initiatives now exist throughout the country. They are inadequately funded and their distribution is patchy – but they are there. Almost all of these services derive in one way or another from the well-spring of the women's movement.

Women's Liberation in the 1960s and 1970s was characterized by political activity, demonstrations and active campaigns. It attempted to build a new politics for a new future for women. Its basic building block was the small consciousness-raising group in which groups of mainly white, often (but by no means solely) middle-class women met together to share their lives and experiences and to build a grass-roots political analysis of male domination and female subordination.

Groups and campaigns started up in many towns and cities, some connected in Britain to the long-standing socialist movement, and often with acknowledged or unconscious links to national liberation struggles in the Third World and to the New Left movements in North America and Europe – the Black Liberation movement, the anti-Vietnam War struggle, the worldwide student rebellions and the oppositional 'counter-culture' of the time. These were heady days which transformed the lives of many who were part of them.

By the early 1970s, the consciousness-raising and the rapidly mushrooming analysis and understanding of women's oppression had started to encompass the subject of male violence in the home. It began when women who had suffered violence started coming to the new women's centres requesting help and the women working in them did not know what to suggest. Meetings and political actions began to be held about the issue, involving women who had experienced violence and others who had not. Out of these meetings came the idea of setting up safe houses or refuges to which women who had suffered violence could escape, and from which they could perhaps begin to construct new lives, free of violence.

The idea was more or less a new one. Apart from the few precedents which we have noted and about which little is known, it had rarely been done before. However, we do know that, whenever refuges for women are established in societies dominated by men, it seems to be a challenge to the status quo, and this was also the case in Britain in the 1970s. The initiative confronted in a concrete and undeniable way men's rights and power within the family, the heart and bedrock of society. Women were taking action to leave violent marriages and partnerships, often without warning, to live with groups of other women in safe houses run by women. In a small but significant way, the very fabric of sexual politics was being challenged.

To some extent it is common knowledge that the first refuge of the period was set up by a women's group known as Chiswick Women's Aid, whose spokesperson was Erin Pizzey. Public consciousness was moved in a profound way by the media publicity and hype surrounding Chiswick – so much so that even today, twenty years later, references to the original Chiswick Women's Aid refuge occur in media coverage of domestic violence. In fact, however, refuges were more or less simultaneously being fought for and established up and down the country, and some may have opened before Chiswick. It was not long before Erin Pizzey, whom the Dobashes have called 'the visible moral entrepreneur launching the issue', had quarrelled with the rest of the Women's Aid movement over her views as to the cause of the violence, which she developed along the lines that some women are 'violence-prone', and her antipathy to collective and co-operative ways of working. Chiswick Women's Aid split away from the rest of Women's Aid to go it alone – a situation which remains to this day, although its successor, Chiswick Family Rescue, relaunched in 1993 as 'Refuge', has repudiated Pizzey's more women-blaming perspectives on male abuse.

It is hard now, in a decade comparatively lacking in political action, to visualize the speed of almost daily change which characterized the Women's Aid movement and the wider women's liberation movement of the early 1970s. Women put much energy, work and commitment into trying to get refuges set up, often pitting themselves against local resistance and opposition. More than forty refuges had come into being by 1974, with new ones being set up all the time.

As well as providing safe and secure accommodation for women and children escaping violence in the home, the new Women's Aid groups campaigned about and publicized the issue of domestic violence. In 1974 they established two refuge federations, the National Women's Aid Federation (NWAF) for England, Wales and Northern Ireland, and Scottish Women's Aid for Scotland. (It was in fact at one of the very first conferences of NWAF that the split with Chiswick Women's Aid was dramatically finalized.) By 1975 more than eighty groups were part of NWAF alone. The federations co-ordinated local groups and mounted national campaigns around domestic violence. In 1978, to encourage regional autonomy further, NWAF divided into three separate federations, Northern Ireland Women's Aid, Welsh Women's Aid and WAFE, the Women's Aid Federation (England).

Throughout Britain as a whole, local groups worked tirelessly on a volunteer basis setting up more and more refuges for women and children, usually with no funding at all. Many used short-life properties with very little in the way of facilities. As a result, conditions were often poor. All of the houses were continually overwhelmed with women and children needing refuge space. The extent of the need was painfully clear. The new refuges filled up as fast as they opened, but everyone involved knew that this was merely the tip of the iceberg of domestic violence. In 1975 a government Select Committee on Violence in Marriage (set up due to the surge of interest in and publicity about the subject) recommended that refuges should be established throughout the country to provide an initial target of one family place per 10,000 of the population. This remains the aim today, even though it is widely recognized as itself an inadequate estimate. Nearly twenty years later, we have fewer than one-third of those places. The tip of the iceberg remains just that.

From the first national conferences up until the present time, the Women's Aid movement has had to struggle with dilemmas and contradictions. A major issue from the beginning was how much an organization could be simultaneously both a political campaigning body and a provider of services to abused women. There is plenty of left-wing literature saying it cannot be done, as well as right-wing opinion saying it should not be attempted. Providing services almost automatically entails a degree of negotiating with the establishment, in order among other things to secure funding, which is likely to be unacceptable to those in a campaigning movement who are dedicated to opposition, resistance and political action. In the Women's Aid movement of the 1970s, the debate crystallized around how to provide sensitive, independent services to meet the needs of women and children, while obtaining much-needed funding through central and local government bodies. The federations attracted some grant-aid more or less from their inception, and by the end of the decade many refuges had some sort of funding, although this funding was, without exception, inadequate and precarious.

Throughout the late 1970s and early 1980s, the Women's Aid movement continued to develop services for women and children. More and more refuges obtained properties and funding from official government bodies and programmes. Some examples are the Urban Programme, local authority housing and social services committees, and housing association special projects and joint funding schemes. All the refuge federations campaigned hard (in conjunction with other women's organizations) on behalf of women and children escaping domestic violence. Some of this campaigning energy was directed towards the legislature. Women's Aid was instrumental in the drafting of various pieces of legislation, such as the Domestic Violence and Matrimonial Proceedings Act 1976, the Domestic Violence and Magistrates' Courts Act 1978, and the Housing (Homeless Persons) Act 1977, now Part III of the Housing Act 1985.

The Women's Aid federations have continued this work in the 1990s, representing and co-ordinating the growing network of refuges, and lobbying and campaigning for legal and policy measures and for comprehensive services to meet the needs of abused women and children. None of the federations has centralized management structures which directly control local groups. Affiliated refuge groups agree to accept certain conditions and principles but remain autonomous. The federations all have regional structures of different kinds and hold annual member conferences. National advocacy work, lobbying and service provision are co-ordinated by the national staff, together with voluntary national working groups.

Women's Aid as a whole continues to function as an independent advocacy agency and service provider outside the statutory social services. In this deliberate pursuit of political autonomy, it has been more successful than refuge movements have been in some other countries. Some shelters in North America, for example, have become closely associated with conventional social service agencies, and this has tended to result in workers becoming 'professionalized' and in a loss of grass-roots feminist practice and principles. In some countries of the world, refuges, where they exist at all, are run by official government agencies or under the auspices of religious groupings. In Britain, however, the refuge movement retains a specifically feminist identity as a national movement of women committed to self-determination, and relatively independent of both church and state. Although not of course without its fair share of problems and internal disagreement, this movement can in some ways act as a challenge and a model for women in other countries where no independent women-run services exist. And it can learn from countries where policies against domestic violence and services for abused women and children are better developed.

Beliefs, principles and policies

Women's Aid services are based on four principles:

- The central importance of the abused woman's perspective in the provision of support and services.
- The need to empower women and to enable them to regain control of their own lives. Women's Aid services are provided by women and for women.
- The value of the mutual support of other women who have similar experiences.
- A commitment to caring for the emotional, developmental and educational needs of children affected by domestic violence.

The work and standards of Women's Aid groups affiliated to the four federations are bound by policy statements and codes of good practice which encompass these principles, together with policies on the following:

- Self-help and self-determination.
- 'Open door' policies – all women are found a safe place to go.
- Equal opportunities and anti-discrimination.
- Confidentiality.
- Provision for children.
- Education and liaison.

These values and principles underlie all the work of the refuge network and of many other services provided for women experiencing domestic violence and their children. Self-help, self-determination and empowerment are particularly important principles. They have always formed the foundation stones of what the Women's Aid movement stands for, and they inform the other principles and policies as well. What, however, do they mean?

Self-help for women means what it says – women helping themselves and other women to establish independent services to combat male violence. Empowerment has become a popular word in the 1990s. It came mainly from the political left wing originally, but now the political right wing is using it as well. The notion has also been adopted by some establishment agencies. It is currently heard quite a lot in social work circles, for example, in relation to social work clients. Good social work practice is now seen to consist of empowering people – although presumably such empowerment only goes so far, since social workers also have to act as social controllers, as in cases of child protection. One of the aims of empowerment, however, is that those who are empowered might choose to become resistant to the status quo, or might even try to challenge those who have power. The women's movement has been developing the idea for years as a way of resisting male control and power over women, and also as a means to oppose other sorts of discrimination on the grounds, for example, of race or social class.

Empowerment for abused women means becoming more powerful on a personal and psychological level so that they have the strength and emotional resources to break away from or to change violent relationships, if they choose to. Importantly, it means having the economic and other resources to do so, which is why the provision of adequate financial support through the welfare benefits system and access to permanent housing options is so important for abused women and children. Empowerment also means women being able to help each other in refuges and support groups to deal with violent relationships and live violence-free lives. One of the basic tenets of refuges has always been that women can assist each other to grow strong.

Like empowerment, self-determination is a term which has usually found its home in left-wing and feminist social movements, but which is often used these days by the political right as well. As a result it can lose its political edge. National liberation movements in colonized or occupied countries and people living under oppressive conditions commonly use the concept as a principle of organization. At its most basic level, it means that people should be able to determine their own lives and their own futures. For women who have been in abusive relationships with men, self-determination means taking control back from the abuser, and gaining self-esteem, self-confidence and the financial, material and emotional resources to control their own lives, rather than living under the influence or control of a violent man.

Over the last twenty years, the refuge network has developed various ways of putting empowerment, self-help and self-determination into action, of working out some practical 'how-tos', rather than allowing these principles to remain in the realm of lofty rhetoric. First and foremost, refuges are empowering by their very existence. Women facing violence in their homes find it strengthening just knowing that there is somewhere to escape to, knowing that there is somewhere where they will be given help and support. It can never be emphasized enough just how much the provision of refuges has transformed the lives of abused women and their children. Having options means having a bit more power and control, and having a choice rather than being trapped. It means knowing that you are not alone. Women's Aid operates an 'open door' policy, which means that no woman or child needing refuge will be turned away without assistance. Women can refer themselves to a refuge, rather than having to be reliant on an official organization, and Women's Aid refuges do not require women to offer proof of the violence and abuse which they have experienced. A woman's word is enough.

Within the refuge itself, the main way in which empowerment works is through the help and sustenance which both women and children can draw from each other, by offering mutual help and support and by sharing similar experiences. Finding out that other women and children have been through the same thing, that you are accepted and respected despite everything that has happened – that everyone is in the same boat and there is even the possibility of rowing that boat somewhere – these seemingly simple realizations are crucial. Women in refuges share life together on a daily basis. They frequently share the anger and pain which they may feel about what they have been through, and often support each other in each new challenge. This sort of sharing can lead to women becoming stronger both individually and collectively. Anyone who has lived or worked in a refuge can attest to this. Of course, it does not happen that way all the time. Women in refuges, like anyone else, can behave badly towards each other and there can be rows and disputes, often caused by the crowded living conditions. But it happens often enough to confirm the belief that women sharing together at their time of greatest crisis can be empowered by the experience.

A women-only organization

Women's Aid is an organization of women working with women for women. Women in general, and women who have suffered violence at the hands of men in particular, may be intimidated by the presence of men. And many women can attest to how men can often try to take over, to dominate in mixed situations, to speak on women's behalf – often without even realizing it. For abused women, it can be particularly recuperative to leave these problems behind. Most important of all, women who are homeless due to male violence need to feel safe and secure. Many request specifically to be placed in an all-women environment. They may need to know that they are far removed from male aggression in order to have the space to start to take control of their own lives, to begin the process of recovery. Women living in refuges who have previously been facing domestic violence isolated and alone often say how wonderful it was to find out that there were other women who would help them, that women could stand firm together. For these various reasons, it is empowering in itself that there are no men involved in Women's Aid groups affiliated to the federations.

At the beginning of the Women's Aid movement some refuges employed committed anti-sexist men as childcare workers to act as models (particularly perhaps for the boys) of how men can be gentle, non-violent and involved in looking after children. But in the late 1970s, the decision was made to become a women-only organization and to affirm the ability of women together to oppose male violence. The 'no men rule' has been and continues to be a strategy of empowerment. Women attending gatherings of women who have suffered domestic violence are often profoundly moved by the strength of women together. However, excluding men has, on occasion, caused problems with funders, and it has also resulted in some refuges remaining unaffiliated. A small number of general refuges have wished to have men on their management committees or to employ male workers, and a few refuge groups for black women feel at the present time that, because of the effects of racism, they need to work in conjunction with black men.

Autonomy and equality

While accepting common principles, each group running a refuge is an independent and autonomous organization. Many groups are committed to developing participative management structures and aim to operate as collectives. This is a tall order in a society dominated by hierarchies, but it is an empowering way to work. Most refuge groups are committed to making decisions by consensus. The employed staff frequently work together collectively, although some groups now employ refuge managers or co-ordinators, and workers may have specialized roles and responsibilities within the overall staff team. Staff try to work as equally as possible with refuge residents. The national federations are also autonomous, and their national staff members work together on a collective team basis, without national directors.

One of the main policies of the Women's Aid network is to strive to pursue equal opportunities for all. Equal opportunities in employment have become a popular subject in the late 1980s and early 1990s, and many employers now claim that they are equal opportunity employers – a large percentage of local authorities, for example. While this claim is often accompanied by little concrete action, there are signs now that the government and the business world are intending to pull back from pursuing equal opportunities altogether in the future, saying that they cannot afford it. Women's Aid, on the other hand, is actively committed to equal opportunities and to combatting oppression and exploitation of all types. This means that the federations and the individual refuge groups within them strive not to discriminate against any woman on the grounds of class, race, disability, age or sexuality. Refuge groups are expected to develop equal opportunities policies and monitoring processes to cover the services offered to residents and to other women seeking advice, the employment of workers, the recruitment of volunteers and the operation of the management committee or support group.

In addition, Women's Aid attempts to work in a way which is anti-discriminatory. Refuges often take an active role in combatting prejudice and injustice. The federations expect refuge groups to initiate regular discussion about equal opportunities issues and to provide appropriate training and services for both women residents and workers – for example, anti-racism and disability awareness training. These are hard matters to take on, however, and involve struggle and debate within most refuges and Women's Aid groups.

In common with the rest of the 'white' women's movement, Women's Aid was slow to take up issues of racism, and some refuges are only now doing so. Partly as a result of these failures, some black women have decided over the last ten years to organize separate provision. However, Women's Aid as a whole now operates anti-racist policies, and many refuge groups previously dominated by white women have taken positive action on racism and have profoundly challenged their own previous practices. WAFE has a national Black Women's Group which meets regularly. Both inside and outside Women's Aid, black women have set up specific projects and refuges. The majority of these are for Asian women (including young women). They are run and managed by Asian women, and provide safe accommodation, free of racism, specifically designed to meet the needs of Asian women who have suffered domestic violence and their children. Various other refuges now exist either for black women in general or for black women of specific heritages, and also for women from other ethnic minority communities, such as those of Latin American origin.

In a study of refuge provision in London in the late 1980s called *Taking Stock*, it was found that, at least in London and possibly elsewhere, refuges for black women were significantly underresourced compared with other refuges. This is a direct example of institutionalized racism in the provision of funding. It remains the case today, even though some progressively minded housing associations and other bodies have made attempts to address this shortfall.

The Hidden Struggle, Amina Mama's influential book on violence against black women in the home, explains how the egalitarian nature of refuges frequently means that one of the main ways in which racism is displayed is at the level of interpersonal conflict. Although clear anti-racist policies (which include the provision of anti-racism training) now exist in refuges, it is often the case that white workers are insufficiently committed and are ineffectual in challenging racism among both white residents and themselves. This failure can seriously undermine the safety and security of black residents. Mama suggests that the refuge federations must continue to develop effective ways of challenging racism in refuges, of providing on-going anti-racism training for all white residents and workers, of extending and monitoring their anti-racist policies, and of translating the policies into effective action.

Black women have not been alone in mounting challenges and confrontations about questions of discrimination. Lesbians, working-class women and to a lesser extent women with disabilities have also challenged the refuge network to improve its practice. These challenges have led to the adoption of some relevant policies by Women's Aid – for example, on heterosexism and anti-lesbianism. 'Heterosexism' is a term which refers to the way in which heterosexuality is upheld throughout society as the only true and real sexuality. Consequently, lesbians and gay men experience disadvantage, exclusion, harassment and prejudice as part and parcel of the social structure. Refuge groups are expected to confront anti-lesbian and heterosexist attitudes and actions both within their refuges and their group, and in society as a whole when they can. Within WAFE, there is a national 'Lesbians in Women's Aid' group for lesbians either working in the organization or using the services provided. This group meets regularly and has produced training material for internal use within the refuge network.

Access to refuges remains poor for women with disabilities, due partly to the general problem of inadequate conditions and low funding throughout the refuge movement, and partly to a lack of commitment to the issue. The situation is now improving a little as more refuges take up the matter and some obtain purpose-built, fully accessible accommodation. Welsh Women's Aid, for example, is in the process of developing at least one family space in a refuge per county which is fully accessible for women with disabilities or physical injury. There are few refuges for abused women with mental health special needs and, due to the lack of overall mental health provision, women in this situation who may or may not have suffered violence quite often get referred inappropriately to general refuges which are not able to offer the level of services required.

The Women's Aid federations, and perhaps Welsh Women's Aid in particular, attempt to highlight the difficult position faced by women experiencing domestic violence in rural areas. Women often live in isolated communities where everyone knows each other. In such a situation, escape can be virtually impossible. The distances involved in rural communities and the lack of public transport and of information and support services mean that rural women are in a particularly vulnerable position. The strategy of Welsh Women's Aid and of the other refuge federations is to attempt to improve service provision, to help to organize transport, and to make information available in isolated communities. Women from rural areas, interviewed by ourselves for a recent study, have talked about how empowering they found it when they gained access to such information, after years of thinking that there was no way out, and when they were assisted to make use of the services available in other areas.

Class issues can reveal themselves starkly in refuges where most of the women may be working-class, and some of the staff and voluntary management members may be from middle-class backgrounds. Women's Aid has always been committed to breaking down class barriers, although this endeavour has sometimes led to conflict and difficulty. In practical ways, though, Women's Aid refuges have routinely attempted to challenge discrimination on the grounds of differing educational experiences and class background.

Employment strategies and working practices

The refuge network has always held that it is women who have suffered violence who are the experts on the experience, rather than professionally qualified social workers or therapists. In developing policy, therefore, the views of abused women are sought as a matter of principle. In the past, women who live in refuges have had the opportunity to be full members of the collective along with workers and support group or management committee members, although this is now changing in some groups. Women who have lived in refuges or who have experienced domestic violence have always been encouraged to apply for refuge jobs. Many Women's Aid groups consider specific life experience to be of great value in choosing workers, while also valuing specific skills, qualifications and training. Qualified social workers and counsellors do sometimes work in the houses, but they are not considered to be necessarily more expert than anyone else. They would be accepted rather as having a particular set of skills to offer, different from, but not superior to, other skills that women might have to contribute.

These employment strategies can be empowering for the women concerned providing that they are accompanied by adequate support and access to training possibilities. Some women without educational qualifications or job experience who have escaped violence and become Women's Aid workers have then gone on to do vocational training or degree courses, or to develop successful new careers. In recent years, refuges have become somewhat more 'professional' with the development of financial accountability to funders, training programmes for workers, more efficient management methods and equal opportunity employment practice.

The working practices of refuge staff also reflect the overall commitment to self-determination and empowerment. Women seeking shelter, support and advice from Women's Aid are encouraged to make their own decisions, to take control of their own lives, and to determine their own futures, whether this involves starting a new life elsewhere or returning home. On a practical level, workers attempt to ensure that women and children have access to the best possible services and resources. On an emotional level, women have a chance to talk about their experiences and their feelings, and to be taken seriously, sometimes for the first time in their lives. A woman who has suffered domestic violence very often feels that it was her fault, that she brought the violence on herself or that she did not work hard enough to keep the family together. Refuge groups consciously oppose the view that male violence towards women is the fault of the woman experiencing the violence, or that blame can be equally shared between the man and the woman. Such notions are empowering and strengthening for the women concerned. Two women whom we interviewed in refuges in 1992 put it this way:

> The advantages of getting support from the workers and living with other women is that you give each other strength. You know, why it all went on, you talk about all the experiences you've been through. And you find that it wasn't you, it wasn't you. That it was the men who had the problems really. That it wasn't the women.

> I'm really grateful because I can be who I want to be here. All the workers and the volunteers are really supportive. They do a lot for you and they build you up. They encourage you to make your own decisions and decide what you want to do. There is no pressure on you. You learn to be strong here ... You need support and you need to know that it's not your fault. While you're here, you get strong.

Women's Aid refuge groups try at all times to treat abused women and children non-judgementally and with respect, and to make sure that other agencies do the same. They counter the myths about domestic violence, and publicize the issue as much as they can, given extremely limited resources and woman-power. Refuge staff deliberately 'interrupt' views expressed by other agencies which pathologize women who have suffered violence, or which are blaming, judgemental or patronizing.

The stated commitment of Women's Aid to combat discrimination against children, as well as against women, means that refuges believe in self-determination and empowerment for children as well as for women. In the Women's Aid view, children are not in general given much control over their own lives. They are frequently ignored, patronized, lied to, betrayed and 'spoken on behalf of'. As a conscious commitment, refuges try to combat this sort of general discrimination. It is expected that children using refuge services will be treated with respect and equality, and the federations encourage a 'no smacking policy'. Childworkers offer support to mothers on issues that affect their children, and are committed to caring for the children's emotional, developmental and educational needs. They also engage in anti-discriminatory work with children, encouraging anti-racism among children and working with boys and girls in different ways to meet their different needs and to counter the effects of sexism.

As we have seen, many Women's Aid groups offer supportive outreach and advice services to women who have suffered violence but who do not wish to come into the refuge. Such services can play a vital role in enabling a woman to deal with the situation of abuse and violence which she is facing. Follow-up support for women who have left refuges can also be empowering, and in some areas women in this situation have set up their own self-help groups.

Finally, building international co-operation, and supporting other political struggles on both the international and the national stage, can assist self-determination. Welsh Women's Aid, for example, hosted an international conference in 1988 which resulted in the setting up of some informal international links between movements against domestic violence throughout the world.

Inadequate resources

While Women's Aid and the refuge network as a whole does its best to provide responsive and empowering services for abused women and their children, the whole enterprise is hampered by inadequate funding and poor resources. The Women's Aid federations would like to see a commitment from the British government to the systematic financing of refuges and to the improvement of standards across the board. This would include the provision of funding not only for refuges, but also for the linked services which are essential to meet the needs of women who have suffered violence and their children. These include outreach, community development and follow-up, together with improved services for children (see Chapter 9). The all-party Home Affairs Committee which reported in the spring of 1993 recommended that funding for refuges should be systematically improved. This recommendation has been widely welcomed, but we have yet to see how it will be acted upon. Any national funding strategy would include the specific provision of specialist refuges for black and other ethnic minority women, many of which are currently even more underfunded than general refuges.

At the moment, however, some refuges have no grant-aid at all and are dependent on the payment of rents by women residents and on private fund-raising. Refuge groups and other services for women and children disappear regularly as funding is withdrawn or cut back. Workers are often underpaid and chronically overworked. Many regularly work at least double their official working hours, and this can lead to stress between workers, to exhaustion and illness. The houses tend to be crowded and under-equipped, with insufficient resources to decorate as often as is necessary or to replace outdated or broken equipment. The lack of privacy and facilities can breed tensions and difficulties between women and between children.

All of this could be avoided by proper resourcing, by proper recognition of the problem, and by the political will to do something about it. At the moment, policy and practice changes are taking place in some agencies, such as the police and various local authorities, to improve responses to women and their children who suffer abuse. However, without the provision of sufficient, good-standard refuge accommodation and linked support services, these changes will run aground. To be effective, all civil and criminal legal action depends on adequate service provision. The lack of systematic national funding for refuges will remain a severe problem until the new recommendations are implemented.

At the moment, all refuges have many times more women wanting to move in than they can accommodate. London Women's Aid, which co-ordinates referrals to the London refuges, noted in their 1990 Annual Report that, while they received over 5,000 phone calls from women seeking refuge (or from agencies working on their behalf), they were able to find space for only 40 per cent of that number. And also in London, the *Taking Stock* report on refuges estimated in 1989 that the level of refuge provision within the capital should be increased sixfold to meet the need. In 1992 a refuge group in the south-west was able to house temporarily only 142 of the 490 women, most with dependent children, who were referred to them in desperate need of emergency accommodation due to domestic violence. In another local authority with a population of over a million people, there are currently just 19 refuge spaces. Despite some improvements, in a male-dominated world the traumas experienced by women and children fleeing male violence still have very low priority.

3
Why does it happen? Attitudes and explanations

Attitudes towards domestic violence and explanations as to why it happens are critical in deciding what kind of support women will get from family, friends and neighbours, and from state and voluntary agencies. This chapter will look at explanations of domestic violence and how they relate to the way in which different agencies approach it.

Traditional attitudes

In the past, the overriding attitude to domestic violence was the belief that it is a private affair between husband and wife, and that nobody should interfere unless it is happening constantly and causing serious and visible injury to the woman or, more importantly, injury to the children. This attitude went along with reactions which tended to excuse the violence and blame the woman. Traditionally, if people were concerned at all about the man's violent behaviour, they would often put it down to drink. This was the most common explanation favoured by professionals in a study called *Marital Violence* by Margaret Borkowski, Mervyn Murch and Val Walker in the early 1980s. Yet the Scottish study by the Dobashes for their book *Violence Against Wives* had found that alcohol was a factor in only 25 per cent of the relationships studied, and was important only in a very few cases. However, putting it down to drink meant that there was no need to ask any further questions about why the violence happened. People might then ask, 'Why doesn't she leave?' or 'Why does she put up with it?', or else they would wonder what it was she should have done to avoid it.

Often the explanations that the man gave for his violence would be accepted. He might say he was jealous because he thought the woman was paying attention to other men, so the woman might be advised that she should make sure that she did not give him any cause for this. His other 'reasons' could include: 'She spent too much time outside the home, with her family or her friends.' 'She was a bad housekeeper.' 'She spent too much of my money.' 'She was too independent.' 'She answered back.' 'She nagged me.' 'She wouldn't have sex with me.' 'She did not control the children properly.' Professionals might add that she tried to be too 'controlling' or, the complete opposite, that she was too timid and invited aggression because of her passivity. Since women often feel that the violence is their fault, such attitudes intensified the guilt that they already experienced.

A group of women writing an account of their own experiences as survivors of domestic violence, *Breaking Through*, list a number of these explanations and comment: 'Explanations that blame the woman go on and on. Sometimes they are the excuses given by the man for his behaviour, sometimes they are explanations given by perfectly "well meaning" people – doctors, social workers, friends, family.' They see these explanations as part of what women are up against when they are trying to survive domestic violence or to escape it. They also point out that this often comes on top of women blaming themselves for the violence anyway. So we need to look at why it is that domestic violence has traditionally been either taken for granted or blamed on women.

One of the most important reasons is that, as we saw in Chapter 1, men were historically given the right in law to discipline their wives, children and servants. So physical punishment of a wife was acceptable provided that it was not 'excessive'. In their book *Women and the Law*, Susan Atkins and Brenda Hoggett, who are both lawyers, give a brief history of what they call 'the breadwinner's legal authority', which makes it clear that these attitudes persisted in the courts into the 1980s.

Violent men *still* believe in their right to control their wives and partners, and so probably do many men who are not themselves violent. The most recent survey carried out in Islington in 1992 by researchers from Middlesex University reported that only 37 per cent of men did not see violence against their partners as an option, and 19 per cent of men admitted that they had struck their partners. Men are also traditionally 'excused' for violence including murder if they are 'provoked', one of the most common reasons for 'understandable' violence being that they know, or suspect, that their wives or partners are unfaithful. This tradition remains very strong both in the courts and among men themselves. In the Islington survey, 50 per cent of those men who admitted physically attacking their wife or partner gave infidelity as the reason. Women in the Dobashes' Scottish study, on the other hand, described the major occasions of violence as arising from unreasonable possessiveness or anger because household tasks were not performed to the man's liking.

Explanations of domestic violence in terms of the privacy of the home and the right of a man to be in control of his household, providing he does not go too far, often lie behind the more formal and theoretical accounts which sometimes concentrate on attempting to explain 'excessive' violence. Such accounts may also look to individual deviancy and pathology in men, and to women's behaviour, as reasons why men lose control.

In the recent past, traditionalist explanations like those mentioned above tended to hold sway, not least in the courts and in the police force. There are, however, a number of alternative types of explanation, some of which overlap and which emphasize different key ways of analysing or describing violence against women by their partners.

Individual pathological models of explanation

This kind of explanation is based on the idea that the individual using violence suffers from a pathological condition which leads to deviance from a non-violent norm. In practice it might only be quite extreme forms of violence or repeated violence that would be included in this kind of diagnosis. A certain kind of 'low-level' aggression might be seen as 'normal' at least in some families. Pathological deviance, however, might be thought to be based on either psychiatric illness or faults of temperament of one or both partners. Often it has been regarded as a sign of inadequacy, of an inarticulate person who had not learned to assert himself in non-violent ways.

When violence within families began to be perceived as a major problem in the early 1970s, it was in the context of medical evidence of the physical abuse of children in the United States. Initial explanations of violence within families at that time arose from concern about child abuse and focused on 'abusive families'. Women, as mothers, were viewed as colluding in the abuse of their children and also colluding in, or provoking, violence against themselves. The early research into 'family violence' in the United States in particular, where most of the large-scale studies have been carried out, was often based on this kind of assumption.

Such ideas are still current in psychiatry and psychology. They also persist in certain kinds of therapeutic social work, most notably in family therapy, where individualistic explanations shade over into theories of group pathology in which those who experience the violence are themselves often seen as helping to cause it. Certain kinds of psychotherapy too involve the idea that violence arises from 'issues' which the individuals concerned have not 'worked through' in their relationship. In recent years, some researchers with such views have been moving towards other types of explanation as they have asked more sophisticated questions.

Cycles of violence

The 'cycle of violence' theory suggests that there is a direct transmission of violence down the generations by learned behaviour, creating a cycle in which the violence continuously reproduces itself. This theory has a variant in which it is argued that the behaviour is learned by children who either witness or experience violence within an individual family. There is also a 'sub-cultural model' in which the use of violence is learned as part of a wider way of life, either in neighbourhoods in criminal sub-cultures or gangs, or in certain professions such as the police and the army.

There is certainly some evidence that violence can be learned, but these theories cannot explain why some individuals who observe such behaviour or live in such environments are not violent, or why some people are violent who do not live in this kind of family or social setting. Nor can they explain why, according to a rather indiscriminate lumping together of different kinds of learned behaviour, it ends up that boys both observing and experiencing violence should, according to the theory, become perpetrators of violence whereas girls apparently learn to choose violent partners and 'enjoy', or passively put up with, violent assault.

The theory rests ultimately on assumptions about the natural aggressiveness of boys and men, and the passivity of girls and women. This kind of explanation also loses force if violence, and violence against women in particular, is both very common and often accepted in the whole society, as suggested by Elisabeth Wilson in *What's to be Done about Violence Against Women?*:

> If you are one of only 500 [abused] women in a population of 50 million then you have certainly been more than unlucky and there may perhaps be something very peculiar about your husband, or unusual about your circumstances, or about you; on the other hand, if you are one of 500,000 women then that suggests something very different – that there is something wrong not with a few individual men, or women, or marriages, but with the *situation* in which *many* women and children regularly get assaulted – that situation being home and the family.

Yet, as we will see in later chapters, the cycle of violence is still a very popular kind of explanation. One possible reason for its popularity is that it seems to suggest that those men who attack their wives or partners, and those women who experience violence, are not 'people like us' – but rather belong to a special deviant group of 'violent families', who are completely different from the rest of us. Even if the violence happens more often than we would like to think and is much worse than we ever imagined, it has been explained. And, using the theory, it can be dealt with, perhaps by removing children from the violent family or violent sub-culture – and thus 'breaking the cycle'.

As to the adults, it might be too late to change the ingrained pattern. Perhaps all you can do is to recognize that, or perhaps you can help the women and children to get away. Perhaps you prosecute the man, or break the cycle by re-educating the parents or the perpetrator (in more optimistic variants of the theory which think it is actually possible to change what happens). Ultimately, though, if you believe that this is why domestic violence takes place, all you can probably hope to do is to minimize the transmission of violence, because it is all a result of some unexplainable situation in the violent past. It is not about the present situation of many families, as Elisabeth Wilson suggests. Some people are 'just like that', even if there are a large number of them.

Biological explanations

Biological explanations offer a set of causal theories about domestic violence which are based on sciences such as biochemistry or genetics, and which are regarded as scientific, although there appears to be no systematic research to establish whether they are firmly based as they apply to men's violence against their partners.

Medico-biological explanations often incorporate notions of addiction to violence. This can take a conventional psychiatric form, which rests on a description of symptomatic 'types' of personality. An example of this was that developed by Jasper Gayford in 1975 from interviews with a small number of women in Chiswick refuge (see Chapter 1). Other explanations of addiction rest on ideas of chemical imbalances of adrenalin or cortisone, for example, or other hormonal disturbances. These usually involve the application to domestic violence of medical research on the relationship between chemical substances and aggression, mood changes, deviant behaviour and mental illness. They are often based on interviews with very small samples, of women rather than men, and not necessarily carried out by trained scientific observers.

Socio-biological explanations are rather different. They have much in common with the traditional viewpoints described at the beginning of the chapter. The supremacy of men over women is seen as a social necessity dating from the evolutionary past. In this view, there is an evolutionary need for men to be dominant, and modern society ignores this at its peril. These sorts of explanation often base themselves on comparisons with selected non-human species, particularly the primate apes, but ignore research on other species or anthropological studies of hunter-gatherer societies which often do not confirm their views. For example, works like those of Desmond Morris in *Naked Apes* and of the aptly named Lionel Tiger and Robin Fox propose that modern man is a frustrated version of 'man the hunter', blocked by modern social organization and egalitarian ideas of relations between the sexes from a productive evolutionary path. This school of thought is called 'the Tarzanists' by Elaine Morgan in her book *The Descent of Woman*, which puts forward an alternative evolutionary model.

In the view of the socio-biologist, dominance by 'man' and submission by 'woman' is good for all our futures. Fortunately, there is little evidence that these ideas hold sway in any of the agencies called in to help women experiencing domestic violence, at the official level at least, though they can give comfort to violent men and those who would support men's claim to dominance in the family.

Social-structural explanations

This is another kind of explanation of 'family violence'. It bases itself on the stress caused by lack of access to money, housing and education common to both men and women in the family. This view was expressed very succinctly in a discussion document drawn up by the British Association of Social Workers in 1975:

> Economic conditions, low wages, bad housing, and isolation; unfavourable and frustrating work conditions for the man; lack of job opportunities for adolescent school leavers, and lack of facilities such as day care (e.g. nurseries), adequate transport, pleasant environment and play space and recreational facilities, for mother and children were considered to cause personal desperation that might cause violence in the home.

This kind of explanation usually assumes that violence occurs mainly in working-class and poor families. There is a 'middle-class' version in terms of financial pressures and stressful careers, but more commonly in this view the greater resources of middle-class families or, in some cases, the ability of middle-class men to maintain dominance without resorting to violence are thought to explain what is believed to be the relative lack of violence in these families.

However, as Michael Freeman and others point out, it is likely that violence in middle-class families can more easily remain hidden from neighbours and public agencies like the police and social services. Borkowski, Murch and Walker found in their study *Marital Violence* that the more significant class differential was not in whether violence occurred but in the kind of agencies consulted, the middle class being more likely to use lawyers and the divorce courts than the police, social services or women's refuges. Although it seems very likely that the pressures of poverty might increase the occurrence of violence or make it worse, this type of analysis fails adequately to account for the predominant direction of serious violence from men towards women or the fact that it occurs in all social classes.

Academic researchers

Academic researchers sometimes develop a unifying theory to explain violence in general, and 'family violence' or domestic violence in particular. However, social scientists, at least those who do research into domestic violence using surveys, have tended in the past to explain domestic violence as resulting from a combination of many factors, none of which is necessarily any more important than the others. This is the case, for example, in the study quoted above by Borkowski, Murch and Walker. Others may highlight certain factors, but in the end they rest their explanation on a general characterization of the entire society. In this way, for example, Murray Straus and his co-workers have often referred to family violence, and with it violence by men against their partners, as a consequence of the violent character of the whole society in the United States. There may be some truth in this view, but it still shifts the focus away from the fact that so much of this violence rests on the power of men over women in the family (which Straus and his colleagues also acknowledge to some extent).

Such studies can nevertheless be very useful because they are often based on extensive investigations and have access to funding that it can be difficult for less established researchers to obtain. They can provide factual information from which it is possible for others to develop explanations which may be different from those adopted by the researchers themselves. Sometimes such research just adds up all the possible explanations or avoids explanation altogether. In some cases, however, this 'adding up' of potential explanations is a genuine attempt to take into account the complexity of human motivation, without avoiding the problem of identifying the more important causal factors. In quite significant cases these academic studies have moved closer to feminist explanations as they have considered more fully the nature of the evidence.

Moralist explanations: the breakdown of the family

Violence in the family can be explained in terms of a number of different historical perspectives. One, based on the historical disabilities of women before the law, has already been mentioned. It is an important component of feminist explanations of domestic violence and will be discussed again briefly below. But there is another explanation based on an argument from history which has been very influential in government circles by way of the writings of Ferdinand Mount, Norman Stone, Roger Scruton and others. It is based on the idea of a current crisis in the family caused by a decline in morality and family values in this century and, more particularly, since World War II.

This kind of explanation fails to account for evidence of widespread cohabitation outside of marriage, and of widespread violence towards wives and female partners, in the 'golden past', notably in the Victorian era. Legislation giving women greater civil rights was passed in the second half of the nineteenth century because women at that time, though lacking the parliamentary vote, were able to convince Parliament that some husbands were abusing their powers to control the property and income of their wives, and were often violent towards them. It was for these reasons that the first legal separation was allowed to women in the Matrimonial Causes Amendment Act 1878, if their husbands were convicted of aggravated assault against them; and the Married Women's Property Acts were passed to allow women control over their property and their earnings after marriage. Previously the husband had a right to control his wife's property and earnings even if they were legally separated.

As in other cases, moralist explanations can overlap to some extent, depending on differences of emphasis. So there are traditional, democratic and radical models to explain family violence based on moral failings and the breakdown of the family. Some rest on the failure of the 'nuclear' family consisting of the couple and their children, and see the traditional extended form of family as superior. Others would argue that the nuclear family is potentially better. What they all tend to have in common is the notion of an ideal family form to which we should all aspire. Often this is thought to have existed in the past and to have been capable of satisfying the needs of all family members without conflict.

The emphasis, then, is on the family grouping, on the inter-relationships and bonds that hold it together, and on harmonious divisions of responsibility (or 'roles') along gender and age lines within it. Ideally, the family is thought of as a symbiotic whole in which each member functions for the good of the others and on behalf of the 'good society'. But it is important to remember that what some see as both natural and right, or as mere differences in the functional 'roles' of people within the family, others see as inequalities of power. In addition, these ideas about family forms refer only to western societies and to white family forms. They have little to say about the variety of ways in which relationships between people are organized in different societies, cultural contexts and ethnic communities.

Feminist explanations

Feminist explanations of domestic violence, like those of the socio-biologists, focus on the central importance of male dominance, but they see that as precisely the problem to be overcome, rather than as an ideal to be restored. In the feminist view, domestic violence arises out of men's power over women in the family. This male power has been built into family life historically, through laws which assume that men have the right to authority over both women and children within families, where this does not conflict with public policy and the interests of the state. Rebecca and Russell Dobash in *Violence Against Wives*, for example, describe the inferior historical position of women in British and North American society and in marriage, which arose from laws and customs which excluded women from public life and placed them under the authority of their husband or their father within the private sphere of the family.

As Susan Schechter has pointed out in *Women and Male Violence*, this does not necessarily mean that feminists are 'dismissing psychology or ignoring violent individuals'. Rather:

> They are stressing the need for a psychology that analyses wife beating in its proper contexts, accounts for power differentials, and asks why women have been brutalized. Rather than label battering as pathology or a family systems failure, it is more conceptually accurate to assume that violence against women, like that directed towards children, is behaviour approved of and sanctioned in many parts of the culture. Extreme cases in which women are mutilated by psychotic men are only one end of a continuum of violent behaviour the more moderate forms of which are viewed as normal. Many in this culture approve of hitting women.

Many feminists would use the kind of explanation which stresses the need to examine the historical position of women in particular societies and the way in which it was, and still is, embodied in law and custom. However, some forms of feminist explanation, basing themselves on the male-dominated nature of most known forms of society, come close to arguing that inherent biological differences between men and women are at the core of male violence and female non-violence. Others argue that there can be no such definite, undifferentiated categories as 'men' and 'women', but that we live among conflicting or intersecting sets of inequalities and differences in power.

Most feminist accounts draw attention to the economic position of women. They point to the way in which the responsibility that society assigns to women for looking after children often places them in a position of enforced financial dependency on their partners or ex-partners, a situation which will be reinforced in Britain by the new Child Support Act. It is also used as an excuse for paying women low wages or minimal state income support. Some feminists would also want to argue that class and racial oppression, and social stresses such as unemployment, bad housing and poverty, are likely to increase violence and make it harder to escape. Yet they would point out that this does not explain why it is that it is predominantly men who become violent in these circumstances, or why so much of the violence is directed towards women whom the men would profess to love.

Black feminists in particular (such as Amina Mama in *The Hidden Struggle,* and Parita Trivedi in 'Many voices, one chant') emphasize the need to develop perspectives that take into account the specific histories of different communities, particularly black communities. They point especially to differences that the experience of racism and colonialization make to the situation of black people, both women and men, in Britain, to say nothing of recognizing the need for analyses that are sensitive to racism worldwide. In criticizing writers who talk of a 'public'/'private' divide, authors like Amina Mama show that under slavery, and in colonial regimes, state agencies have shown themselves far from reluctant to intervene very directly to regulate or destroy the personal lives of black families. They would argue that this remains true in Britain today, while black women are still not protected from domestic violence. This analysis suggests that the problem is not so much one of overcoming a general reluctance to intervene in family life, as one of ensuring that what agencies do is sensitive to the needs of the women concerned and is not based on repressive models of control.

Despite differences, however, what unites all forms of feminist explanation is the belief that domestic violence arises from the power and control that men exercise over women, and from the unequal position of women in society. All feminists argue that there is a need to develop strategies to enable women to challenge that abuse of power, and the power itself, both individually and collectively. Part of this strategy rests on challenging the views of state agencies and their reluctance to provide appropriate backing for women experiencing domestic violence.

Agency responses

Traditionally, it has been difficult for women to get help from state and other agencies when facing domestic violence. There are a number of reasons for this and many of them arise from traditional assumptions about women's place in society and the home, and the continuing inequality of women before the law. One important influence is the fact that the violence takes place in the home, a private domain, and one in which men are still seen as the 'breadwinners' and heads of household. This feeds the view that women are people with lesser rights in general within society.

In the case of the police and the courts, these influences can be related to observable differences in attitude to offences and offenders across a number of dimensions, which can be useful as an index for testing the reactions of society, and of other social agencies. Reactions are affected by who the aggressor or offender is and who the 'victim' is; by where the offence takes place; and by the degree of violence or the seriousness of the damage or loss. All these are independent variables, which can intersect in various ways. So, for example, violence against someone who is of a higher social status, or violence in a public place, is likely to be treated more seriously. In contrast, violence by a person of higher social status, in a private place, especially his own home, against a social inferior or someone over whom he has authority – for example, his children or his wife – has often been taken less seriously. The attitude of state agencies, therefore, may relate back to the fact that traditionally the husband/father had the right and obligation to discipline, within reason, those under his control, and that such matters were not normally the concern of the public authorities.

In this kind of view, the role of the wife and mother was to care for her husband and their children, under his general authority, so that the family thrived as a healthy part of the social organism. She, therefore, essentially lived for and through other people and gained her fulfilment through their happiness. Since it was assumed that this was the normal and natural state of affairs, the focus, as we have pointed out previously, was often on the woman's failures if things went wrong.

In the last few years – because of the work of women's groups, of Women's Aid refuges and the national Women's Aid federations, and of feminist researchers and writers – many professionals, including those in state agencies and even government bodies, have come to accept, to some degree at least, the argument that domestic violence is an abuse of the power of men over women in the family. Of course, this still means that the focus is on the abuse. Only feminists, including some who work in state agencies, are seriously questioning the legitimacy of the power relationship itself. The following chapters will look at the ways in which the responses of statutory and other agencies to domestic violence have been changing, beginning with the police and the legal system.

4

Policing domestic violence: crime prevention and the public/private divide

In theory, assault is a crime wherever it happens and whoever does it. There should be no difference whether it is committed in the home or outside, by a husband or by a stranger. In practice, it has made a great deal of difference. The law and the police have been of little help to women who are attacked by their husbands or partners – or by former husbands or partners – especially within their own homes.

Most crime prevention advice to women highlights the danger from strangers in public places. Yet despite the very real and frightening vulnerability of women to attacks in public, especially at night, it is men, especially young men, who are most in danger in the street from other men. Women are most at danger in their own homes from the men who are closest to them. However, only slowly and uncertainly is domestic violence being recognized and incorporated into strategies to protect women.

The police and hospital casualty departments are the only agencies available 24 hours a day, and the police alone have the responsibility to keep the peace and to prevent crime. Although police have traditionally played down the seriousness of domestic violence, many women have continued to ask them for help in an emergency. On the other hand, the evidence reviewed by Lorna Smith in her Home Office study, published in 1989, suggests that calling the police is often seen as a last resort after repeated violent attacks.

The most recent large-scale survey, conducted in Islington in 1992 by researchers from Middlesex University, shows that, while one in ten of the women in the survey had experienced an attack from her partner in the past year, only 22 per cent of these had contacted the police at some time for help. In general, women had only ever reported 28 per cent of the assaults they had experienced. The survey confirms earlier research showing that domestic violence is very common, but that much goes unreported. These results are of particular importance because Islington is one of the areas that has pioneered a new approach to policing domestic violence in Britain since the mid-1980s, setting up a domestic violence unit, and more recently a civilian Domestic Violence Intervention Team with special funding from the Home Office. The survey discovered that many women were not aware of these developments.

Police attitudes and the need for change

From the early 1970s women began to highlight the problem of sexual and physical attacks both in the street and in the home, and the failure of the police to help them when they reported these assaults. Women coming to refuges would often describe how the police were reluctant to protect them, or to help them get clothes and other belongings from the house if they had been forced to leave. Women's Aid activists have for many years, therefore, been involved in attempts to change police practice, to develop a more sympathetic and helpful attitude among police when called to incidents of domestic violence. One aspect of this has been the attempt to have domestic violence, as well as other forms of violence against women, taken seriously as 'real crime', 'real violence'.

Individual police officers have sometimes been helpful, and some refuges have developed good relationships with the local police, but at first the attempts to change police responses to domestic violence appeared to have little impact on general police practice or public policy, although the concerns about police responses spread far beyond the feminist movement. First the Select Committee on Violence in Marriage in 1975, and later the Women's National Commission in 1985, broadly endorsed the viewpoint of grass-roots women's campaigns. It was also backed up by research in the 1970s and early 1980s, such as that of Jan Pahl and Susan Edwards in London and various locations in the south of England, of Jalna Hanmer and Sheila Saunders in West Yorkshire, and Rebecca and Russell Dobash and Fran Wasoff in Scotland.

This concern about the policing of crimes of violence against women was first acted on at governmental level, mainly in relation to rape and attacks against women in public, especially following the horrifying murders of women in Leeds by Peter Sutcliffe. The fact that murder statistics showed that many women were murdered by their husbands in their own homes did not have the same impact.

At about the same time, questions of policing in general also became a focus of attention in some local authority areas. In the early 1980s there was a series of local government initiatives examining police practice from the Greater London Council and some other councils, mainly in London. These involved Women's Units, Civil Rights Committees, and Police and Community Safety Units, which began monitoring police activities because of a concern about bad police–community relations, oppressive policing and poor service to black people and women. The work of organizations like the Police Monitoring Research Group, set up by the Greater London Council, and of Camden Council's Women's and Civil Rights Units also fed into a growing concern in some police forces and the Home Office itself about public criticism of police practices, and of their failure to deal adequately and fairly with women and with black and minority ethnic communities.

The need for changes in police practice on domestic violence was accepted in Parliament in November 1986 by the under-secretary of state at the Home Office, following a circular from the Home Office in 1986, and the report of a Metropolitan Police Working Party in the same year. Although their report was never published in full, the Metropolitan Police in 1987 issued new Force Orders on procedures to be followed by its officers in cases of domestic violence. Finally, there was a substantial Home Office circular in 1990 which was issued to give guidance to chief officers of police throughout Britain. Details of these moves and their results are given later in this chapter.

There is much to be changed. Women calling the police for help have often found them unsympathetic and unhelpful. There is considerable evidence that serious assaults have been treated as minor or even disregarded altogether. Independent research studies into police practice carried out by Susan Edwards, Alan Bourlet and Ian Blair in the early 1980s suggested that this was systematic practice which amounted to policy in the areas studied. Local studies like that by Jill Radford in Wandsworth, others in Manchester and Camden, the Islington crime survey in 1986 and many small-scale surveys of women in refuges confirmed both the prevalence of violence against women and the lack of an adequate response if it was reported.

Police officers have generally felt that domestic disputes are private matters and have been uneasy when dealing with them. In the research on police practice, male police officers, who make up the vast majority, expressed their strong dislike of dealing with 'domestics'. These offences have been widely regarded in the past as not 'real' crime or proper police work by both beat officers and their superiors up to chief officer level. For example, it is reported by the London Strategic Policy Unit's Police Monitoring and Research Group that Commissioner Newman of the Metropolitan Police suggested in 1983 that domestic disputes should be hived off to social services.

Until recently, domestic violence has been invisible in crime statistics. Often no record has been kept of requests for help. Even where an assault has been recorded, it might have been simply entered in the incident book as a minor assault even if it was more serious; or, if recorded as a criminal offence initially, it was often not proceeded with and 'no crimed' (i.e. not entered in returns for inclusion in the official Home Office crime statistics). Many police officers called to intervene would see the attack as largely the woman's fault. Often they accepted the husband's version of events or made their own moral judgements about the woman. Sometimes, if the man was a heavy drinker, the woman would be blamed for not having left him before, or else the alcohol seen as an excuse for the violence and the woman told that it 'would be all right when he was sober'. Women's Aid refuge workers have often been told that 'women have only themselves to blame' because they are bad housewives or have provoked the man in some way.

Typically, police have not intervened to arrest the man and protect the woman. Even when faced with clear evidence that a crime has been committed, they have seen it as their job to mediate, to calm things down as far as possible and then leave, without taking any steps to ensure the safety of the woman. At best, they might give the man a 'talking to' or take him to the end of the road to cool down, and perhaps advise the woman to take out an injunction or a private prosecution for assault, even when the attack had caused her injury.

Studies of police records have shown that this minimizing of domestic violence happened even where women were visibly injured. Assaults which resulted in broken skin, cuts and bruises, which should be classified as causing actual bodily harm (ABH), or those causing

even more serious injuries (GBH) might be described as common assault and the woman told that she herself would have to prosecute in the magistrate's court or apply for other civil remedies such as an injunction or exclusion order to protect herself. Although in fact they had the same powers under the Offences Against the Persons Act 1861 in domestic violence as in any other assault, the police would often say that they had no power to arrest the man unless there was a civil injunction in force with a power of arrest, and even then they were often unlikely to act. In some cases they maintained that they could not arrest him unless they themselves had witnessed the offence. Even where the attack was so serious that the man was arrested, normally either no charge was laid or it would be withdrawn, usually on the grounds that the woman did not want to proceed. Since in so many cases no crime report was ever filled out, repeated serious offences would not necessarily leave any trace in the records.

Where police have been called to deal with an attack on a woman in her own home, she has often found that it is treated as her husband's home only. Where the man has smashed up the house and furniture, it has often been seen as no crime because it was his house and his furniture. Moreover, women in refuges give accounts of being assaulted in public places by their husbands or partners, and the assault still being treated as a private matter. In *The Boys in Blue*, a book discussing policing in the 1980s from the point of view of women, an example is given of a woman whose husband attacked her in a public car park, attempting to strangle her. She was picked up by a passing police car which took her home. Although the police called a doctor to attend to her injuries, they took no action against her husband. Police are much more willing to press charges if they themselves have been insulted or attacked, or if the man is 'known' to the police or suspected of other criminal activity.

Black women in particular have faced the problem that police either might not act or else might overreact, because of their racist perceptions of black people. In some circumstances, following the 1983 Immigration Act, calling the police has resulted in the deportation of women or their husbands if they were immigrants. Black women in Camden and Islington responding to surveys in the 1980s said that they were especially reluctant to contact the police for these reasons. Amina Mama in *The Hidden Struggle* gives accounts of women who were themselves assaulted by the police or threatened with arrest when police were called to the scene of domestic violence.

In general, criticism of police practice on domestic violence has centred mainly on failure to act: failure to log calls for assistance; failure to respond quickly; failure to take the assault seriously; failure to arrest or charge the attacker, or even to remove him from the home; failure to consider prosecution, or to record the assault as a crime; or a subsequent downgrading of an attack to 'no crime' even following charges, if a prosecution was not being proceeded with. Police also failed to give women advice and support in the majority of cases where they were not going to press charges, and showed little knowledge of what support was available in the community. They were rarely able to refer women to a Women's Aid refuge or to give her advice about her right to apply for emergency housing from the local authority. Nor did they usually have an accurate idea of the nature and scope of the protection orders available in civil courts. If there was an injunction with powers of arrest in force, they would often not act on it. Occasionally, however, they might remove the man from the house or offer to take the woman and children to a refuge or another safe place. Often no separate interviews would be carried out with the woman and her attacker to try to discover what had happened. Moreover, it was rare for a woman to be interviewed by a woman officer – and because there are still so few women in police forces, currently somewhere between 10 and 13 per cent, this is still likely to be the case.

Police reluctance to prosecute has been justified by the unreliability of women and their tendency to withdraw charges or to refuse to act as witnesses. The studies of police practice show that the police have often given women no support in reaching a decision in the first place and that women have been given little help in proceeding when they were willing for the police to prosecute. Where the woman has wanted to press charges, the police have sometimes themselves suggested that she should not proceed, or have not charged the man immediately in order to allow a 'cooling off' period – which is a time of great uncertainty and danger for the woman. If the man has been arrested and charged, they have rarely tried to get bail conditions to prevent him returning to the house and intimidating her.

Little recognition has been given to the fact that, except in the most serious cases, or where they leave their homes, women will often have to go on living with their attacker while waiting for the case to come to court, during the proceedings and even afterwards if he is not given a custodial sentence. In *Breaking Through*, written by women experiencing violence, the writers wonder whether policemen have ever had to share a house with someone they are in the process of prosecuting for assault!

Many of the studies document a lack of sympathy or backing for women, lack of understanding of a woman's frequently justified fears of making the violence worse by taking action or of her concern at the effects of prosecution. In many cases women may want the attacks to stop and the attacker to be removed, temporarily or permanently, but they may not wish to send him to gaol, perhaps because they love him or because they and their children might then face the public stigma of having him declared a criminal. Even where this is not the case, there seems to be little understanding by police officers that the man's imprisonment or even the imposition of a fine means that the whole family might suffer financial hardship, especially where there are children and the woman is financially dependent on her partner.

One of the barriers to change in police practice is the traditionalist masculine culture of the police. As an overwhelmingly male organization, they have developed what has been described by the Policy Studies Institute as 'an occupational culture of their own'. This culture has not often been welcoming to women, as recent surveys showing the prevalence of sexual harassment and sexual assault against women police officers have demonstrated. The existence of such attitudes, both now and in the past, has increased the possibility that police officers would side with the man more easily and believe his story. However, this tendency to excuse the man did not always occur when he was black, or not someone the police officer could have a fellow feeling for.

As we have seen, the belief that it is sometimes reasonable or excusable for a man to discipline his wife, or to use violence when provoked, is not confined to the police. The approach of the police reflects many conventional social attitudes which will not be easily changed, but need a careful response at a variety of levels.

Recommendations and guidelines for improved practice

By the mid-1980s, as a result of women speaking about their negative experiences of police responses, because of the activities of Women's Aid and other organizations and the development of research and monitoring of police practice, the need for change was becoming clear. A number of detailed recommendations were developed, such as those listed in the comprehensive report of the London Strategic Policy Unit's Police Monitoring and Research Group in 1986. The group had worked with Women's Aid and refuge groups and the London Women and Policing Network in drawing up their proposals. At about the same time, similar proposals were put forward by the Women's National Commission, which appear to have had considerable influence on government thinking.

The recommendations of the LSPU included the ending of discrimination in police recruitment to ensure that women officers would be available in cases involving domestic violence. They also pointed out the necessity for women interpreters speaking appropriate community languages, and wholly independent of the police, to be available for women needing or requesting such a service. In dealing with incidents of domestic violence, the LSPU report recommended 'positive intervention, instead of inaction and/or conciliation, both of which may have dangerous consequences'. There were a number of detailed recommendations to ensure that all incidents would be recorded in a retrievable form, that crime reports would be completed for all criminal offences and that attacks would be correctly identified rather than recorded as common assault. It was also recommended that reports should record gender and 'specify the relationship between victim and assailant'. Where charges were not pursued, the offence should be included in the statistics as 'detected, not proceeded with' and should not be 'no crimed'.

The LSPU report recommended that there should be an immediate response to a woman's urgent call, and repeated calls should be treated with equal urgency. Officers should interview the woman separately, tell her about Women's Aid and other local agencies (without telling the man), and give her accurate information about her legal position. Recommendations were also made that the police should provide the woman, if required, with transport to a place of safety such as a Women's Aid refuge after making suitable arrangements. They should also be prepared to accompany her back to the house if necessary – for example, to collect belongings.

Importantly, the report recommended that the police should be prepared to arrest and charge the man with an appropriately serious offence, rather than minimizing the assault. They should consider taking preventive action using other powers of arrest for breach of the peace or under the Police and Criminal Evidence Act 1984 (which came into effect in January 1986). The LSPU also recommended that police should not discourage a woman from pressing charges or allow a lengthy 'cooling off' period between arrest and charge. They should recognize that she may be afraid to proceed and be prepared to prosecute without her testimony, if necessary, but not against her wishes. Where appropriate, bail conditions should be imposed and enforced in order to protect the woman, and police should also be aware of the intimidating effect of harassment such as pestering letters and phone calls.

Where there is an injunction with powers of arrest, the report recommended that the police should arrest the man on the woman's statement when there is a breach, not only if they themselves witness it. Injunctions should be kept on file and easily accessible, and officers should be co-operative in servicing them. Records of reported incidents of breach of injunctions should be made available for civil court proceedings, and officers should be prepared to attend court to give evidence.

It was also recommended that full training should be made available not only to probationers but to officers in service, and also to judges and magistrates. As well as involving training in how to take the appropriate action and to give correct legal advice, this should include training in awareness about racism and sexism, in the effects their own attitudes may have, and in the pressures created by other legislation, such as immigration laws.

As a result of these and similar recommendations, a start was made after the mid-1980s in developing better police practice, first by individual action in a few police forces – Bedfordshire, West Yorkshire and Tottenham in London being notable examples. This was followed by influential policy directives from the Home Office in 1986 and the Metropolitan Police in 1987. These recommendations were picked up and strengthened in the advice given to chief officers of police forces by the Home Office in 1990 (see below).

As we have seen, a major problem has been police reluctance to act against domestic violence using their powers under the Offences Against the Person Act 1861. In 1986 they were reminded of these powers by the Home Office and advised also to make use of their powers to make an arrest under the Police and Criminal Evidence Act 1984, where there was a reasonable suspicion that a crime of domestic violence was about to be committed. They were additionally reminded that a woman could (once more) be compelled under that law to give evidence against her husband in criminal trials involving his violence against her. As Lorna Smith points out, this restored the position that had existed before the House of Lords judgment in the case of *Hoskyn* v. *Metropolitan Police Commissioner* in 1978, although wives had remained compellable witnesses in such cases under common law. (The question of the use of compulsion in these cases remains a matter of debate and we will return to it later.)

The 1986 circular accepted a number of the recommendations contained in the Women's National Commission report of 1985, including a request to chief officers to review training, record-keeping arrangements and instructions to officers on arrest, on providing women with information and on liaising with local support groups, including Women's Aid. The circular rejected, on cost grounds, the recommendations of the Women's National Commission on the collection of data on domestic violence. There was some emphasis in the circular on the 'difficult and sensitive issues which may be raised for the family and for the police' in cases of domestic violence, and a reiteration of the idea that difficulties were caused for the police by the reluctance of women to provide evidence.

The circular was an important step forward because it stated clearly that 'there must be an overriding concern to ensure the safety of victims of domestic violence and to reduce the risk of further violence both to the spouse and to any children who may be present'. However, it did not appear to accept criticism of current police practice or regard change as a matter of policy. Rather the implementation of the recommendations was seen as 'an operational issue'. It was to be left to the discretion of chief officers to decide 'the extent to which the recommendations of the Women's National Commission may appropriately be implemented in their area'. The initiative was therefore passed back to chief officers and local police forces.

At this time, the Metropolitan Police already had the report of their Working Party, which had carried out a review of policy and practice on domestic violence between 1984 and 1986. This report examined international evidence, including a research report by Sherman and Berk on pro-arrest policies from Minneapolis in the United States and the experience of pro-arrest policies combined with multi-agency support services in Duluth, Minnesota, and in London, Ontario. The recommendations of the report became very well known because they were made public by Chris Smith MP in a House of Commons debate, although the report itself was never published in full. It apparently endorsed many of the criticisms that had been voiced by the Women's National Commission, by the various police monitoring reports, and by voluntary organizations including Women's Aid.

The report was followed up with a Strategy Statement and new Metropolitan Police Force Orders in 1987. As well as the changes in practice and recording procedures described earlier – for example, an emphasis on an active approach to arrest and prosecution where appropriate – there was a commitment to the introduction of training which would work on changing entrenched attitudes. There was also an emphasis on the fundamental principles which should be applied. The guiding instruction was that 'an assault which occurs in the home is as much a criminal act as one which may occur in the street'. The definition of violence was to be expanded to include 'threats or attempts to cause physical harm to another family or household member'. There was a call to respond more positively by giving 'enhanced support, care and concern to victims of crime, including the victims of domestic violence'. A beginning was made, too, in developing a multi-agency approach to providing support and information, with more effective liaison between police and supporting agencies. A number of police stations in the Metropolitan Police area and elsewhere developed specialized Domestic Violence Units, which were often staffed by women officers, on the model of those which had been set up earlier to improve the treatment of women reporting offences of rape and sexual assault.

These developments were further encouraged by the issuing in 1990 of new Home Office guidelines in Circular 60/90. This followed the publication of a comprehensive review of the literature on domestic violence by Lorna Smith, which gave serious consideration to the view that domestic violence had deep historical roots and was grounded in the inequality of power between men and women in marriage and in society at large. Her report reviewed the critical analyses by researchers of police attitudes and practice in Britain. It examined the North American literature on crisis intervention and the influential but disputed research into the impact of pro-arrest policies in Minneapolis.

The 1990 circular adopts a much wider perspective and a much less piecemeal approach than earlier circulars. It commends the adoption of explicit force policies on domestic violence, and approves the establishment 'where practicable and cost effective' of special units to deal with it. It also makes a clear statement of the approach to be taken and the expectation of a national response to the advice which it contains:

> The Home Secretary regards a violent assault, or brutal and threatening behaviour over a period of time by a person with whom the victim lives, as no less serious than an attack by a stranger. The Government's view has been made clear in Parliament and the purpose of this circular, which has been agreed with the Association of Chief Police Officers, is to offer guidance to the police on their response to the problems of domestic violence and to encourage the development and publicizing of force policy statements and strategies to deal with it.

The circular emphasizes the need for the police to ensure that they make a speedy and effective response to calls to incidents of domestic violence. It reminds officers that domestic violence is a crime and that it is their primary duty 'to protect the victim and any children from further abuse and then to consider what action should be taken against the offender'. The immediate protection could include 'referring or taking her to a shelter' as well as liaising with other statutory or voluntary agencies which can supply longer-term help and support. Agencies mentioned include 'doctors; health, social services and housing authorities; voluntary bodies such as victim support groups and refuges for battered women; and citizens advice bureaux, and legal advice centres'. Surprisingly, there is no explicit reference to Women's Aid as a key source of long-term support nor, interestingly, to referring women to local offices of the Department of Social Security, which could well be crucial to their ability to survive financially.

Chief officers are reminded of the interest of the Crown Prosecution Service and the courts in police policies on domestic violence, and they are advised to discuss evidential and other matters with their local Chief Crown Prosecutor before finalizing their policy, to ensure consistency of aims and approach. Chief officers are also urged to consider setting up Domestic Violence Units with specially trained officers 'where it is practicable and cost effective to do so', or at least to ensure that all officers have up-to-date knowledge of suitable referral points in other agencies. The circular then goes on to specify the central features that should be included in force policy statements: the overriding duty to protect victims and children; the need to treat domestic violence at least as seriously as other forms of violence; the use and value of powers of arrest. It also emphasizes the dangers of seeking conciliation between assailant and victim, and the importance of comprehensive record keeping to allow the effectiveness of the policy to be monitored.

The process of responding to an incident is spelt out in detail from first contact. The need to check records of previous incidents and any injunctions in force, and the importance of keeping these records, are stressed. There is a detailed description of possible action at the scene of the incident, reminding officers that physical signs of violence may not be initially obvious. There is also a reminder that it is desirable for a woman officer to be present, and that a woman should be interviewed separately and should never be asked in the presence of the assailant whether she would be prepared to give evidence against him. Removal of the woman and any children to a place of safety may be the immediate priority.

Regarding the assailant, there is a repetition of the need to consider using the power of arrest and detention, both because of the indication from experience in other countries of its possible deterrent effect and because of its importance as a means of showing the woman that 'she is entitled to, and will receive, society's protection and support'. There is a reminder of the importance of establishing whether there are witnesses, in view of the difficulties of bringing a prosecution in cases of domestic violence.

Further detailed advice is given on action after the incident, with a warning against making a decision not to initiate a prosecution because of a belief that the woman may not be prepared to give evidence in court. The advice is that the same factors should be considered as those relevant in attacks by strangers, and that women may gain in confidence with proper support and recognize that prosecution is in their own interests. There is also advice to consider the use of police bail if further inquiries are needed to make a decision about prosecution.

Detail is also given on the information needed by the Crown Prosecution Service, on the need for support and written information for the woman prior to trial, and on questions to be considered if she wishes to withdraw, including the possibility that she might be compelled to give evidence. There is also a reminder that action can be taken against the man if she is being intimidated into withdrawing. Where the man does receive a sentence, chief officers are advised that the woman should be informed of his release from custody. Finally, they are advised that all officers likely to be involved in incidents of domestic violence should receive training in their powers under the law and in understanding force policies and procedures, particularly as they involve working with other agencies.

Has police practice changed?

Writing in 1989, Susan Edwards stated that many police forces in England and Wales were currently reviewing their policies and procedures in dealing with domestic violence, but that policing priorities differed in each of the 43 police forces. Alan Bourlet found that only nine forces had any specific policy in his study published in the same year. Although no systematic study has been carried out of changes since the issuing of Home Office Circular 60/90, there is evidence that the impact has been uneven. It does seem, however, that there has been a gathering momentum in drawing up force policies and in providing information booklets for women seeking police help, with forces such as Nottinghamshire and Avon joining the pioneering areas such as West Yorkshire and London.

In a survey of refuges carried out by WAFE in 1992, to which 102 refuges responded, a series of questions were asked about the police response to domestic violence and liaison with Women's Aid. Seventy-five of the refuges said that they had regular contact with the police, of which 72 had a specific liaison or contact officer, and 42 were involved in police training (but only 11 received any payment for this). Sixty-seven refuges said that the policy of their police force on domestic violence had changed within the last five years. Fifty-nine said the response had actually changed practice on the ground. The main practical changes were that in 15 cases the police were said to be more sensitive or sympathetic and in 12 cases this included more follow-up work by the police and the involvement of Domestic Violence Units. In only 11 areas had the change resulted in quicker responses, giving domestic violence higher priority and/or the introduction of a pro-arrest policy. Five refuges commented that the top ranks of the police force were much better but that there was little actual improvement in police practice, while others said that the police now asked their advice, were much better at telling women about Women's Aid and carried information cards. Those refuges which said that the police were more sensitive also said that there was room for improvement and that attitudes within the local force were uneven. In only 35 cases had the police consulted Women's Aid groups on changing their local policy following the issuing of the 1990 circular.

Fifty-three of the refuges had been involved in liaison with the police through a multi-agency forum, and in 36 cases this was part of a regular process. There were a variety of other agencies involved, of which the most common were victim support, rape crisis and housing agencies, black women's organizations and other organizations from black and minority ethnic communities, citizens' advice bureaux and the Samaritans. (Inter-agency initiatives will be discussed further in Chapter 8.)

In the WAFE survey, 49 refuges said that there was a Domestic Violence Unit in their local area; but, reflecting the fact that women in refuges come from a variety of different areas, more than this number had experience of contact or consultation with a DVU. A majority had found the units helpful in improving the overall response to domestic violence; however, 13 had not found them helpful and the same number were uncertain.

These responses broadly confirm other experience that suggests a significant number of police forces have not set up a specific unit to deal with domestic violence, although more are being developed all the time. Some forces have more general Family Protection Units, and in others domestic violence work may be grouped with work on non-domestic rape and child sexual abuse. However, Women's Aid experience suggests that such units will tend to give priority to rape or child abuse rather than to the support of women experiencing domestic violence.

There are other problems that can arise. In some cases Domestic Violence Units appear to have seen their role as one of conciliation. This has had tragic results in the case of the murder of Vandana Patel by her husband during a meeting organized by a Domestic Violence Unit and held in its premises within the police station concerned. In other cases it is a matter of resources. Frequently, there are only one or two officers working in the unit, and because of the pressure of demand they are often out of the office. The telephone is then switched to an answerphone most of the time, so that officers are not available when needed. Given the evidence of women's hesitation to contact the police, or indeed any other agency, for help, this places important limitations on the effectiveness of the service they can offer.

Domestic Violence Units cannot be independent advice and advocacy services because they must be bound by the policing priorities of the force they belong to, and, as a result, they may face possible conflict with other areas of police work. They can still be seen as less central and less important by other police officers or units, and can come under pressure to do proper 'criminal' work even where this is not necessarily appropriate to the situation they are dealing with. However, where charges are laid they can also act as support for the woman through the prosecution process, explain the law and the court system, inform her what is happening in the investigation, and act as a reassuring presence in the hearing itself.

Officers in Domestic Violence Units can also act as a point of liaison with the community, with Women's Aid and with other services, and can develop a high level of expertise and effectiveness in the right circumstances. In other situations, they can be relatively isolated and their ideas may not necessarily feed through into the policy process or into general police practice. Nevertheless, they can act as a catalyst within the police and may keep up pressure for training and policy and practice discussions with other police officers. It is important that Domestic Violence Units should not be regarded as a substitute for general police training and awareness on issues involving domestic violence – or an excuse for inaction by patrol officers called to deal with this kind of assault, on the grounds that it is the responsibility of specialist domestic violence officers. The Metropolitan Police are currently reviewing the work of the Domestic Violence Units in London and their report is expected to be completed soon.

Assessing the impact of the changes

There has been no research yet to monitor the overall changes in police practice, so evidence on the general impact of recent policy changes is still unclear. As we have seen, the survey of WAFE refuges suggests that the change may have been more in the degree of contact and liaison than in any dramatic increase in prosecutions. Out of 74 refuges, 56 said that there had been no increase in the number of women in refuges with prosecutions pending, yet a clear majority of the respondents indicated that they believed that arrest and prosecution could help women.

It is possible, however, that there has been an increase in the use of arrest and detention for a short time to ensure the woman's safety without a corresponding increase in the prosecution rate. One of the features of the Police and Criminal Evidence Act 1984 is the power it gives the police to arrest on 'reasonable suspicion' that an offence may have been committed, or may be about to be committed, which then may not necessarily lead to prosecution. It was this increase in police powers to arrest on suspicion that gave rise to widespread concern about possible abuse of police power under the Act and its implications for civil liberties. Such concerns are not entirely absent in situations of domestic violence, especially for black people and anyone who might be a focus of police suspicion for other reasons, but it is probable that in most incidents of domestic violence the power of preventive arrest will act, if at all, mainly to overcome the general reluctance to intervene in such cases.

When it comes to prosecution the situation is little changed. While the Police and Criminal Evidence Act gives increased powers to arrest and detain, prosecutions for assault still have to be processed under the previously existing law and rules of evidence. The main change is in the possibility of compelling the women to give evidence, or alternatively, as the Home Office circular suggests, using the woman's original statement to the police as evidence under section 23 of the Criminal Justice Act 1988, possibly along with the evidence of police officers and any other witnesses.

Compelling a woman to give evidence when she may be under threat of retaliation remains a difficult and controversial subject. While some police officers believe that compulsion could relieve a woman of some of the guilt or apprehension she might feel in participating in the prosecution of her husband, it has also been suggested that the Crown

Prosecution Service would be reluctant to proceed in this situation, or else that the judge might dismiss the case. It is also true that the change in the law makes no difference where the couple are not married. In these situations the woman has always been a compellable witness and yet the prosecution rate has remained low.

Disquiet about the possible impact of compulsion on women was increased by the case of Michelle Renshaw, who was committed to prison for contempt of court by Judge James Pickles at Leeds Crown Court in 1989 when she refused to testify against her partner who had been accused of wounding her. Although initially willing, she had refused to give evidence because she had been followed and had received threatening telephone calls. This case suggests a danger that the compellability provision might be used, or not used, according to perceptions of the needs of the criminal justice system rather than for the good of women experiencing domestic violence. All commentators agree that compellability is rarely used at present and that there will probably be little change in the future. (As yet there has been no systematic investigation of compellability, although research is currently being carried out by Antonia Cretney and Gwyn Davies at Bristol University.)

There is some suggestion – for example, in the WAFE survey – that even where there is no prosecution there has been an improvement in the more general protective role of the police, in giving the woman information about Women's Aid, referring or transporting her to a refuge, or helping her to collect clothes from home after leaving. It is also possible that it is still easier to get effective support if women leave and are backed up by Women's Aid or some other agency when they seek police help. The WAFE survey makes it clear that the participating refuges played a significant role by supporting women in seeking police help with a number of important matters, including trying to get their children back or bringing complaints or charges against their partner. They were also very likely to be in contact with the police when necessary to assist the women in making a complaint about the police response, or to complain about racist or discriminatory treatment of black women or women from minority ethnic communities.

It is possible that police attitudes have been changing more rapidly at a senior level. For example, the new Commissioner of the Metropolitan Police has made public statements on issues of policing relating to women, on the treatment of women within the police force itself, following published evidence of sexual harassment, and on racism within the police force. The WAFE survey suggests that liaison, contact and consultation have been increasing, even though only a minority of the refuges responding felt that there had been significant changes in the police response to domestic violence itself.

Why have these changes taken place?

The hard work of Women's Aid and other women's organizations in Britain, and the research and monitoring work described earlier, have had an important impact on changes in police practice, but other factors must also be considered. A change took place at the level of central government guidance between 1986, when the Home Office circular was at pains to emphasize the discretionary powers of chief officers of police over operational matters, and the 1990 circular, which made the wishes of the Home Secretary very plain and embodied a clear message that chief officers were expected to respond as a matter of course. A major factor may have been the influential action taken by the Metropolitan Police and the publicity which that received.

Other influences were international. The British government was a signatory to the United Nations Convention on the Elimination of All Forms of Discrimination Against Women, which is now being strengthened by a Declaration on the Elimination of Violence Against Women, currently in draft form. By 1990, the government was overdue in reporting on action it had taken to implement the Convention. It is possible that the Home Office circular and other government action – for example, the funding of development projects and the evaluation of these under the Safer Cities Initiatives – resulted partly from the need to show progress on this subject. Other international bodies such as the Council of Europe, the European Commission and the European Parliament were also active, and possibly influenced the climate of opinion within government towards a more interventionist position.

This might also help to explain the central position occupied by questions of policing in British government actions. A number of the countries which had played a leading international role in action against domestic violence had highlighted action in the field of policing and pro-arrest policies in both the civil and criminal justice system. Although policing has been regarded as an important issue by activists and researchers, it was seen within a context which included not only the provision of refuges for temporary safety, but the involvement of local housing authorities in the provision of safe permanent housing for women made homeless by domestic violence. This was an emphasis not present in many countries because Britain was unusual in the extent of its publicly owned housing, much of which has now been sold or is under pressure from the government's public expenditure restrictions (see Chapter 6).

It may be, therefore, that the awakening interest of the British government in policing domestic violence, in crime prevention measures such as Safer Cities Projects and in inter-agency initiatives linking statutory and voluntary agencies, arises from a reluctance to recognize women's need to have access to alternative housing in the many cases involving persistently violent partners. However, this is not to say that arrest, detention and prosecution may not be important to ensure the woman's safety in the short and intermediate term, and to give a clear signal that society regards domestic violence as both unacceptable behaviour and a crime which is as serious as assault of any other kind.

Britain can also learn from other countries. Legislative changes, policing practice and liaison with voluntary agencies in such countries as Australia, Canada and the USA have much to teach. But, until recently at least, it was also the case that these countries had much to learn from the United Kingdom, both from the Women's Aid movement and from the possibility for women to be safely rehoused in public sector and social rented housing, and to benefit from other social welfare provisions.

It is the erosion of these possibilities that gives rise to fears among domestic violence workers that the current preferences of the British government for private solutions are being reflected in their emphasis on policing, prosecution and the use of civil remedies in the courts. It is feared that these will be viewed as an alternative to government action in funding more adequate and safe emergency, temporary and permanent housing for women escaping from domestic violence, and to the provision of other important public welfare measures, such as reasonable income support, which involve public expenditure. Fears are also aroused by this emphasis on court action when the legal aid programme is being made increasingly inaccessible.

Even accepting the importance of the policy changes on policing, arrest and prosecution through the justice system, and even leaving on one side the question of housing, the weakness of the government's policy is that it seems largely to rely on policing and police–community liaison alone. Much less attention has been directed at the courts, the judiciary, the Crown Prosecution Service and the Probation Service, which has to deal with offenders who may be on suspended sentences. There is scope for these to draw up their own practice guidelines and develop their own training programmes, as suggested by the LSPU report in 1986. As we will see in Chapter 5, the Probation Service in consultation with WAFE has already drawn up a position statement with some practice guidelines on dealing with issues arising from domestic violence, including those involved in working with offenders and their families.

Police action alone will not be sufficient to deal with domestic violence. Even if the police fully carry out all of the recommendations for good practice, there is still a lot more to be done within the justice system itself. Without changes in attitudes in the Crown Prosecution Service and in the courts, serious assaults may still be treated lightly or excused. Prosecution is certainly not the whole answer, and it is not always what is needed in every case, although the real possibility of prosecution under criminal law must be part of an overall process in which domestic violence is taken seriously and the safety of women and children is the primary objective. In fact, prosecution will only work effectively, or at all, if it is just one part of such an overall community response. The civil law also has an important role to play in conjunction with a range of other support services. The most important recommendation of all was summed up in the evidence given to the House of Commons Home Affairs Committee by the Women's Aid Federation (England) in 1992: 'The safety and well-being of the woman and her children should always be the first priority.'

5
Legal remedies and the court system

When the network of women's refuges grew up in the early 1970s, the lack of protection for women experiencing domestic violence became very apparent. Although remedies against assault existed in both the criminal and the civil law, they were often not easy to use or not adequately enforced. As we have seen, the police commonly failed to use the remedies that existed to protect women from assault under the criminal law. It was possible to obtain protection as part of an action for damages or in divorce proceedings, but only where the woman was married to her attacker, and where she had decided that she wanted the marriage to end.

Many women who came to refuges had left home as a last resort, sometimes in order to give themselves a breathing space, and perhaps to bring home to their partner the effect that his violence was having on their relationship and the family. Yet often the only way they could escape from repeated violence was by staying away and finding a safe, permanent place to live. Often they could not go back home even if they wanted to, since there was no easy way of getting protection against continuing assault, or of getting their violent partner removed from the house.

The Women's Aid movement therefore began to campaign for changes in the civil law so that women could apply for the protection available under matrimonial law, but on grounds of domestic violence alone and without the action having to be linked to any other legal proceedings. The intention was to give women some degree of choice in deciding whether or not they wanted to try to preserve their relationship. Changes in the law to give a woman the right to apply for a court order for protection from domestic violence, including both assault and harassment, were also recommended by the Select Committee on Violence in Marriage 1975.

Domestic violence and the civil law

Largely because of these developments, the Domestic Violence and Matrimonial Proceedings Act 1976, which applied to action in the county courts, was introduced as a private member's bill, though with government support, by Jo Richardson MP. It came into force on 1 June 1977 and was followed by the Domestic Proceedings and Magistrates' Courts Act 1978, and by further changes to the law on occupation of the matrimonial home during and after divorce, in 1983. These laws introduced important new possibilities for women to seek legal remedies against domestic violence. They gave some women protection, in the short term at least, and a chance to think about what long-term steps to take. In practice, though, they have proved to have limitations.

What follows is a brief introduction to this legislation. There is a more detailed description of the civil legislation on domestic violence in *Not Worth the Paper?* by Jackie Barron, which reports on the results of a research study undertaken for the Women's Aid Federation (England) examining the limitations of the law in practice. The nature of the legislation and its application is described in a number of other publications, including *Women and the Law* by Susan Atkins and Brenda Hoggett, and in two Law Commission reports, published in 1989 and 1992.

The Domestic Violence and Matrimonial Proceedings Act 1976 (or DVA) made important changes to existing law. One of its most far-reaching innovations was that it could be used if the couple were 'living in the same household as husband and wife' at the time of the incident of abuse or assault, whether or not they were legally married. It was also very important that applications for protection did not have to be linked to any other proceedings, such as divorce or damages.

The DVA provided for two types of order (or injunction). The first, a non-molestation order, was aimed at preventing further abuse or harassment, and providing emergency protection for the applicant or any child living in the household. The second, an exclusion order, or ouster, would exclude the violent partner from the home (or part of it) for a specified period, or prevent him from returning if he had left. He could also be ordered to keep away from certain areas, such as those surrounding the home, or particular places, such as the children's school or the woman's workplace. Both types of injunction could in some circumstances be initially obtained 'ex parte', without the man being present in court, and an order could be backed up with police power to arrest the man if he disregarded it.

This was the first time that married and unmarried women were treated as equals in legislation affecting their shared home or their relationship. It was regarded as contentious by some judges and other lawyers, and was soon to be challenged in the courts. The power of arrest was also contentious, even though it could only be used in cases where it had been demonstrated that a defendant had caused actual bodily harm to the applicant or to a child in the household, and if the judge was satisfied that the violence was likely to be repeated.

A power of arrest can be particularly important as a protective measure for women and children experiencing violence: it means that the police can arrest without a warrant if they have cause to believe that an injunction has been broken, even if no other arrestable offence, such as further violence, has occurred. An injunction without a power of arrest only allows the police to arrest for offences under criminal or common law. A power of arrest also means that, if arrested, the man must then be brought back to court within twenty-four hours for the case to be heard. Without this, the woman, or her solicitor, must apply to the court for a committal for contempt of court. A court summons then has to be served on the man, who is often able to avoid being served and may disappear, evading the summons and the court appearance indefinitely.

Many problems have arisen with the enforcement of this law, not least because judges have been reluctant to attach powers of arrest or to interfere with the property rights of the men concerned. Problems also arise from ambiguities in the Act itself, resulting from the speed with which it was introduced. The DVA has, like other legislation, been modified by case law following appeals, and by practice directions from the President of the Family Division of the High Court. We will return to these issues later in this chapter.

The second Act passed to deal specifically with domestic violence was the Domestic Proceedings and Magistrates' Courts Act 1978 (DPMCA). Magistrates' courts have traditionally been regarded as cheaper and more accessible, especially to working-class women, than the county courts or high courts. The purpose of the DPMCA was to bring matrimonial and family law in the magistrates' courts into line with that in the county courts (except for the power of divorce itself). The DPMCA permits magistrates to grant 'personal protection orders' and 'exclusion' or 'ouster' orders that are very similar to the injunctions of the county courts. Powers of arrest may also be attached to these orders, but the law is restricted by the fact that applicants to the magistrates' courts must be legally married to their attacker, and magistrates are only empowered to make personal protection orders against physical violence and not against other forms of molestation or harassment. This will change if the proposals of the Law Commission in 1992 are adopted into law (see below).

Procedures for enforcing orders when they are broken are also different from in the county courts, but may in some ways be more effective. Magistrates have the power to impose direct penalties for actual breach of the orders made in their courts rather than for contempt of court. The applicant herself can also apply for an arrest warrant for the breach of an order which has a power of arrest attached, and if this is granted the man can be either kept in custody or released on bail until the hearing. Under the DVA the county court has no power to remand in custody in proceedings for breach of an injunction with arrest powers attached, nor can the county court issue a warrant for arrest for breach of a civil order. Again, if the Law Commission's proposals are adopted similar powers will be available to all courts.

The Matrimonial Homes Act 1983 (MHA), the third piece of legislation which provides for civil injunctions against domestic violence, only applies if a couple are married, as with the legislation in the magistrates' courts. The powers of the county court or the High Court under the MHA are not primarily intended to offer emergency protection, but are aimed at the more long-term resolution of disputes over the occupation of the matrimonial home following divorce. The court has the power to prohibit, suspend or restrict the right of either spouse to occupy the family home, or to require either to permit the other to exercise that right. These orders can have the same force as exclusion orders.

Since the House of Lords' judgment in the *Richards* case in 1984, if a married woman is applying to exclude her husband from the home, the judge must apply the criteria laid down in the MHA in deciding whether or not to grant the order, even if the application is made under the DVA. This has meant that criteria that are intended to apply to temporary procedures on the way to a permanent property settlement between married partners are also used in deciding whether or not a woman and her children can be protected in the family home in the short term. The judgment had a very restrictive impact on the use of ouster and exclusion orders when it was first made, and it has continued to make the issuing of these orders more difficult than before.

By raising the question of the conduct of both partners, this judgment threw the emphasis on to considering the seriousness of the violence rather than the need of the women and children for a safe home. Since the *Richards* case, according to the Law Commission's Working Party Report in 1989, there appear to have been no reported cases in which a man has been ousted unless there had been physical violence. Susan Atkins and Brenda Hoggett have pointed out that the multiplication of the issues to be considered also gave greater opportunities for the man to use delaying tactics to stall the making of an order.

The domestic violence legislation assumes that the woman and her partner are living together in the same home, but as we have seen, some domestic violence originates outside the home. The legislation can apply when former partners or former husbands continue to assault or harass women after they have stopped living together, but not when violence is directed at a woman by a man with whom she has had a close relationship but who has never shared a home with her. The domestic violence legislation does not apply when it is a close male relative – a father, son or brother – who is the attacker, whether or not these men are living in the same household as the women they are assaulting, so women must use other laws to seek protection.

If the children need protection from attack and the couple have never lived together, the Children Act 1989 can be used to obtain an injunction to protect both the mother and the children in proceedings for residence and contact orders (formerly custody and access), but not to oust someone who has a right of occupation. Injunctions may also be granted to protect children in the course of Wardship proceedings. Where violence is coming from outside the home and children are not involved, or a family member other than the spouse is the abuser, the only possibility in civil law is to apply for an injunction under action for damages.

Some general aspects of civil legal proceedings and orders

A woman seeking civil legal remedies will normally consult a solicitor and have legal representation in court, although she has the right to present her own case if she chooses, or if she is unable to instruct a lawyer for financial or other reasons. It is easier for a woman to present her own case in the magistrates' court because the clerk to the justices has a duty to help her and there is no need to present typed and sworn affidavits. In the past women have often been eligible for legal aid, but this will be more difficult to obtain in future because of government measures to restrict the numbers eligible by using stricter means tests.

In an emergency all injunctions under the DVA, in matrimonial proceedings or in action for damages may be applied for *ex parte*. If the assault is likely to happen again or if the woman has nowhere to go, this should mean that there will be a court hearing the same day, or the next day at the latest. In practice, though, the county courts are very reluctant to make *ex parte* exclusion orders, and the magistrates have no power to make exclusion orders in an emergency under the expedited proceedings, although they can make expedited non-molestation orders. Powers of arrest are very rarely attached *ex parte* in either court.

In the county courts it is a common practice to substitute an 'undertaking' for a court order. This may happen when the man or his lawyers suggest to the woman's legal representative that he is willing to 'undertake' not to assault her, and perhaps also to promise to leave the home by a particular date. This means that none of the evidence will be heard and no judgment will be made on the truth of the allegations. The woman will usually be advised by her lawyer to agree because it will simplify the hearing. Her application is then withdrawn or adjourned, and the man is asked to sign an undertaking instead. Magistrates, on the other hand, have no power to accept sworn undertakings. An undertaking signed in court is, in theory, similar to a court order, and a breach of an undertaking carries the same penalties as any other breach of the court's directives. However, in practice it is not regarded as seriously, and no power of arrest can be attached because the man has signed the undertaking willingly.

If a man leaves shortly after attacking his partner, it can be difficult to serve an injunction or a notice on him to attend the court. This can mean that further assaults occur and that the police and representatives of the court are unable to catch up with him. The inability to serve notice can delay a full hearing for at least four days in the case of the DVA and two days in other proceedings. If the case is heard *ex parte*, any order will probably be temporary, usually for a week, and the woman will have to return to court when it expires. She is also unlikely to be granted an exclusion order. Courts do have the power to rule that service is 'deemed good', if, for example, the woman is prepared to swear that she has told the man of the hearing date, but courts are reluctant to do this until several attempts have been made to hold a full hearing.

The most serious problem in this situation is that, in general, no court order is in force until it has been served. Ideally this should be done by handing it to the person concerned – and injunctions cannot be delivered by post. If the man has disappeared or is evading service, it is possible to serve the documents on someone else who is known to be seeing the man regularly, but solicitors often seem unaware of this possibility. Evasion of service can prevent a woman and children being able to stay in their home because of delays in hearing dates, and can allow further violence to take place without remedy, even if an *ex parte* order has been made.

Problems with civil protection in practice: the WAFE research

In looking at the effectiveness of injunctions the WAFE researchers considered three main questions: first, how likely women were to obtain the kind of order they asked for; second, whether orders lasted for as long as women needed; and third, how effective court orders were in protecting women from further abuse. The evidence from their interviews and the court hearings they attended suggested that, while almost everyone was successful in obtaining a non-molestation order or an undertaking, it could be difficult to get stronger protection. A number of women were unable to obtain exclusion orders even though they saw them as vital for their protection. Even in cases where there was a long history of violence, judges and other lawyers appeared to believe that it was perfectly safe for a woman to return home once she had a non-molestation order or an undertaking that her partner would not molest her.

The reluctance of courts to grant ouster and exclusion orders seems to arise because they are unwilling to interfere with men's property rights, especially where the couple are not married. Although the DVA is specifically intended to give the right to exclude the man from the family home where there has been physical violence, this has been subject to much dispute and several appeals. The most important case was that of *Davis* v. *Johnson*, where an appeal to the House of Lords ruled that even when those concerned were not married, an exclusion order could apply in cases where the man had rights in the property – for example, a joint tenancy with his partner. As the Law Commission has pointed out, however, there is still uneasiness and confusion in the courts, especially where the woman does not have a clear legal right to occupy the family home. This has led to a general Practice Direction that an exclusion or ouster order should not operate for longer than three months.

On several occasions in the course of the WAFE research, judges referred to Appeal Court rulings that exclusion orders were 'draconian'. A number of judges also said that they were unable to make an exclusion order unless the man was present to argue his side of the case, which is not actually the position in law. This reluctance could be overcome if the situation was seen as very serious – for example, if the woman was severely injured, or where serious criminal charges were being pursued. In other cases, if there had been a failure to serve notice of the hearing or if the man had failed to attend, the case was usually adjourned.

Men were sometimes given several weeks to make arrangements to move out, especially when the woman had left the home after a violent incident. Sometimes the judge might refuse an exclusion order altogether, on the grounds that the woman had a place to go, even if this was temporary accommodation, whereas the man did not. This was especially likely to happen if the woman had left the children behind and there was a dispute over custody. In one such case the woman concerned told the researchers that the man had dropped the custody case once the exclusion order had been refused. In these cases women who had not left previously would either have to remain in situations where they were likely to experience further threats or physical danger, or else have to move out, with or without their children, often into overcrowded temporary accommodation. Courts were also reluctant to grant orders excluding the man from an area surrounding the home, on the grounds that they were difficult to enforce. And judges and magistrates were very often unwilling to attach powers of arrest even in cases of very serious assault, particularly in some courts and some areas.

This concern for the legal rights of the men, particularly their right not to be deprived of their home without a hearing and except under the most extreme circumstances, frequently involved a denial of the rights of the women to live in *their* home. It could lead to the woman, and possibly the children too, being forced out as a result of illegal actions on the man's part. It appears to be a quite serious negation of the original intention of the law.

In some cases identified in the research, a non-molestation order alone was sufficient to calm the situation down, or an exclusion order was enough to make things reasonably quiet while the man made arrangements to move out. Women themselves were often able to anticipate this. However, where they were afraid of further violence without a strengthening of the basic order, their knowledge of the man concerned was rarely taken into account.

Injunctions of all kinds are usually granted for three months under the domestic violence legislation. Occasionally they may be for six months, and they can be extended further on application. In divorce proceedings in the county courts, they may be granted until divorce is finalized and a property adjustment order made, or for an indefinite period. In some cases in the WAFE research, women did not realize that their original injunctions would expire on divorce, or that there was an expiry date at all. Divorced husbands returned to assault and harass their ex-wives in several instances, and in other cases men moved back in when the exclusion order expired. Some women did not know they could apply for an extension or another order, and lawyers did not always give adequate advice.

One of the chief problems with civil protection orders is their enforcement. In the WAFE research, half of the women interviewed said that their partner had disobeyed the order or undertaking on at least one occasion. Some of these breaches were more serious than others, but even where they were serious and repeated, neither the police nor the courts seemed able to to prevent them. The effectiveness of the orders seems to rest mainly on the extent to which men are prepared to respect the court judgment. From the WAFE research it seemed that the women's solicitors often acted as a filter, resisting action on breach of injunctions according to their own view of what a court would take seriously. Cases are quoted in which assaults following an injunction or undertaking were not taken back to court, including one in which the woman's finger was broken and her partner was constantly threatening her.

It was apparently a common practice for solicitors merely to write a letter warning that further breaches would be taken to court. In some cases this might happen many times and the solicitor would not act because anything less than 'a split lip, black eye, something really showing' did not seem to be enough: 'they aren't really bothered about bruises'. Women also found they got little help from the police when the injunctions were broken, even when they had been physically attacked. In one case quoted, the man came back to the house on the day the injunction was granted. When the police came the man had hold of both the women's arms but the police only told him to let her go. The woman told the police she had an injunction and asked them what they were going to do. 'And they said, "Nothing. We'll just let him go ... we haven't seen nothing happen." '

This research was carried out before the issuing of the Home Office Guidelines in 1990, but there had been earlier guidelines in 1986 from the Home Office, and the Metropolitan Police Force Orders of 1987 had received national publicity. As it happens, the police force in the main research area had adopted Force Orders which recommended that officers take domestic violence seriously. However, women were still told by police in the area that they could only act if there were powers of arrest attached to the injunctions.

Police apparently fail to recognize that the courts are reluctant to grant a power of arrest in the first place except where the violence has been both repeated and extremely severe. Then, in addition, when the courts do attach powers of arrest after there has been severe assault, the police have often refused to use these arrest powers, which are purely permissive in any case. And courts have also been unwilling to commit a man to prison for contempt even where there have been frequent and serious breaches of injunctions or undertakings. The WAFE research describes a failure to act which stretches from solicitors through the police to the courts themselves — which appear simultaneously to insist on the sanctity of court orders in words and to collude with the man's contempt for court orders in practice.

The Law Commission's proposals for change

For a number of years now, the Law Commission has been considering the question of domestic violence and the occupation of the family home. A report was published in 1992 which made recommendations for rationalizing the civil legislation on domestic violence and drew up a draft Family Homes and Domestic Violence Bill. These proposals were endorsed, in the main, by the House of Commons Home Affairs Committee in 1993. It is likely that the draft bill will form the basis of legislation to be considered by Parliament in 1994. This proposed legislation would introduce a unified law on the civil remedies available for protection against violence and harassment, and for regulating the occupation of the family home where a relationship has broken down, whether or not that breakdown is violent.

The Law Commission's first recommendation is that the new law should provide, as the current legislation does, for two types of civil remedy, a non-molestation order and an occupation order, the first being designed to prevent violence or molestation of another family member, and the second to order one partner to leave or stay away from the family home. The occupation order would not necessarily imply molestation or harassment, but would regulate the occupation of the family home in either the short or the long term where the relationship had broken down. A decision to make an occupation order would be based on the 'balance of need' and decided in the interests of whoever had the most need to occupy the family home, taking into account the welfare of any children, but not the conduct of either partner.

The Commission also proposes that non-molestation orders could be used for a much broader range of people and relationships than at present. This would mean that many women who are currently only able to apply for injunctions in connection with other court action would be able to make direct applications for non-molestation orders under the proposed legislation. Another proposal is that non-molestation orders should be able to be made for any specified period or indefinitely for as long as it is needed – beyond the end of a relationship if necessary. The current normal limit for exclusion and ouster orders of three months is seen as too short to allow a proper examination of housing options and to find alternative accommodation. This initial period has already been changed to six months in Scotland because it led to too many applications for extension.

The proposed orders would have a very broad scope. The potential applicants would include both those who were already legally entitled by ownership or tenancy to occupy the family home and those who were not, but the rights of those who were not legally entitled would be more limited. This would mean that, as in Scotland, cohabitants with a right to occupy the family home would be treated in the same way as married people with occupation rights.

The Commission makes proposals to strengthen and broaden the scope of orders in other ways. It is proposed that all these orders should be available, as now, without any other proceeding being necessary, and also in the course of any family proceedings, with or without an application being made first. The Commission also recommends that magistrates' courts should have the same powers to make non-molestation and short- and medium-term occupation orders, though not permanent property settlements, for the same range of applicants as the county courts.

The Commission stresses the need for caution in making *ex parte* orders because of possible unfairness to the respondent, but considers that they could be necessary in cases of imminent physical violence and where it is suspected that the man is deliberately evading service of a summons. They propose to give all the courts similar powers within a law which lays down criteria to be considered in granting *ex parte* orders.

A number of recommendations are made on the enforcement of orders. The commissioners see a power of arrest as a 'simple, immediate and inexpensive means of enforcement which underlines the seriousness of the breach to the offending party'. They recommend that a court should be required to attach a power of arrest to specified provisions of an order 'unless in all the circumstances the applicant or a child would be adequately protected without such a power'. Where the respondent is not present, the court should not be required to attach a power of arrest, but should be able to do so if it is satisfied that there is a risk of significant harm. The Commission also recommends that the power of the magistrates' court to remand a man in custody or on bail in the course of committal proceedings be extended to other courts.

The Commission's proposals are an important step forward, and the endorsement of most of the recommendations by the House of Commons Home Affairs Committee and their call to the government for early legislation is very welcome. However, the history of the original domestic violence legislation of the 1970s suggests that changing the law in itself will not be enough. Unless the judiciary and the rest of the legal system take on board the spirit of the legislation, the way will be open to a limitation of its scope in appeal judgments, the muffling of its impact by the use of discretion, and the filtering out of enforcement applications by solicitors when injunctions have been broken. In its evidence to the House of Commons Home Affairs Committee Inquiry into Domestic Violence, WAFE broadly welcomed the Law Commission's proposals, while expressing reservations about giving the court discretion, in *ex parte* hearings, to decide whether the applicant or any children would be adequately protected without a power of arrest. WAFE also considered that the Commission's proposals did not go far enough, especially in failing to stress that a breach of injunction should be responded to severely, whether or not powers of arrest exist.

The criminal law

The law on assault is in theory the same for domestic violence as for violence of any other kind, and is largely contained in the Offences Against the Person Act 1861. This Act deals with all forms of assault from common assault to murder – and includes sexual assault, although this is also covered in the Sexual Offences Act 1956 and the Sexual Offences (Amendment) Act 1976. The four sections of the Offences Against the Person Act which are most likely to be relevant to domestic violence are those covering common assault, assault causing actual bodily harm (ABH), malicious wounding, and grievous bodily harm (GBH). There is also the possibility that the man may not actually attack the woman or the children personally, but may break windows or furniture, destroy her clothing or even burn down the house. These actions are also clearly subject to legal sanctions for criminal damage or other criminal charges under laws which have long been on the statute books. Action under common law for breach of the peace is also possible.

Although sexual assault and rape are often involved in domestic violence, women are less likely to report these than other kinds of assault. Until a House of Lords' judgment in 1991, it was regarded as impossible in law for a man to rape his wife because of the assumption that sexual intercourse within marriage could not be unlawful. An offence of sexual assault was legally possible where there had been violence, but ruling attitudes in the justice system tended to make charges unlikely unless the violence was extreme.

As we saw in Chapter 1, the murder of women by their husbands has been seen as a lesser crime than the killing of other people, or the killing by women of their violent partners. The question of justice for women who kill their husbands or partners after experiencing years of violent abuse has been brought out sharply in the last few years. As we will see in Chapter 9, campaigns on behalf of a number of women who have killed their violent husbands or partners have taken up issues arising out of the legal definitions of provocation, diminished responsibility and self-defence, and have proposed a new defence of 'self-preservation'.

Public attention has focused mainly on the way in which the defence of provocation has been interpreted by the courts. This appears to have worked to the advantage of men who have killed their wives and who plead successfully that this has been provoked by a succession of comparatively trivial acts, the last of which has caused them to kill in a moment of 'sudden loss of self-control'. As we have seen, a resulting conviction for manslaughter can lead to a light sentence of a few years' imprisonment, or even no imprisonment at all. Yet for women the defence has been rejected – or in certain cases not put forward by the woman's lawyer – where the provocation has consisted of repeated and extreme acts of violence, but where the woman's retaliation has been delayed. This leads to a supposition of premeditation and a conviction for murder which carries an automatic life sentence.

In its report on domestic violence the House of Commons Select Committee on Home Affairs endorsed the recommendation of a new statutory definition for the defence of provocation made by the Law Commission in its Draft Criminal Code for England and Wales in 1989. However, Southall Black Sisters, who have been closely involved in the women's campaigns for justice, see the Law Commission's proposals as a step backwards from the position that was established by Lord Taylor in his judgment in the appeal of Kiranjit Ahluwahlia in 1992. This stated that the question of self-control should be examined in the light of the evidence in the case, rather than relying on the concept of 'suddenness' as a rule of law.

The Home Affairs Committee rejected changes to the current definition of 'sufficient force' in self-defence to allow for women's lesser physical strength, and also rejected the introduction of a new defence of self-preservation which would differ from self-defence because it would not require a life-threatening act immediately to precede it. This was because the Committee feared the possibility of 'revenge killings committed while defendants were fully in control of their emotions resulting in convictions only for manslaughter'. Yet, as we have seen, it is clear that very few women commit homicide of any kind, while a significant proportion of homicides are committed by men against their wives or females partners. It therefore seems very unlikely that a change in the law would lead to an outbreak of revenge killings by women. However, a careless redrafting of the law might lead to an even greater toll of deaths among women, which could be successfully defended on the grounds of provocation. Whatever changes may take place in legal definitions, there is no short cut to changing the culture and climate in which the law operates.

Enforcement of the law and the nature of the legal system

Many legal and feminist scholars and researchers have seen the organization of the law and the legal system itself as part of the reason why women who experience domestic violence find it difficult to get justice. Susan Edwards, for example, concludes that the law in the widest sense 'subverts rather than facilitates protection for women'. These defects in the legal system interact with the perceptions of those within the system that violence against wives or female partners is both distinct from, and less serious than, violence against other people.

Susan Edwards herself sees the distinction between public and private law as part of the problem, and regards as mistaken those feminists and others who see civil remedies as in some ways more useful than criminal proceedings. For her the use of the civil law reinforces the public/private divide and the cultural fabric which sees men as 'possessed of a natural entitlement to correct, chastise and sometimes batter justifiably'. She points to the fact that, even where there was evidence of criminal behaviour, the police would often direct women into a private prosecution for assault, where it is the victim who must make the complaint and press charges.

The second fault with the legal system, according to Edwards, is that until 1984 it created significant differences between assault against a wife and assault against any other person, a female partner or a cohabitee or stranger of either sex, because a wife could not be compelled to give evidence against her husband when he had assaulted her. This is a relic of the times when a wife was not regarded as a competent witness against her husband because their interests were held to be identical in law. However, as Lorna Smith points out, this difference was reimposed by a court judgment only in 1978, specifically in cases of assault by a man against his wife.

Another general problem in relation to prosecuting an assault under criminal law is in assessing whether a case is strong enough to proceed. In Chapter 4 we described the past reluctance of the police to prosecute in cases of domestic violence, even where the woman was willing for a prosecution to take place. Now that the police are being advised by the Home Office that prosecution should be considered seriously in a wider range of such assaults, the actual decision to prosecute rests no longer with them, but with the Crown Prosecution Service. The police are advised in the Home Office circular of 1990 to consult with the CPS on the criteria to be considered in these cases before sending a case forward. This requirement to anticipate the views of the CPS in relation to the strength of the evidence, the likelihood of a conviction and whether such a prosecution would be in the public interest is likely to influence the nature of the cases that the police refer to the CPS.

As with other such bodies, the attitude of the CPS in different areas is likely to vary. Therefore the recommendation of the Home Affairs Committee that the CPS should gather regional and national figures on prosecution, and remedy existing regional disparities, is very important in trying to ensure that there is some consistency in prosecution policy throughout the country. When dealing with the possibility that a woman might withdraw her complaint, the 1990 Home Office circular drew the attention of the police to the powers of the CPS, under the Magistrates' Courts Act 1980 and the Police and Criminal Evidence Act 1984, to compel a spouse or cohabitee to attend court for the purpose of giving evidence.

The question of the compellability of witnesses is very complex, as we saw in Chapter 4. On the one hand, policies of dropping prosecution whenever a police officer or prosecutor feels that a woman may be reluctant to proceed are not at all helpful. On the other hand, a decision to call the police for protection should not set off an unstoppable juggernaut in which a decision to arrest and detain a man in order to prevent further violence progresses inevitably to prosecution, despite the wishes of the woman. This could be especially dangerous where the woman is the only witness, and might be compelled to give evidence despite threats of retaliation, or be imprisoned for contempt of court if she refuses.

It is very commendable that the Home Affairs Committee recognizes the danger of the intimidation of witnesses in these cases and recommends the prosecution of men responsible. It is also welcome that the CPS is asked to explain decisions directly to the women concerned, including giving reasons for downgrading charges. However, both the police, in the stages leading up to the decision to charge the man and send the details to the CPS, and the CPS itself, in deciding whether to proceed with a prosecution, should be able to consult the woman concerned and to make decisions jointly with her about when and how to proceed, especially when she is reluctant to testify. Such consultation is not possible in the present system, especially in the case of the CPS. The Home Affairs Committee has drawn attention to the possibility of proceeding with a prosecution on the basis of a woman's previous statement, under Section 23 of the Criminal Justice Act 1988, without the need for her to testify. Even here, there is a need to appreciate the dangers a woman may face and to provide adequate support and protection if a prosecution proceeds. However, most commentators expect that few prosecutions will go forward on this basis.

Women concerned in domestic violence cases need to have access to informed, independent advice throughout the period in which prosecution is being considered or carried forward. Models for such support, consultation and advocacy are described in more detail in Chapter 9. One model, the Domestic Violence Crisis Service (DVCS) in Australia, is described in a book called *Working for Change: The Movement Against Domestic Violence*, by Heather McGregor and Andrew Hopkins. This is a system pioneered in South Australia and put into effect in Canberra and the Australian Capital Territory in 1988.

The DVCS is fully funded by government, but arises from a feminist initiative and has feminist objectives and a radical agenda, including working closely alongside the police while remaining an independent advocacy service for women. Public funding and close liaison with police and government services does not prevent the DVCS retaining control over the nature of the service it should provide, the structure in which it should work and the type of intervention that should occur when police are called to incidents of domestic violence. After considerable negotiation it was decided that crisis service workers would be notified when police were called to domestic violence incidents, and would wait nearby during the police visit to the house so that they could be invited in if any occupant wished it. The invitation usually comes from women, and the DVCS sees the major focus of its work as supporting women who are subjected to domestic violence; however, the service also takes on the problem of children and young people subjected to violence from parents, and it will act as a referral point for perpetrators seeking counselling.

The relationship between the police and domestic violence service workers in the DVCS is one of greater equality than it is possible to imagine in Britain at present, while the degree of liaison with the courts and other statutory agencies is beyond the wildest dreams of the British Women's Aid network or of other organizations, such as Southall Black Sisters and Justice for Women, who are campaigning for changes in the law of provocation and self-defence. Although the recent work of the Law Commission and the report of the House of Commons Home Affairs Committee suggest that the climate of opinion at official level may be changing, there is still a considerable distance between official attitudes and those of Women's Aid and other grass-roots campaigns and organizations working in the area of domestic violence.

The nearest British equivalent to the DVCS, the experimental Islington Domestic Violence Intervention Team, suffers from the disadvantage that it is sited within a police station and its workers are not independent of the police force. Whether or not this means that they are subject to pressures to conform to police policies and priorities, they have no independent base or telephone number and are therefore not likely to be seen as independent by women who may need their help. In particular, this will limit the access of women who may not want to call in the police, for whatever reason. Women experiencing domestic violence need accessible advice and advocacy services, available twenty-four hours a day. These should be adequately funded and should work in conjunction with the police and other statutory bodies, while remaining fully independent.

Prosecution and after

In looking at possible action in the legal system, it is important to stress that arrest will not always lead to prosecution and prosecution will not always result in a prison sentence. Even if police forces do follow a pro-arrest policy, a preventive arrest under the Police and Criminal Evidence Act will not necessarily lead to a prosecution. The use of 'preventive arrest', however, can be seen as something which might protect women and help to overcome the complications, and the work involved for the police, if a prosecution is started and not proceeded with.

As we saw in Chapter 4, there are many reasons why abused women might not wish their partner to be prosecuted or imprisoned. There is also the problem of a lack of protection for women in the process of prosecution, and following the release of a man who is given a custodial sentence. The advice of the Home Office that the woman should be informed when the man is about to be released only deals with part of the problem. In our recent research study on domestic violence and housing, we found that the release of a husband or partner from custody could lead to a woman becoming homeless either from a well-founded fear of further violence, or because of actual attacks on her or the house following her partner's release.

In fact, it is less likely that a man will be imprisoned in cases of domestic violence than for other kinds of assault, and as for any other crime, there are debates in any case about the effectiveness of imprisonment. However, even though imprisonment is not always desirable, it is very important that the offence is not trivialized by being treated more leniently than other offences of similar seriousness. Women's Aid workers are often frustrated by the sentencing policy of judges in these cases. After the trauma involved for a woman in going through the prosecution process, and the filtering that operates to divert all but the most serious cases from prosecution, a fine or a suspended sentence, and the kind of remarks sometimes made by judges in the process, can give a man the impression that his attacks on his partner are being condoned by the justice system.

It is therefore particularly important that the Association of Chief Officers of Probation (ACOP) agreed a comprehensive position statement on domestic violence in 1992. The statement is very clear that when the probation service is supervising offenders or working with families in either the criminal or the civil side of their work, probation officers should take the issue of domestic violence very seriously. It signals the danger of probation officers colluding with offenders by accepting their common argument that the violence was the result of a momentary loss of self-control, or by believing the myths that exist about domestic violence. It accepts that the criminal justice system has not been sufficiently responsive to the needs of abused women in the past. The statement suggests that the encouragement to the police to take domestic violence seriously, contained in the 1990 Home Office circular, is beginning to have an effect, and that as a result an increasing number of perpetrators will find their way into the courts. In this situation, it is thought that the probation service will need to develop a deeper understanding of the causes and effects of domestic violence, and more effective practice in the supervision of offenders.

The statement describes the reasons why many women stay with their abusers as ranging 'from love to terror'. There is a recognition that agencies need to give a woman time and space to talk, without pressurizing her into taking immediate action. The statement acknowledges the special difficulties likely to be faced by black women and women from ethnic minority communities. It also looks at the practical difficulties a woman may face in leaving a relationship, especially when she has children, and recognizes that it is often only when all strategies for saving the relationship seem to be exhausted that she will begin to contemplate ending it.

The implications for practice are considered in detail. The position paper states firmly that domestic violence is an abuse of male power over women and requires male attitudes towards women to be addressed. It underlines the need for flexibility and openness in dealing with the problems of abused women. Stereotyping, and especially racial stereotyping, is warned against. Reiterating the need for advice on the choices open to an abused woman, the statement suggests that this may best be provided by another agency such as Women's Aid, or perhaps by a solicitor, law centre or housing advice centre. If a woman chooses to stay, the statement points out that her decision should be respected, and that she should be given the same standard of help if she returns for aid in the future. Where a woman and her partner are both supervisees, it is pointed out that they should normally be allocated to different officers, because it is difficult for the same supervisor to offer help and support to both partners. Posters advertising sources of help to abused women are recommended for display in offices, to show women what help is available and that the probation service takes violence seriously. In looking at working with violent men, the statement warns against the use of anger management courses on their own, noting the danger that anger management may simply lead to more effective domination and control of his partner by the abuser. These and other issues involved in programmes for perpetrators of domestic violence are discussed further in Chapter 9.

Imprisonment is seen as an opportunity for both partners to take stock. The position statement emphasizes the need for careful sentence planning, in which the safety of the abused woman is central to planning the man's release and subsequent supervision. The woman should be given support in deciding what she wants to happen on the man's release, and what support systems she may need. Work with the man by both prison and probation staff in preparation for his release should focus on his offending behaviour and the development of attitudes and skills that will minimize its recurrence. The statement assumes that in most cases women will have their partners back on their release. Staff are told that they need both to challenge the power imbalances that may put pressure on a woman to do so, and also to respect the choice she makes.

The statement also contains advice on dealing with situations where men on bail or remanded in custody may put pressure on abused women to withdraw their co-operation with the prosecution process. While probation staff should do their best to ease contact where this is desired, they must also be aware of the dangers. The ACOP statement presents a possible practice model to be considered by other sections of the criminal justice system, such as the CPS, magistrates and the judiciary, when considering their actions in cases of domestic violence.

Limitations on using the legal system in domestic violence

There is a continuing debate as to whether domestic violence falls most appropriately within the scope of the civil or the criminal law. On the one hand, there are those like Susan Edwards who regard the 'diversion' of domestic violence protection into civil courts as an error because it 'reinforced popular family ideology, reaffirming a belief that marital violence was indeed different from other violent crime'. On the other hand, the WAFE research report by Jackie Barron describes the criminal legislation as being mainly concerned with punishment of the offender; and, while not denying the symbolic importance of prosecution, it also points to the fact that custodial sentences are rare, and that any protection given to the woman and children by bail conditions no longer operates after the hearing. There is also the problem that the woman herself is not legally represented in criminal prosecution and has no control over the process of the case or the outcome, as she does to some extent in civil actions.

It is important to recognize that neither civil nor criminal sanctions can offer a solution to domestic violence, or deal adequately with its consequences for those who experience it. Only a comprehensive approach involving many different services and agencies, and including adequate, independent advice and advocacy services and emergency, temporary and permanent alternative accommodation, will even begin to deal with these consequences. The Law Commission Report of 1992 sees limitations in all forms of legal action:

> Domestic violence is not simply a legal problem which can be eradicated by appropriate legal remedies. It is also a social and psychological problem which can be eliminated only by fundamental changes in society and in attitudes to women and children. While legal remedies are an attempt to alleviate the symptoms of domestic violence they can do little to tackle the causes.

Yet, as the Law Commission itself recognizes, the alleviation of symptoms is important. The same judgement applies also to the actions of other agencies such as social services and the health services, and in the provision of housing, which will be discussed in the following chapters. If a comprehensive and co-ordinated attempt were made to alleviate the symptoms, it might at least make tackling the causes a little easier.

6

Finding somewhere safe to live: housing options

One of the most important needs of women leaving home due to violence is access to safe, secure permanent housing. The refuge movement provides a network of refuges, but the accommodation is available on a temporary, emergency basis only. Legal remedies, especially if strengthened as the Law Commission proposes, can assist some women in returning safely to their former homes. But for very many women, the protection offered is insufficient or ineffective. In any case, perhaps the majority of women who have left home because of violence do not wish to go back to the same property even if the man has been effectively excluded.

Thus, for very large numbers of women in this situation, the only way to be really safe is to make a fresh start far away from their home area and in a place which their violent partners do not know about. Women fleeing violence are usually quite clear about the dangers they face. They may well know that if they are found by their partners it will all start up again, that the only safe possibility is to disappear and begin again somewhere else. Such a dramatic life-move takes great courage, but many women and children take the enormous step, often with only a suitcase or perhaps just the clothes they stand up in.

To get clean away from a violent relationship in this way means first and foremost having somewhere safe and permanent to escape to. Temporary accommodation in refuges becomes merely a dead end, the hope it offers a charade, if there is no permanent accommodation available afterwards. For many women in Britain, applying to get rehoused by local councils or housing associations is often their only option. However, privately rented accommodation can sometimes help, and some women are able to become owner occupiers in their own right.

Private accommodation: owned or rented

Some women may be able to find private rented accommodation. This can have the advantage, if furnished, of providing furniture and facilities which can be helpful for women who have been forced to leave all their possessions behind. It can be a particularly useful option for women without children. However, renting from a private landlord does not offer a good source of long-term, permanent accommodation. Private tenancies are almost always insecure. This is particularly so since the introduction of the shorthold tenancies which many private landlords currently offer, and which are often for as brief a period as six months. In addition, privately rented accommodation can be very expensive, priced outside the range of people on low incomes.

In the cheaper tenancies, conditions are sometimes poor and the accommodation is often limited to bedsits with little comfort and no security, leaving women fleeing domestic violence particularly vulnerable. Tenants' rights have been eroded over recent years, so it can be hard to get such properties improved. But even these cheaper options may cost more than women can afford, especially in the capital. Jenny Muir and Mandy Ross of the London Housing Unit have produced a book called *Housing the Poorer Sex*, published in 1993, which details how difficult it is for many women in London to make use of private rented accommodation. On average, women have lower incomes than men and therefore find it harder to gain access to housing in the private sector. Only 19 per cent of women can afford to rent a bedsit in London without assistance from housing benefit, as compared with 57 per cent of men. The London Housing Unit book demonstrates that privately rented housing, in London at least, is only slightly more affordable than owner occupation.

Rented accommodation can also be hard to find. The British government is currently encouraging an expansion of the private rented sector, but it remains very small in comparison with similar countries. In many areas, private tenancies are extremely scarce, and the competition to procure them may be fierce. In major cities, for example, such tenancies are often taken within hours of being advertised. Crucially, a very large number of private landlords refuse to take children. For these various reasons, the private rented sector does not offer a satisfactory permanent solution for many women fleeing domestic violence, especially those with dependent children.

Many women who have left their homes due to violence may be in a position to buy their own accommodation, most commonly after a property settlement with their ex-partner. Owner occupation is frequently used as a housing option and can work well for abused women and their children who have some financial resources, especially when property prices are not prohibitively high as they became in the late 1980s. The legal and housing issues involved are complicated, however, and can work to a woman's disadvantage. It is essential for women in this situation to seek advice both from a good solicitor experienced in matrimonial work and, if possible, from a housing adviser in a housing advice agency. To settle property matters can take a long time and, at the end of it, the settlement may be insufficient to enable a satisfactory purchase of another property of the size required. For a woman who has fled to a safe location, divorce and property settlement can be particularly traumatic and may become almost impossible if it is not safe for either her or her representatives to have any contact with the male partner. Women in this situation may be able to disguise their location by making an arrangement to be represented by solicitors in a different part of the country. Nevertheless, they will need somewhere safe and permanent to live during the process. Refuges are not suitable for the lengthy stays which may be involved; they very often have a time limit on residency.

Thus owner occupation, though a satisfactory solution for many women homeless due to violence, can also be a problematic housing option. And even where it is a possibility, the well-documented poverty trap which often awaits women who leave their partners and become single parents may preclude it. Women without children are also likely to find it difficult to become owner occupiers due to financial consider-ations. The London Housing Unit found that only 15 per cent of women, as compared with 49 per cent of men, earned enough to qualify for a mortgage for a one bedroom flat in London.

While both owner occupation and private renting have a role to play in meeting the housing needs of women who have left home because of violence, many women turn to the social housing sector, which includes both local councils and housing associations. *Housing the Poorer Sex* points out that women rely on public sector housing to a greater extent than men do because they are less likely to be able to use the private market, especially if they have children or other caring responsibilities or are elderly. Getting rehoused by the local council or by a housing association may therefore be the principal viable options. It is vital that these possibilities remain open to women and children who are homeless due to domestic violence.

Council housing

During the twentieth century, a large and solid heritage of public sector housing was gradually built up in Britain. Every town and city, and almost every village, has – or had – a stock of council houses in it. Until recently, we have all been so familiar with this scenario that it has sometimes been a shock to find that such estates of housing owned by the local council do not exist in many other countries. While poorly built or run-down estates exist with all their attendant problems, British council housing has provided decent and well-built accommodation for many millions of citizens at affordable rents. In the past at least, there has been so much of it that tenants have not felt as stigmatized and 'labelled' as people often have been in public or welfare housing projects in other countries.

All this, however, is changing. Over the last few years, the British government has been attempting by a variety of means to break up the solid stock of publicly owned housing which has previously been such a benchmark of British policy. Funding and spending restrictions on local councils coupled with the introduction of right-to-buy legislation, under which many council tenants have been enabled to buy their homes, have resulted in a large decrease in the amount of council housing, and in under-investment and poor maintenance. Many housing authorities have lost half or more of their units – and of course it is always the best stock which is sold. The properties which people have bought are the houses with gardens, the units with three or four bedrooms, the older properties with period features which have been recently renovated at council expense. Councils are often left with a disproportionate number of smaller units, maisonettes and flats, commonly the high-rise ones that nobody wants.

Thus, the supply of council housing has been substantially diminished and the remaining stock is usually of poorer quality. During the 1980s, council building programmes were wound down almost completely under the impact of government restrictions and cutbacks in public expenditure. The result is a crisis in the availability of social housing at reasonable rents despite government encouragement of the housing association sector to fill the gap. There is now a chronic shortage of such accommodation coupled with a mushrooming growth in homelessness.

The national housing advice service, Shelter, has produced an emergency contingency plan to attempt to halt the decline. Together with other housing experts, it estimates that at least 100,000 additional homes per year are required in the social rented sector even to begin the process of meeting the need, and it proposes that these are provided by a variety of means including bringing empty properties back into use. However, nothing like that number of extra homes is available despite various government initiatives. The shortfall remains massive. The housing market is stagnating and the building industry is in crisis, beset with losses and bankruptcies. Many in the construction trade estimate that the trade has contracted by 50 per cent. Meanwhile homelessness keeps on growing. Women and children who have left home because of male violence and who have no other permanent housing options can be disproportionately affected by this situation.

At the same time that Britain has a chronic shortage of public sector housing, there is also legislation in place which says that local councils must secure accommodation for certain sections of the homeless. The result is, in the words of a council housing officer we interviewed recently, like being 'crushed between a rock and a hard place'. The homeless continue to knock on the council's door, but the accommodation to meet the need keeps disappearing.

Before 1977, there was some confusion as regards homelessness. Under the National Assistance Act 1948, homelessness was seen as the responsibility of social services departments, but under the Housing Act 1957, it was the duty of local housing authorities to provide housing. The homeless families' accommodation which social services provided often carried a stigma with it. Meanwhile homelessness was growing and there was beginning to be an awareness that people were homeless not because of their own poor conduct or personal inadequacy, but because there was not enough housing. By the mid-1970s, women who had suffered domestic violence and the newly formed refuge movement were putting particular pressure on the government to improve the permanent housing options available to women homeless because of violence. Over several years, there were moves from a variety of quarters to pass fresh legislation on homelessness.

In 1977, under the Labour government of the day, the Housing (Homeless Persons) Act was passed. A private member's bill put forward by a Liberal MP, Stephen Ross, this was essentially a government measure, reproducing a former Department of the Environment draft bill. The idea of it was to give housing departments of local councils the principal responsibility for homelessness. In fact they were given a formal duty in law to house certain categories of homeless people. The original bill was meant to be very wide-reaching, but several limitations were introduced before it made it through Parliament. Due to these amendments, some commentators have suggested that the Act was a 'confidence trick' from the start. And many housing experts claim that, throughout its life, the legislation has been hamstrung, since it has never been accompanied by the resources necessary to allow local housing authorities to do the job properly. Nevertheless the Act is there, and councils break the law if they fail to follow it.

The original Act is now Part III of the Housing Act 1985. It is brief, general and ambiguously worded in places, and so is open to a wide range of interpretations. However, it is constantly being modified by case law, and it is accompanied by a Code of Guidance issued by the government from time to time. The most recent version was issued in 1991 after extensive consultation. It provides guidance on each section of the Act, and recommends that housing departments of local councils interpret the Act quite generously. Local authorities are expected to take note of the Code and to be guided by it. However, they do not have to act on it; it does not have statutory force. The Women's Aid federations and a variety of research studies, including the study of domestic violence and housing conducted by our own research group, have recommended that the Code should be given the force of law, but there seems little chance that this will happen. Many councils do not follow the Code of Guidance as a result.

Neither the Act itself nor the Code of Guidance covers all the homeless. Most notably, they omit almost all of the single homeless who have become increasingly visible on the streets of British cities in recent years in the wake of the housing crisis. Being homeless, literally without a roof over your head, is not sufficient. To be eligible for rehousing under the Act, you have to pass various 'tests'. The housing departments of most councils have special sections, sometimes called 'homelessness sections' or 'homeless persons units', which employ trained case workers to assess whether or not applicants have passed these tests and should be accepted for rehousing.

Now that public housing has been put under such extreme pressure, due to under-investment in the social housing sector and to the chronic depletion of council housing stock, local authorities are placed in an almost impossible situation in their attempts to operate the Act and to follow the Code of Guidance. The serious lack of permanent accommodation of a reasonable standard is accompanied in many areas by a shortage of adequate temporary accommodation. One result of this is that some councils have been forced to interpret the homelessness legislation much more stringently than they would like to, while others have always adopted a policy of what is often called 'minimal legal compliance' on principle. Housing officers in homelessness sections and homeless persons units often suffer high levels of stress and exhaustion, due to the large workloads involved and the almost impossible rationing job which they are expected to do while dealing with people who are homeless and often desperate. Managers usually do what they can to support officers, but are often in high-stress situations themselves. This is the backdrop against which the following discussion of how councils actually deliver their housing services must be understood.

Delivering housing services

The first test which housing authorities must apply to applicants under the legislation is to ascertain whether they are homeless or not according to the terms of the Act. Second, applicants must be in 'priority need'. This is defined as including people with dependent children, pregnant women, people homeless due to emergencies such as flooding, and people who are vulnerable because of old age, disability, handicap or for any other 'special reason'. The person must also be homeless unintentionally, which means that they are not homeless through any deliberate act or omission of their own. And in general they should have a 'local connection' with the authority they apply to.

Under the Act, local councils have a responsibility to secure temporary accommodation for an applicant while they investigate the case, if they judge at the initial interview with a homelessness officer that the person is both homeless and in priority need. The officer concerned then makes enquiries into the case and is expected to come to a decision as quickly as possible about whether the applicant is to be accepted for rehousing. The enquiries are expected to be 'thorough but not over-elaborate' according to the Code, and to be completed within 30 working days whenever possible. If the person is accepted for rehousing, there is a legal duty for the authority to secure temporary accommodation for them until an offer of permanent rehousing is made. A place in a refuge usually counts as 'securing temporary accommodation'. In consequence, some councils make funding grants to refuges under a special section of the homelessness legislation.

For women who have suffered violence, there are special points to consider about the legislation. Importantly, being homeless due to domestic violence counts as 'homelessness' and not as 'intentional homelessness' under the Act. The Women's Aid movement and others active in the domestic violence field at the time that the Act was originally passed lobbied hard for domestic violence to be included as a reason for homelessness. The good news is that it was. However, there have always been problems, in certain areas, of women fleeing violence being regarded as intentionally homeless.

Quite soon after the Act was passed, it was established in case law that women living in refuges are also to be regarded as homeless, even though they do have a roof over their heads. Until recently, however, women were only regarded as homeless because of domestic violence if they had suffered violence from someone actually living with them. The reality is that women frequently experience domestic violence from men whom they do not live with. They may be abused by ex-partners, estranged partners or boyfriends who have their own accommodation somewhere else. In *The Hidden Struggle*, Amina Mama suggests that some black women – and in her study, women of Caribbean descent in particular – have long-term 'visiting relationships' with men who do not actually live with them. None of these women would have been eligible for rehousing following violence under the original Act.

The legislation was amended by the Housing and Planning Act 1986. The amendment added that an applicant should be considered as homeless if it was not reasonable for the person to continue to occupy their former property. In 1989, it was established in case law that this clause could be used for domestic violence following a case in Broxbourne (*R.* v. *Broxbourne, ex parte Willmoth* 1989) which involved domestic violence from outside the home. The ruling was that such violence made it unreasonable for the woman to continue to occupy the property. The new Code of Guidance now recommends that violence from outside the home should be included as a cause of homelessness under the Act. Not all councils follow this guidance, however, although increasing numbers do so.

The Women's Aid federations and concerned housing bodies have pushed for the definitions of domestic violence, which councils use in determining whether they view someone as homeless, to be expanded to include psychological and sexual violence. The councils with the most generous interpretations of the Act have done so. But many others tend to include severe sexual violence but to exclude emotional or psychological abuse. In these authorities, women who have suffered sometimes quite extreme mental and emotional violence are then excluded from the possibility of being rehoused into council property. In any case, homelessness officers tend to vary in how they deal with psychological and sexual violence. Some take it more seriously than others. Many officers ask for more evidence of psychological violence than they do for physical violence.

The categories used in assessing whether an applicant is in 'priority need' also affect women fleeing domestic violence. Both the previous and the new Code of Guidance recommend that women without dependent children who have suffered domestic violence should be included as being in priority need. This recommendation, if followed, radically changes the position for women without children. Without it, it is almost impossible for such women to get rehoused by their local council unless they are 'vulnerable' for some other reason. They then face a very uncertain housing future unless they can afford to buy a property of their own. The Code in theory at least remedies all that, and offers good tidings to child-free women. Again, however, many local authorities, especially those with small stocks of single-person housing, do not follow the Code in this respect.

As the crisis in public housing continues to bite, some local councils have introduced policies to ask women fleeing domestic violence to go and see a solicitor before they may be considered as homeless. The idea is that if a woman is able to take out a non-molestation or an ouster injunction against her partner, she may be able to return to her former home. Women may then be told that they are intentionally homeless if they do not go back. Some local authorities take this hard line even if there is previous evidence that injunctions have not worked and the woman herself is adamant that she does not wish to pursue this course of action. In the recent study of domestic violence and housing which we conducted, we accumulated a great deal of evidence of the devastating effects that such policies can have on the lives of women homeless because of violence. The Women's Aid federations, the National Inter-Agency Working Party and other concerned bodies and reports all recommend against the use of legal remedies in this way. The Code of Guidance warns against it, but not strongly. Women's Aid also recommends that the Code is strengthened on this issue.

Local connection is another area of difficulty. Women fleeing domestic violence frequently apply for housing in local authorities far removed from their own home area. If a woman homeless due to violence does not have a local connection, the authority she applies to should disregard this factor providing that she cannot be referred to any other authority where she does have a local connection because of the threat of violence. Many authorities follow this course of action, but others, particularly perhaps in London and in rural areas, may dispute cases strongly and make every effort to refer women elsewhere. In some areas, councils use a variety of methods which together have the effect of making it almost impossible for women without a local connection to be rehoused.

It should be obvious by now that local councils vary widely in how they interpret the homelessness legislation. The use of discretion is built in, so it is not hard to see how inconsistencies and anomalies can arise. In our own study, we found a wide variation not only between local authorities but also between the practice of individual homelessness officers working in the same authority. This means that whether women who have suffered violence get rehoused or not can depend on the luck of the draw – on which authority they happen to apply to, or even which officer they happen to see.

The way in which housing departments process applications also varies widely. Some ask very few questions about the violence and conduct few or no enquiries into it. In others, homelessness interviews are quite adversarial in nature, and women are subjected to detailed questioning about the violence which they have experienced. This is often the case in authorities which are trying to ration access to small amounts of stock, but it can also be related to the political complexion and commitment of the council in question. In such authorities, the maximum possible amount of evidence may be required before a woman stands a chance of being accepted for rehousing. For many women, however, there is little corroborative evidence available. Having to produce police and medical reports to prove domestic violence works against women who do not have such reports, who may be too embarrassed or frightened of repercussions to approach other agencies for help. Women visiting doctors or casualty departments with injuries often pretend that the injuries were not caused by violence. And black women in particular may be suspicious of involving the police and may not wish to expose their partners to police intervention. They will be disadvantaged if the housing department then insists on the production of reports as evidence of violence.

Homelessness applications in such authorities are often contested strongly, especially where stocks of council housing have been depleted. Women applicants are likely to be successful only if they have active support from voluntary sector and housing advice agencies, and from legal representatives working hard on their behalf. This can be exhausting for the women concerned. Many lose heart and give up on their applications. It is also a considerable drain on the limited resources of refuges and voluntary organizations, and on the time and energy of solicitors.

In other authorities, applications may proceed in a straightforward manner and officers may be as helpful and sympathetic as they can. However, it seems from all the relevant research that, in most authorities, some women complain of intrusive and insensitive questioning when they are being interviewed by officers. Women fleeing violence want to be treated with dignity and respect, and to be believed. What they do not want is to be forced to go into embarrassing and distressing detail about their violent experiences. One woman fleeing violence put it this way:

> I felt in a way like I was being judged and it was all my fault, my failings, and that's how he made me feel. I came out very upset ... you just feel stripped afterwards ... You shouldn't have to give a detailed account of [the violence], I mean you don't want to recall it at the best of times ... Because you feel like a failure anyway. You feel awful having to sit there and say it all. And to have to say it to a total stranger, it's really demoralizing. It makes you feel degraded. It makes you feel dirty ... And it's your life. And you don't want to put it all on the table for discussion. You don't want that ...

The investigations which are conducted can also be a source of anxiety and insecurity to women who have fled from violence and who are living in secret locations to avoid discovery by their violent partners. Local authorities attempt to be as careful as possible about confidentiality issues and about protecting women's safety, but most refuges can report incidences where breaches have occurred. The practice of contacting husbands is particularly nerve-wracking for women in hiding because of violence and appears to serve little useful purpose. Encouragingly, the new Code of Guidance recommends that violent perpetrators should not normally be contacted, and many local authorities now follow this advice; but many others do not. Some still follow the largely discredited practice of contacting friends and neighbours for information.

The Code of Guidance recommends that women who have suffered violence should be interviewed by a woman or by a specialist officer. A large number of women are very grateful if this option is offered, even if it means coming back for another appointment (providing this can be done safely). Many, however, are quite happy to be interviewed by a man. Thus, offering a choice does not necessarily place undue pressure on women officers. A considerable number of authorities now operate policies of this sort. Similarly, many authorities offer black women the option of being interviewed by a black officer, preferably a woman and of a similar racial and cultural heritage. In this context, various housing officers and workers in the field have noted that, for some black women and women from minority ethnic communities fleeing violence, interview by a male officer of the same ethnic or cultural background might be particularly inappropriate. The possible

choices of officer need to be offered actively so that women are aware of their options and can make informed decisions. It is no good merely providing such a choice only if a woman is confident enough and sufficiently knowledgeable about council policies to take the initiative and request it. During our research, we were told of various authorities where a choice of officer was available but women applicants were unaware of the policy and so could not take advantage of it.

Even where authorities have such policies in place, there can be a problem regarding the attitudes and opinions which housing department staff hold about women who have suffered domestic violence. One woman whom we recently interviewed summed this up as follows:

> They never take me seriously. Because I've got a ring in my nose. They just dismiss me, don't believe me ... They should stop looking at us as 'those women'. We get labelled because we've suffered violence ... They are really shocked when they find I'm doing a degree.

The attitudes which officers hold can be crucial in determining how a woman is treated. In 1985, a research study of the policies and practices of four local authorities in Scotland by Mary Brailey found that such attitudes often spring from traditional notions about what a family should be and about a woman's place within it. Things have probably improved in many authorities since this study was done. Nevertheless, many women in our own housing study reported that they felt judged by their interviewing officers on a wide variety of grounds – because they were black, for example, or older, or young and pregnant, or living unconventional lifestyles. They often felt that they were not taken seriously. Some felt that there was a division in many officers' minds between abused women whom they thought of as being deserving of assistance and those whom they thought of as non-deserving. Such views take many forms and hark back to the Poor Law. They take a long time to eradicate.

Potential racism and other discrimination

Many commentators and researchers have highlighted the need for councils to be aware of potential racism in the delivery of their services and to operate anti-racism policies. In her study *The Hidden Struggle*, Amina Mama found that black women who were interviewed for the research tended to underreport racism in their contacts with housing authorities. Even so, it was clear that the women in the study had faced a variety of bureaucratic obstructions, and sometimes inaction and discrimination. Mama concludes:

> [Black women] are very often not only denied access to decent housing away from extremely violent men and kept in the half-life of homelessness for very long periods, but also subjected to the emotional traumas of racism, made all the more damaging because of the insidious ways in which it can operate over the months and even years of homelessness and powerlessness.

Black women in both Mama's study and our own sometimes faced questioning in homelessness interviews which was insensitive and ignorant of cultural issues, and in which racist attitudes were only lightly veiled. The provision of interpreting for women who have suffered violence and who do not speak English as their first language can be particularly crucial due to the delicacy of the issues involved. Interpreting services for locally spoken languages are, however, ad hoc and piecemeal in many authorities. While a few provide comprehensive and efficient interpretation and translation, many offer either fragmentary services or none at all.

Women fleeing violence need access to interpreters who are women and who have some grasp of the issues involved. As in the case of black interviewing officers, the use of male interpreters can be particularly inappropriate for some women, especially if they are of the same ethnic community or heritage. Interpreters should be trained and properly paid for their services. All too often in local authorities, the provision of interpreting depends on the goodwill and generosity of refuge staff and council workers who are fluent in the language concerned. It is never acceptable to use a woman's children to interpret, especially when traumatic personal issues involving abuse and violence are being discussed. While this should be obvious to all concerned, it still happens time and time again.

There are few black officers in post in many homeless persons units or homelessness sections outside major cities, and even fewer in senior managerial or policy-making positions. Thus, the interests of black people, and perhaps of black women in particular, are often overlooked. Some researchers have noted that black women may wait longer in temporary accommodation than white women in some authorities. The areas where rehousing is offered can also be a problem.

Due to the omnipresence of racism and, for some women, the presence of extended family networks, black women and women of minority ethnic heritages have to be particularly careful about areas of rehousing. As it is, the National Association of Local Government Women's Committees, among many bodies, has pointed out that black women tend to be rehoused in black communities in the poorest accommodation and the most deprived inner city areas. An African-Caribbean woman whom we interviewed said that:

> Black women's choice of area must be respected. The women know what support they will need and choose their areas accordingly ... Black women shouldn't be put all in one area. Then you get the 'ghetto' effect and it becomes a 'no go' area for whites. Then the streets aren't cleaned as often, the bins aren't emptied. It happens ... And women shouldn't be housed in a white racist area either. We would like to see people being housed where they want. Black people usually want to be near other black people – want to be near friends – but they might not. They want to make the choice though. Not have it pushed on to them ...

Immigration and nationality issues should not get tangled up with housing matters, but they sometimes do. In some authorities, abused women with properties in other countries may face being told that they are intentionally homeless if they do not return there. For immigrant women whose immigration status may be dependent on that of their husbands, the process of seeking rehousing after leaving home due to violence can be particularly traumatic, especially if intensive enquiries are carried out. It should be noted that under immigration law applying as homeless counts as having 'recourse to public funds'.

Lesbians, older women, very young women, and women with disabilities, among others, can all face specific difficulties in getting rehoused. These problems often revolve around judgemental attitudes held by housing officers. For example, in the housing study which we conducted, some older women whom we interviewed felt as though they were being brushed to one side. They felt that housing officers neither understood nor empathized with their problems. Young women also had trouble in being taken seriously as genuinely homeless due to violence. If they did not have children, they faced great difficulty in being accepted for rehousing even if they had suffered quite severe sexual or physical abuse. Most of the young women whom we talked with, in both our pilot and main studies, remained homeless or moved into special projects. A recent piece of research by the Housing Campaign for Single People (CHAR) and the Joseph Rowntree Foundation found that as many as four in ten young homeless women may be homeless due to sexual abuse. While this problem is beginning to be addressed in some areas, it remains a cause of grave concern.

Lesbians face both invisibility and a lack of concern for any difficulties they have, coupled with prejudice and discrimination. Applying as homeless therefore presents specific problems, and there is little support or help available. Some authorities have policies to treat lesbians and gay men fleeing violence exactly the same as heterosexuals, but many do not recognize the issue. Women with disabilities also face difficulties. They are rarely catered for adequately by housing departments and are excluded from much housing provision. Shelter has pointed out in its good practice guide, *Homelessness*, that very few housing departments keep specialized records or information about disability. In addition, disabled women who are abused face a general ignorance about the effects of violence on their lives, or about the fact that they might experience domestic violence at all. Women with disabilities who have suffered violence may have great difficulties in approaching the housing department in the first place, especially if their carer is also their abuser, and may need specialized support and help. There is also a need for councils to address mental health issues and domestic abuse. At the moment, provision for abused women with mental health special needs is woefully inadequate.

Some local housing authorities do operate specific anti-discrimination policies for people with disabilities. They may also operate such policies for lesbians and gay men, which may cover homelessness due to violence. These developments are to be welcomed, although they rarely go far enough. The majority of authorities do not have policies of this sort, however, and many which do have been publicly ridiculed by the Conservative right and by members of the government. Recommendations have been made – for example, in the *What Support?* research report about Hammersmith and Fulham, and others – that more research is specifically needed into the experiences of black women, lesbians, older and very young women, and women with disabilities in seeking rehousing. They also recommend strongly that such experiences should be included as an integral part of all domestic violence training in housing departments and elsewhere.

Effects of the legislation

There are many points which could be made about the homelessness legislation, only some of which we have touched on here. A fuller consideration of the issues involved can be found in the various publications about housing available from the Women's Aid federations. Although the most recent Code of Guidance improves the position for women homeless due to violence, the operation of the legislation is beset with problems. Some of these are about the use of discretion by authorities, the lack of clarity and public information about policies, the attitudes and practices of homelessness staff, and especially the impact of shrinking resources. Most of these problems have been there since the legislation first came into force.

Partly due to such problems, and partly as a result of the number of hoops which applicants have to jump through to qualify for rehousing under the Act, many in the movement against domestic violence were doubtful about how useful the legislation would be when it was first implemented. A major study of both temporary and permanent accommodation for women fleeing violence was conducted by the Women's Aid Federation (England) and the Department of the Environment, and published in 1981 in a book called *Leaving Violent Men*. The study was also reported in Jan Pahl's widely used although now somewhat outdated book, *Private Violence and Public Policy*. The authors of the study, Val Binney, Gina Harkell and Judy Nixon, found that, eighteen months after the original Housing (Homeless Persons) Act 1977 came into force, fewer than half the Women's Aid groups of the time felt that the housing prospects of women in their refuges had improved. Many groups felt that the gains of the Act were only temporary and had been subsequently eroded by local authority spending cuts.

Fifteen years later, these spending cuts have become so savage that it can be hard to recollect that we all thought they were quite bad in the late 1970s. However, women who are homeless due to violence probably rely more heavily on the homelessness legislation now, and Women's Aid refuges are more likely to regard the Act as an advance, than they did just after it came into force.

In 1986 Welsh Women's Aid conducted a survey of housing authority policy and practice in Wales. It was published under the title, *The Answer's Maybe – and That's Final*, an apt summing up of many

women's experiences of housing departments. Welsh Women's Aid
drew up a comprehensive list of recommendations which are also put
forward by the other federations. They are included in the *Women's
Aid Housing Resource Pack* produced by WAFE in conjunction with
Welsh Women's Aid and Shelter. WAFE is also producing a housing
charter for women who have suffered violence. Housing organizations
like the London Housing Unit and Shelter, as well as Women's Aid,
produce useful good practice guides on the homelessness legislation
which include material on domestic violence.

Most of these bodies would recommend that the legislation is
amended to improve the position of abused women and others, but
would stress that such amendments would have to be accompanied by
the provision of additional resources to local authorities to allow them
to do the job. Many organizations have recommended that the Code of
Guidance, or sections of it, be given statutory force. For women fleeing
violence this applies particularly to the sections on women without
children, on violence from outside the home, on local connection and
on the inappropriateness of routinely expecting women to pursue legal
remedies.

Meanwhile, housing queues get longer. In the areas of greatest
public housing shortage, many women are turned away or may wait in
temporary accommodation for two or more years. Temporary
accommodation may be in refuges, in council or housing association
projects, in bed and breakfast hotels or in privately leased
accommodation. In our study and in others, the use of self-contained
accommodation leased from private landlords and homeowners was
preferred by women who had been offered it, and the government is
currently showing some renewed interest in this option. The housing
minister recommends against the use of bed and breakfast
accommodation, and many councils are trying to phase out its use – not
before time. For women fleeing violence, such accommodation can be
particularly inappropriate because of the absence of support and the
lack of security in the properties, which can place women in physical
danger. There may also be no facilities at all for children. However,
there are some innovative women-only bed and breakfast projects and
hostels in existence in some areas, for women who choose this type of
accommodation.

The Women's Aid federations and various housing bodies
recommend that women should stay in such emergency accommodation for only a short time and then should be transferred to

self-contained temporary accommodation while they wait. In temporary accommodation of almost all types, however, the needs of children are not catered for adequately. Crèches, play areas and equipment, and support and assistance for children are rarely provided, and children's needs are often ignored in the way in which new temporary accommodation is designed and operated. However, some local authorities and housing associations now attempt to provide good, supportive temporary accommodation in self-contained units, cluster flats and shared houses, including facilities for children.

There are some housing solutions for women experiencing domestic violence which avoid the use of the homelessness legislation. Councils may operate policies to allow women to stay in their original homes, or they may offer emergency management transfers, so that women may be transferred to other properties. Housing officers on council estates can have an important role to play here, since they may be the first point of contact with the housing department which a woman council tenant has when she wants housing assistance to deal with domestic violence. The trend towards the decentralization of housing departments into smaller local units may mean that local housing officers are more approachable in this way, although there can also be problems of security since small neighbourhood offices may be well known to a woman's violent partner. For this reason, many decentralized housing authorities have provisions for women who have suffered domestic violence to approach different offices from their own in order to get help.

Applying for an emergency management transfer can seem the obvious solution for a woman experiencing violence, especially if the man's name is not on the rent book. With the shortage of council accommodation, however, such transfers are becoming more and more difficult to obtain in many authorities. In the study which we conducted, for example, none of the women we interviewed obtained a management transfer. Some authorities include a clause in the tenancy agreement about domestic violence which is usually similar to, but separate from, other clauses on racial and sexual harassment or on harassment by neighbours. Such clauses say that domestic violence is unacceptable in council properties and is an evictable offence. They are rarely used, not least because of the potential danger of repercussions for the woman involved. But they can act as a symbolic statement to all tenants and to the public that the authority will not tolerate domestic violence.

Since the Housing Act 1980, council tenants have had security of tenure. However, the case of the *London Borough of Greenwich* v. *McGrady* in 1982 established that one partner can end a joint tenancy. The *McGrady* ruling was upheld in 1992 by the case of the *London Borough of Hammersmith and Fulham* v. *Monk*. This can be useful for councils wishing to regain a property abandoned by a joint tenant because of violence. But pressure should never be put on a woman to terminate her tenancy in this way, since she may face further violence as a result. The ruling is not used very much in consequence, although some councils have employed it from time to time. Current proposals being developed to introduce new means of bringing a tenancy to an end due to violence, or for transferring it to the woman partner, may mean that the *McGrady* ruling is soon superseded.

Good practice

In a rather bleak scenario of increasing homelessness and housing shortages, there are some bright spots. The Home Affairs Committee recommends in its 1993 report that local authorities should be advised by government 'in the strongest possible terms to put an end to the nonsense' where a woman fleeing domestic violence is deemed to be intentionally homeless. The Committee also recommends that priority should be given to rehousing abused women and children. There is an encouraging trend in some local authority housing departments towards the adoption of written domestic violence policies and good practice guidelines. Some of these policies cover the council's activities as a whole, while some are limited to the housing department. The trend started in London authorities a few years ago, but the accelerating housing crisis in London and, in some cases, changes in political control have resulted in many of the original policies being cut back, or even rescinded. The London Borough of Ealing, for example, cancelled its previously generous domestic violence policy overnight when the Conservatives came to power there in 1990.

Also in 1990, the London Borough of Hammersmith and Fulham introduced an especially pioneering domestic violence policy on homelessness as part of a council-wide initiative. However, many features of the policy were cancelled less than a year after their inception, when it appeared that the resource implications were larger than at first anticipated and the borough faced severe budgetary restrictions. These were caused first by the threat, and then by the reality, of being charge-capped by central government. The authority had never had a large council-owned housing stock, and this stock had been further reduced by the sell-offs of council housing and by government restrictions on the building of new properties. The shortage of permanent council housing stock and rising costs of temporary accommodation were coupled with growing numbers of homelessness applications, a rising proportion of which were made by women homeless through domestic violence. Even though some of the features of the policy remained in place, the situation for women seeking rehousing in the Hammersmith and Fulham area changed quickly from good to poor, although it is still better than that in several other boroughs. Much work has since gone into working out ways to ameliorate the situation and to provide as good a service to abused women and their children as possible, even though rehousing is now so difficult. However, the loss of the main features of the policy shocked the refuge network in London and elsewhere, and is deeply regretted by many local domestic violence activists and workers in the field.

A very small number of London authorities have since developed policies similar to Hammersmith and Fulham's which have remained in place or been trimmed, although not too substantially. However, many London boroughs are particularly hard-hit by local government spending cutbacks. As a result, most of those which operate domestic violence policy and practice guidelines have been forced to retract various of the provisions which they contain. On the other hand, some local authorities outside London have developed excellent new policies on domestic violence in recent years, and are continuing to do so. It is important to avoid the assumption that the best – and the worst – practice is confined to London.

The adoption of domestic violence policy and practice guidelines is recommended by the Women's Aid federations and by housing bodies and research studies. Good practice guidelines help both the council and the public by making details of policy and practice available, comprehensible and accessible. They contribute towards improving services, not only for women and children fleeing violence, but for all women. They also standardize how domestic violence cases are dealt with across the authority, while still allowing for discretion and for each case to be considered on its merits. In addition, an important part of what they do is to demonstrate to the public, to all council members and staff, and to people using council services, the commitment of the authority to opposing domestic violence as a matter of principle. Some of the good practice provisions which domestic violence policies usually include have obvious financial implications, and authorities adopting such policies need to be clear about the extent of extra resourcing which may be required. But many aspects of good practice do not involve additional expenditure. Even authorities facing stringent housing and funding shortages can improve their services in some ways.

In the development of domestic violence and homelessness policies, it is crucial that solid links are built with refuges and voluntary sector groups, with other relevant departments of the council and with the trade unions whose members will have to put them into practice. In any case, policy and practice guidelines are often initiated in conjunction with local inter-agency projects on domestic violence. These types of project are discussed further in Chapter 8. Women's Aid and specialist projects for women fleeing violence – for example, black women, single women or lesbians – need to be involved in the drawing up of such policies and guidelines. And the national Women's Aid federations, which are able to take an overview of the issues concerned, have vital expertise to offer in this area.

The success in practice of any policy depends fundamentally on the full involvement and commitment of homelessness staff, who may be very hard-pressed by the current housing shortage. Such staff need to be fully involved in the drafting and adoption of a policy, and preferably should be offered extra training and support when the policy comes into operation. The importance of taking staff, managers, councillors and unions along with a policy cannot be overemphasized.

Domestic violence policies and good practice guidelines often cover the activities of estate managers and district housing officers as well as homelessness staff, and urge that a sympathetic, supportive attitude is adopted by these officers which will encourage women to approach the housing authority for help. They generally contain commitments to follow or to improve on the Code of Guidance. Usually, this involves such measures as using sensitive, non-intrusive interviewing techniques, adopting a believing attitude to the woman concerned, minimizing enquiries into the violence experienced and accepting a woman's statement about this as sufficient evidence. Domestic violence guidelines are also likely to involve policy commitments to rehouse women who traditionally have not been rehoused under the Act. These include women who have experienced psychological or sexual violence, women without children, women who have suffered violence from outside the home and women with no local connection.

There may be specific policies to refrain from requesting women to seek legal advice, and to offer women who were previously council tenants rehousing of like or better standard. Guidelines may also include specific commitments to address the needs of black women and other women facing discrimination, such as lesbians and women with disabilities. Further provisions may concern emergency management transfers in cases of violence, domestic violence clauses in tenancy agreements, and recommendations to override rent arrears considerations in such cases. Policies often include commitments to prioritize repairs caused by violence, and to increase security in properties rented by women experiencing domestic violence from outside the home.

Domestic violence practice guidelines almost always include the provision of domestic violence training for all housing officers and managers. Interviewing women who have suffered physical, sexual or psychological abuse is a task of skill and sensitivity. Training in how to do it is of critical importance. Such training needs to include material on how to operate domestic violence policies and how to work with women homeless due to violence, and should also cover general issues of domestic violence awareness. The Women's Aid federations recommend that, even where there are officers in post who specialize in domestic violence work, housing department staff in general should be thoroughly trained. It is vital that Women's Aid, as the key voluntary sector agency, and specialist refuges and services for abused women and children, are involved in the training provided. These issues are discussed further in Chapter 8. It should be noted, however, that research by ourselves and others has shown that training on its own changes very little, without associated developments in policy and practice and a commitment by the authority concerned to take on the issue of domestic violence in an active way.

Domestic violence policies need to be monitored and reviewed regularly. They also need to be accompanied by clear public information about both the policy and the services available. How much or how little to publicize a domestic violence policy can be a matter of contention. Various housing bodies and advice centres point out that the financial and political context into which any policy of this type is introduced is critical. The London Housing Unit, for example, says in its 1991 guide to good practice on sexual harassment, *Cutting it Out*:

The constraints under which a council is operating – financial, political or otherwise – should always be acknowledged and taken into account. Policy makers concerned to promote equitable and non-discriminatory service delivery are faced with a dilemma over whether to go for a 'best practice' model, which could later become an obvious target in a round of cuts, or to go for a less ambitious policy, which may have more chance of staying the course.

Housing associations

Particularly since the Housing Act 1988, government policy has been to encourage housing associations to replace local authorities as the principal source of social rented housing. Some housing experts claim that it is hard to see how this could happen. Local authorities still have millions of properties; housing associations only hundreds of thousands. However, the government is trying everything it can think of to make the change happen, and it can be safely predicted that housing associations will become more important as providers of social housing in the future.

Whereas government policies to decrease local authority housing provision have had a profound effect, some of its initiatives to encourage the housing association sector to take over from local authorities have not yet brought results. There are more initiatives to come, however, particularly in terms of how present public sector housing is to be managed and who owns it in the future. 'Large-scale voluntary transfer' involves the transfer of large amounts of council stock to specially established housing associations, and 'compulsory competitive tendering' refers to bidding for the housing management services of local authority stock. How much difference these government initiatives will make in the long term, we do not yet know. Some commentators forecast disaster. They say that the housing association movement will fail to take up the slack, that the provision of social housing will be irrevocably damaged, and that there will no longer be much in the way of accountability to the public for the housing provided. Housing associations, they claim, will become increasingly like private companies.

Others are optimistic. Many in the housing association world are pleased with its management practices and with the freedom and flexibility which it can offer, as compared with bureaucratic local authorities. These officers suggest that housing associations provide a fresh way forward for social housing, open to innovation and more responsive to people's real needs than councils have ever been. But as the housing association sector gets bigger, it may well develop similar problems to local authorities, especially where managements and central or head offices are in locations far distant from housing sites: for some large associations and trusts, this can mean the opposite end of the country.

Much of the housing association movement was set up to provide housing alternatives for people not traditionally eligible for council housing. In the last few years, it has become increasingly large and professionalized, leaving the world of alternatives and entering the mainstream. Nevertheless, women fleeing violence who fail to be rehoused by the council can sometimes get rehoused by housing associations if they apply to them independently. This can work particularly well, for example, for black women applying to housing associations which specialize in housing for black women or black families.

There are a number of housing associations which cater specifically to the needs of women. Some of these were set up many years ago, originally to assist needy women, especially those without children. Others, such as the Tai Havan women's housing association in Wales and the Nottingham Open Door project, have connections with the modern-day feminist movement and may specialize in housing for women who have suffered violence. Innovations like these may develop in other areas in the future.

Many refuges are housed in housing association property and have been established as housing association special projects. They are then managed by the local Women's Aid group or by other organizations. Some of their funding comes through the housing associations concerned, although 'topping-up' grants are required for the majority of the running costs, including the payment of support staff. A few refuges of this sort have negotiated agreements with the housing association in question so that they can be allocated a certain number of permanent tenancies per year for women to move on to. Refuges may also have special quota arrangements with a range of local housing associations for a small number of properties each year for which they can nominate specific women, usually those who are not eligible for council rehousing. Women can also get rehoused on occasion in either housing association or local council properties through the mobility scheme, HOMES. This scheme operates as a kind of clearing-house and brings together several previous mobility schemes for housing associations and local authorities which used to be run separately.

Housing associations now accept more and more people who are nominated to them by the local council. They are meant to offer 50 per cent of their tenancies to the council in this way in order to house the homeless. While some offer considerably more tenancies than this percentage, others offer far fewer. In addition, councils may not use all their nominations to housing associations for people who are 'statutorily' homeless under the Act, but may prefer to put others forward. Housing Corporation statistics in 1992 show that only 17 per cent of overall lettings by housing associations went to households who were 'statutorily' homeless. An article in the March/April 1993 edition of *Roof* claims that housing associations have become the main providers of newly built social housing, but that they seem to be letting little of their stock to homeless families under the Act.

It is likely in the future that larger amounts of housing association stock will be used to house people under the homelessness legislation who would previously have been housed by the council. Women who have suffered domestic violence may not be advantaged by this situation. As we have seen, several studies have shown that housing associations cannot take up the shortfall of council housing, and women who have suffered domestic violence make up as many as 15 per cent of those accepted as homeless by local authorities. This means that their housing prospects could become much more precarious in the future. The Home Affairs Committee, however, recommends that local authorities nominating applicants to housing associations should look sympathetically at applications from women in refuges.

Several housing bodies and research studies have pointed out that housing association rents tend to be high, since associations now have to borrow money on the commercial market in order to raise finance, and in March 1993 this was confirmed by the National Federation of Housing Associations (NFHA). Rent levels look set to rise still higher in the future. Women fleeing violence and others who are rehoused in housing association properties increasingly find themselves trapped into the social security system for the simple reason that they cannot afford the rents if they get a job. In addition, there is the problem that small associations may not be able to provide abused women and children whom they rehouse with the anonymity which they need. Emergency management transfers due to domestic violence may be impossible within a small stock. On the other hand, the large housing associations can offer emergency transfers to other areas, and two unrelated housing associations will also make arrangements on occasion to swap tenants in order to assist women fleeing violence. Accommodation provided by housing associations and trusts is often of a good standard and may compare favourably with local authority stock, although this may change as it ages. Most housing association properties are substantially newer than council properties; and, unlike housing associations, councils are no longer allowed to build much in the way of new stock.

Housing associations, like local housing authorities, are increasingly developing policy and practice domestic violence guidelines. This development is very welcome. Such guidelines are similar to those of local authorities, although they are generally less comprehensive because of the lack of statutory duties involved. They often contain specific commitments to attend to the needs of existing women tenants, which may include making the association approachable and accessible for abused women so that they feel able to reveal problems of violence to housing advisers. Domestic violence guidelines may also include provisions for increasing the security of properties, and for prioritizing emergency transfers due to violence. Housing associations often display information about domestic violence and may make commitments to engage in sensitive interviewing, to provide domestic violence awareness training for staff, and to develop housing strategies which are empowering to women. The NFHA runs an annual national Women in Housing conference. The theme of this conference for 1993 was 'Empowering Women', and it included workshops on refuges and domestic violence. The NFHA is also developing a comprehensive code of good practice on domestic violence which will be of great use to all its member associations.

Thus, there is both good and bad news for women who are homeless due to violence. Many women fleeing violence are rehoused successfully in either council or housing association properties, and are thus enabled to start new lives. For others, the decrease in the availability of socially rented housing, the consequent hoops through which some councils expect abused women to jump, and the lengthening waits in temporary accommodation for both local authority and housing association properties, which can amount to years in many areas, can make the search for permanent housing a nightmare.

7
The caring professions: social and health services

The work of caring agencies like the social and medical services is vitally important for women fleeing violence. How they deliver their services, how easy it is to approach them, their attitudes to domestic violence – all these can affect whether women who have suffered violence make use of them or not. Often a woman delays seeking help, perhaps for years, because of shame about the violence which she has experienced, loyalty to or fear of her partner, and anxieties about the sort of reception she is likely to get. She may wonder, for example, if she will be believed and taken seriously, or if she will be treated in a judgemental, patronizing or pitying way. Most importantly, she may fear that the agency workers she speaks to will not be able to guarantee secrecy and that events will move out of her control. She may well have serious anxieties that her partner will find out and that she will face dangerous repercussions.

Many researchers, activists and workers in the domestic violence field have highlighted the obstacles which women may face in seeking help from agencies. Kath Cavanagh did a piece of research with Rebecca and Russell Dobash on social and medical agencies which is reported in Jan Pahl's book, *Private Violence and Public Policy*, published in 1985. In their study, these researchers found that women were generally reluctant to make contact with official caring agencies because of feelings of shame and guilt, and often because they themselves subscribed to widely held beliefs that marriage is meant to be happy, that it is the woman's job to make sure that it is, and that the domestic sphere is private. These feelings and beliefs often had the effect of making women feel like failures if they reported the violence and hence admitted to the outside world that they were experiencing problems in their personal and intimate lives. However, if the violence became more severe, and with the passage of time, women in the study did seek help.

Many abused women confide initially in women family members, most commonly mothers and sisters. In this study, too, they were likely to turn first to relatives and friends for assistance and advice. Only later and after some deliberation did they approach official agencies. As time went on, however, the number of contacts which women in this and other studies made with agencies increased. In the face of agency unhelpfulness, they often quested around trying to find effective help to alleviate the abuse which they faced, perhaps approaching one organization after another. Thus, women did make concrete efforts to stop the violence. The findings of various studies demonstrate the active and positive attempts which abused women make to change their situation, and counteract theories which stress women's helplessness and passivity, or which suggest that they enjoy the violence to which they are subjected.

Nevertheless, women are sometimes deterred from seeking further help by the negative and unhelpful responses which they often encounter in official agencies. Such responses can be blaming, disbelieving and judgemental towards the woman herself. It seems deeply sad and unjust for abused women that, having quite possibly overcome feelings of shame and self-blame in order to take the enormous step of seeking help, they often encounter further blaming attitudes from the agencies which they approach. In a major longitudinal study conducted in the 1980s by Jan Pahl, more than half of the women interviewed had been in contact with their general practitioner, the police or the social services before going into a refuge. Fewer than half of the doctors and the police officers, and just over half of the social workers, had proved helpful.

Such problems can be experienced particularly acutely by black women, immigrant women and women from ethnic minority communities. In her study, Amina Mama found that black women faced widespread disadvantage in their contacts with a variety of helping agencies. Lesbians may also face difficulties, as may very young and much older women who have suffered violence, or indeed any woman living an unconventional lifestyle. For an abused woman in a difficult situation, getting effective and non-judgemental help can therefore depend on having someone else to represent her and to help her to put her case forward. Women in refuges are usually able to get support and help from refuge staff who will act as their advocates with other agencies if they wish. There is little information available, however, on what happens to women experiencing violence who approach agencies for help without the support of Women's Aid or of other refuge groups. It seems that they fare much less well and are particularly isolated and vulnerable, especially if the agency approached responds in a negative way.

Things have improved in many places since the study by Cavanagh, Dobash and Dobash. As we saw in Chapters 4 and 6, formal attempts are now being made to improve the way that official agencies deal with women who have experienced violence. Various guides and resource packs have been produced. An example is a 1990 Home Office-funded *Fact Pack* which covers the Kentish Town area of London but which was designed to be extended to other areas. It was produced by a domestic violence researcher, Jean Osborne, and includes material on refuges, medical services, police, social services, churches, housing, mental health, alcohol and domestic violence, etc. Cavanagh, Dobash and Dobash suggest that, to improve practice in individual agencies:

> practitioners need to scrutinise their beliefs, actions and policies in order to eliminate those that support the violence. They need to respond in a clearer and more straightforward manner, adopting the role of the advocate in providing positive emotional support and material assistance for the woman while posing a direct challenge to male domination and violence.

In the rest of this chapter, we will discuss how successful the social and medical services are in meeting these recommendations.

Social workers

Of the agencies approached for help by women experiencing domestic violence, the local authority social services department is now one of the most common. Various studies have shown that up to three-quarters of women who have experienced violence over a prolonged period have contacted social workers at least once during the violent relationship. It is therefore vital that social workers respond appropriately. Issues regarding domestic violence and social work are discussed fully in a forthcoming book by Audrey Mullender, entitled *Part of the Problem*.

Women approaching social services for help need to feel safe and secure in doing so, and to be treated sympathetically and with respect. Thus, the social worker's approach is crucial if a woman's trust and confidence are to be established. It is important that social workers are able both to validate and support women experiencing violence and to use their counselling skills to help women talk about what has happened. Women are very often nervous and embarrassed about what they have been through, and may feel unable to speak to a professional about the violence, although they may wish to do so. Social workers can sometimes provide a safe and supportive environment in which women may feel that they can open up, possibly for the first time. The other side of this coin, of course, is that women should not be pressurized to talk if they do not want to. Many women complain that, having gone to see their social workers solely about a practical problem with which they needed help, the social worker 'redefined' the problem and made them talk about their personal lives.

Quite a number of women are not happy talking to social workers at all, due to their much discussed role as a kind of 'soft' arm of the law. Social workers have wide-ranging powers to intervene in people's lives. Working-class women are often strongly aware of general issues about social class and control in relationships between social services departments and their 'clients'. Due to the pervasiveness of racism, black women may feel particularly ambivalent about approaching social workers and may not wish to involve them in their lives. The majority of social workers are white, although more and more black women and men are now entering the profession. White social workers may be unable fully to appreciate and understand black women's experiences.

Social workers themselves, of course, are not oblivious to these difficulties. In the University of North London/Hammersmith and Fulham study on domestic violence in 1989, there was an overall recognition among the workers interviewed that it was more difficult for black and ethnic minority women than white women to approach social services. At the time of the research, however, this acknowledgement was not coupled with many changes in practice or with a full understanding of the specific needs and concerns of such women. Most of the workers had some awareness of the different experiences of Asian women, but this did not extend so comprehensively to other black women.

The power which local authority social services departments have to recommend that children be removed from their parents by the courts acts as a strong deterrent against women, both black and white, confiding in them. Many women in refuges refuse to approach social workers for this reason. And women who have not left violent relationships may lie about the violence, when questioned, rather than risk bringing their families to the attention of the social services. There is evidence that some women have been threatened with having their children removed from their care if they do not leave particularly violent partners. While such situations happen fairly rarely and stem from concern by social services about the welfare of the children involved, abused women hearing such stories are likely to feel nervous and apprehensive about seeking help, even if they are in extreme need. Lesbians, like some black women, may be particularly fearful about contacting social services. If they are mothers, they may be especially wary of doing so due to the possibility that, if they reveal their sexuality, they may risk losing the care of their children. Social services departments need to be aware of these powerful issues in their dealings with women suffering domestic violence.

Social workers, however, are often very experienced in such matters. They may have particular expertise to offer in working with very young abused women who have used the care system and with women who have a disability (although, in the latter case, the Hammersmith study found that social workers at the time of the research had little awareness of domestic violence as an issue for women with disabilities). Social workers often have unique experience and expertise in working with elderly couples where the woman is experiencing domestic violence. In addition, domestic violence frequently comes to the attention of social services through mental health work. Violence in the home is a major source of distress and unhappiness for women. For some, this can result in contact with the psychiatric services, which is often mediated through social workers.

In all of these situations, one of the prime issues is security and confidentiality. This can be more complex for social workers than for other statutory and voluntary sector workers, since they are usually in contact with other members of the family as well. As a result, they may need extra support and supervision to deal with the dilemma of how to negotiate work with whole families where the wife or female partner is experiencing domestic violence. Confidentiality can be particularly important if the woman has left her partner and is in hiding in a refuge.

In order to protect her, it is vital that no details are allowed to slip about her whereabouts, even when, as often happens, the man is pressurizing the worker for information. Social workers can be in a particularly vulnerable position in this respect. They are far more likely than many workers in the caring professions to have to deal with violent men face-to-face. Social workers need to be aware of the possible dangers, and senior social workers and line managers need to do all they can to ensure their safety.

Social workers are a source of information and advice. It is important that they are able to provide women who have suffered domestic violence with correct, up-to-date information and practical help, and that where necessary they can refer them on successfully, for example to Women's Aid. In Jan Pahl's study *Private Violence and Public Policy*, social services departments were the most frequently cited source of referrals to the refuge involved, with one-third of the women mentioning social workers as the people who told them of its existence. It has been widely recommended that social services departments, like housing departments, display posters and other material advertising available services and making it clear that domestic violence is not acceptable, and many now do so. Social workers should be able to give up-to-date and accurate welfare rights, housing and legal advice about domestic violence. The Family Service Units in 1988 produced a booklet entitled *Domestic Violence: A Step by Step Guide for Social Workers and Others*, which gives practical information and advice which women experiencing domestic violence may need. As we discussed in Chapter 6 in relation to housing officers, the provision of sensitive interpreting services is particularly important for social workers working with women whose first language is not English.

The attitudes of social workers to women who have suffered violence vary considerably. Much of what social work is about is to do with families. Social services is one of the few agencies which deals directly with the intimacies and privacies of family life, and which can gain entry into people's lives at the most personal and private level, most often after things have gone wrong in some way. It is quite common for social workers to regard families in which individuals have problems as 'dysfunctional', and, in the past, this analysis has often been applied to domestic violence. The violence has been seen as a symptom of malfunction in the family as a whole, and social workers have tried various measures for improving the way that the family in question works, often involving conciliation between the parties or trying to assist the woman to be a better wife. These types of attitude and social work intervention have led some domestic violence activists to question whether social services can play a useful role in combatting violence in the home. In recent years, since the advent of Women's Aid and of changing awareness about domestic violence, social workers have tended to move away from this traditional approach. Even so, it is still unusual for very much support from social services to be forthcoming solely to meet women's needs if there is not some other factor involved.

Child protection

Most social workers abhor domestic violence and in theory will wish to do whatever they can to assist abused women. In practice, though, what they have the time and facilities to do may be very little. Hemmed in by heavy work burdens and by statutory limitations, they may only be able to offer some advice and information, as we have mentioned, or to refer a woman to a refuge and perhaps support her in getting there. The pressure on social services has been increasing in recent years as public and government concern about the physical and sexual abuse of children has grown. For those social workers who work directly with families and children, child protection usually dominates their work. They have a duty and a responsibility in law to protect abused children. No such duty and responsibility exists to protect abused women. Statutory commitments towards children override all else.

Social workers have come in for much criticism about child protection in the last few years. Frequently, they are severely castigated for not doing enough to stop child abuse, especially if a child dies. They are often further castigated for doing too much if, as in a variety of recent highly publicized cases, they make firm interventions. In addition, child protection work is now very time-consuming and demanding, involving a great deal of paper work and the use of lengthy, formal procedures.

All of this is happening within a changing financial framework in which increasing numbers of care services have to be 'bought in' as local authority facilities decrease. Social work is once again in transition, as it has been many times before. Two new Acts, the Children Act and the Community Care Act, mean that the nature of the work is changing. One social worker, trained ten years ago, described how she felt that the ground was shifting constantly and unnervingly beneath her feet while she juggled with people's lives.

In many ways, social work has become an impossible job, subject to fiercely conflicting demands and to expectations which are unrealizable. It is also a job for which the financial rewards are not high, but the responsibility – for child welfare in particular – is enormous and rather frightening. The penalties for getting it wrong are harsh, perhaps including very public censure, not to mention private anguish. Many social workers experience high levels of stress, anxiety and fatigue. It is small wonder that the abuse of women is not high on their agendas.

It can come as a shock, however, to find that even where domestic violence is clearly involved in a child abuse case, and is quite possibly a factor in the child's experience, it may still be overlooked. A 1993 report to the Department of Health produced by two researchers into child abuse, Elaine Farmer and Morag Owen, and called *Decision Making, Intervention and Outcome in Child Protection Work*, discusses what the authors call the 'missing link with domestic violence'. In an analysis of child protection cases, they found that in 59 per cent of them there was current violence in the family apart from the child abuse. One of the striking findings of this study was that the child protection work done was frequently focused not on the abusing adult but on other family members, such as the mother. Such shifts of focus often allowed men's violence to their wives to be ignored, literally to disappear from view. This study and others have revealed how few social workers regard domestic violence towards the child's mother as worthy of attention in child abuse cases. While such work as that of Peter Jaffe in Canada and of Women's Aid in Britain has begun the process of uncovering the damage done to children by witnessing and being involved in domestic violence, such considerations are usually absent from child abuse work except where the violence is so extreme that it cannot be ignored. There is increasing evidence, however, that child abuse and domestic violence quite often occur in the same family. More research is clearly needed on this interconnection, and social workers need to develop strategies which consider both types of abuse and their relationship to each other.

The American researcher Lee Bowker and his team investigated the relationship between wife-beating and child physical abuse in a large study conducted in the 1980s, and involving one thousand women in the United States who had suffered domestic violence. The study was not a random one and did not claim to be 'scientific' in this way. Bowker found that men who abused their wives also abused their children in 70 per cent of the families in which children were present. The child abuse was generally less severe than the wife abuse in the families studied. The worse the wife-beating, however, the worse the child abuse.

The data obtained substantiated the researchers' hypotheses that the children of women who have suffered violence are commonly abused by their fathers, and that the higher the degree of husband dominance in such a violent marriage, the more severe the child abuse. The research led Bowker to postulate that child abuse by mothers and by fathers was 'cut from rather different cloth'. While maternal child abuse could possibly be explained by poor parental self-control, stress at work and at home, poverty and other similar factors, paternal child abuse was related much more clearly to the need of the men concerned to dominate and control both their wives and their children. Bowker and his colleagues suggest that social workers and other practitioners and researchers should give more consideration to an analysis of power relationships in the family, and to the possibility that different mechanisms are at work in child abuse by women and by men. An understanding of these different mechanisms would probably lead to different types of social work reaction and to the provision of different types of service. Feminist researchers and practitioners have been making these points consistently for many years now. But in spite of calls by feminist theoreticians and practitioners, and by researchers like Bowker, for this sort of analysis, most social workers and social services departments appear to overlook these issues almost completely.

Training

One of the reasons why domestic violence is so often pushed to one side in child protection work is that, traditionally, social workers have not been trained to deal with it. Until recently, social work training often contained little material about it. Social workers whom we consulted who were trained ten to fifteen years ago reported that they had perhaps a half-day session on domestic violence in a two-year course. In addition, courses often demonstrated a somewhat contradictory approach to the subject. They might have included perhaps a contribution from a local Women's Aid group positioning the violence firmly as men's responsibility. And they might also have covered the subject as part of a 'family systems' or family therapy approach which would tend to allocate responsibility for the violence more equally as part of a 'system' of family interaction.

In recent years, feminist criticisms of traditional social work practices have appeared on social work courses. Various books and articles about a feminist approach to social work have been written, and social work students, at least on some courses, now study them. There has been a growth of courses on what is often called 'women-centred practice', which usually include material on domestic violence. Women's studies has become well established as an academic discipline in its own right, and has given rise to an outpouring of intellectual work on women's issues, including material on male violence. Some of this material has filtered on to diploma of social work courses and to a lesser extent into health visitor training and other courses for caring professionals.

The national body which oversees the training of social workers, the Central Council for Education and Training in Social Work (CCETSW), now advocates the teaching of what is called 'anti-racist and anti-discriminatory social work practice'. To be validated by CCETSW and hence to be allowed to run, all social work courses now have to demonstrate that they include such material. Anti-discriminatory social work practice should automatically include material on discrimination against women, including male violence. Thus the situation is improving throughout the social work profession on women's issues, although some social workers and social work teachers have suggested that the improvements are merely a drop in the ocean of negative views about women. However, combatting discrimination of various types, at least on a superficial level, has left the margins and entered the mainstream of social work.

All of this is good news for women experiencing domestic violence. It means that the field is open for the development of improved social services. Newly qualified social workers may well take domestic violence more seriously than their previously trained colleagues. They are more likely to have been trained to listen very carefully to women who have suffered violence, to validate and affirm their choices, and to take a strong line against male violence. Male social work students are more likely than their predecessors to have an opportunity to engage in a sensitive consideration of their role regarding women clients facing violence.

Liaison and good practice guidelines

As we saw in Chapter 2, domestic violence activists and workers in the field have stressed empowerment as a way for abused women to rid themselves of the abuse. Empowerment is currently an important concept in social work too, although social workers often use the word somewhat differently. In an article in 1992 in the journal *Critical Social Policy*, Audrey Mullender and David Ward suggest that empowerment is now in vogue in social work circles much as a concept of community was in the 1970s. It has become something of a bandwagon term. The authors point out, however, that the word is frequently used in a misleading, generalized way so that it becomes almost meaningless, merely a synonym for 'enabling'. It gives social workers who use it an aura of moral superiority and can act to immunize them against criticism. Ward and Mullender claim that empowerment can work as a social work strategy only if it is linked to an analysis of oppression and to action to challenge it. This is also the way in which Women's Aid attempts to use the term. As a result, there are various examples of constructive liaison and innovatory work between progressive or feminist social workers and refuges.

Some social workers take action to support refuges having funding difficulties and to campaign for more refuge provision. Many social services departments run groups for abused women or refer women to voluntary sector groups. In these groups, women may have a chance to discuss their feelings and experiences, and to share them with others in the same situation. Groups may be therapeutic in nature or may be more geared to practical issues. Very often, social workers work closely with local Women's Aid groups, many of whom have now accepted social work students on placement for many years. Some departments employ specialist liaison officers to work with refuges. In addition, social services departments generally participate in inter-agency initiatives on domestic violence, which aim to bring together all the concerned agencies in a locality to improve the delivery of local services (see Chapter 8). There is also a trend, as for housing departments, towards the development of good practice guidelines for working with abused women.

These may include general principles for working with women who have suffered violence as well as practical options. Nottinghamshire Social Services Department, for example, has developed innovative guidelines of this type. They include how to deal with violent partners, how to refer women to refuges, what advice and assistance to offer, how to deal with disputes between the partners about parental responsibility for the children, and so on. They also contain guidelines for male social workers on working with refuges. Nottinghamshire Social Services funds various refuges in the area.

Some councils with a council-wide response to domestic violence produce guidelines and principles which apply to all departments, including social services. Islington Borough Council in London, for example, has produced through its Women's Equality Unit a *Good Practice Guide for Working with Those who have Experienced Domestic Violence*. In common with other similar guides, it includes good practice procedures on the need for confidentiality, safety and security, on how to adopt a sympathetic, supportive approach, and on the provision of sensitive services. It also contains a section on why women leave and the lengthy process which may be involved, possibly involving several returns home. There are sections on black, minority ethnic and immigrant women, older women, women with disabilities, lesbians, young women, children, refuges, housing and law. The specific guidelines for social services include suggestions on empowering and validating the woman, on the importance of believing her and of enabling her to make her own choices. There are also guidelines on domestic violence and mental health issues for mental health workers and for approved social workers who have special responsibilities under the Mental Health Act 1983 for admitting people to psychiatric hospitals.

The Islington document and other similar guides have pointed out the necessity for social workers to support abused women in dealing with the mental health services, which can otherwise be intimidating, and in which people sometimes find that their rights are not protected. Good practice guides also suggest that it is important to be aware of a possible history of domestic violence where an application is being made under the Mental Health Act to admit a woman compulsorily to hospital. The social worker in this situation is obligated to consult the nearest relative, often the woman's husband or partner. While one might expect the nearest relative to have a genuine concern for the person being admitted, it is suggested that social workers should recognize the considerable power which this gives the relative or partner, especially where domestic violence is suspected. In general, women are overrepresented in psychiatric hospitals, more likely than men to be assessed under the Mental Health Act, more likely to be compulsorily admitted, and more likely to be prescribed tranquillizers and anti-depressants.

Other recommendations which have been made by a variety of bodies include the adoption of better statistical methods within social services for recording and monitoring incidences of domestic violence, and the encouragement of greater awareness among social workers of the possibility of violence in the families with whom they work. For example, behavioural problems in children could be linked to domestic violence. It is important that, in responding to such situations, the concern of the social worker is not solely for the welfare of the child, but also for the safety and well-being of the woman.

Most good practice guides and recommendations regarding social work and domestic violence pinpoint the inadequacies of present social work training in this respect, despite the improvements which we have discussed. They recommend that social workers, like housing and police officers, should be provided with domestic violence awareness training on the job. Such training should also include policy issues and practicalities – for example, how to respond sensitively to women who have suffered violence, and what information and advice could be given. Domestic violence training is discussed further in Chapter 8.

Traditional attitudes

Despite these positive recommendations and policy developments, some social workers still harbour traditional attitudes about the family and domestic violence. Certainly in the past, social workers have held views that wives encourage, provoke or even enjoy abusive treatment. The ways in which they have customarily assessed people coming to them for help have been loosely based on psychoanalytic theories developed originally by Freud. If interpreted crudely, they feed into and bolster views of women as often self-harming, weak, passive, and to blame for the violence which they endure. Many feminist psychotherapists have criticized traditional psychoanalytic theories on these grounds, and have attempted to reframe them in a way which is more positive for women; their influence, however, remains immense. Rebecca and Russell Dobash suggest that the idea that women cause male violence is not just common within psychoanalysis, but has permeated western culture as a whole. In *Violence Against Wives*, the Dobashes sum up the psychoanalytic and traditional social work view as follows:

the psychoanalytic idea that violence is a manifestation of individual pathology created by an imbalance in male dominance and female submission and developed through inadequate mothering implies that women (first as mothers, then as wives) are the primary source of violence, including that which is directed at them. Although such ideas have never been adequately supported and have been severely criticized and challenged, the theory has a great deal of appeal ... It is very popular, especially with the media, and underlies much of the training in the helping professions.

Such theories, mixed up with ideas about dysfunctional families, about how women should bring up their children, and about the desirability of the two-parent nuclear family as an ideal, permeate social work despite contemporary challenges by new generations of social workers.

Mary Maynard, in a 1985 article entitled, 'The response of social workers to domestic violence' in Jan Pahl's book, reports how, at that time, ideas about the sanctity of marriage, the privacy of the family and women's role as wives within it still imbued the social services. She describes a study based on an analysis of social work files in a northern town. The study estimated that about one-third of all cases in progress at the time involved domestic violence, although it was difficult to establish this figure since not all instances of domestic violence were recorded and it was not the central focus of most of the cases. The figure was therefore almost certainly an underestimate. The study found that, although women were experiencing quite serious physical assaults, some of which involved the use of weapons, little seemed to be done to assist them.

Of the 103 case files analysed in detail, 34 cases appeared to involve domestic violence. Of these, three couples were referred to the Marriage Guidance Council (now Relate), two women were placed in psychiatric hospital and one was advised to take a holiday. Several social workers had discussions about the violence with the women concerned. But for most of the women, nothing was done. In two instances, women were encouraged to consider separation and divorce, but in seven further cases, they were actively dissuaded from such a course of action. In some of these cases, the welfare of the children and their need for the father was emphasized to persuade the women not to leave with them.

The study found that incidences of domestic violence were described unsympathetically in the records. The social workers continually emphasized to the women their neutrality between the partners and their role to help all members of the family equally. One of the primary concerns of the social services in the study appeared to be to patch up marital conflicts, usually for the sake of the children. Social workers explained in various case records that they had advised women who had suffered violence not to argue with their husbands so much. One recorded:

> It is most important that this couple stick together for the sake of the children and I think this could be achieved more safely by encouraging Mrs Blank to accept her husband's decisions.

Many of the women who had suffered violence were found to be depressed and lethargic, and some became involved with the psychiatric services, but there was little attempt in the case files to explain why this happened. It appeared that social workers were largely indifferent to issues involving domestic violence.

There was, however, an emphasis on domestic competence and cleanliness. Domestic failings were sometimes regarded as understandable reasons for violence, although the violence itself was not regarded as legitimate. Social workers implied rather that 'the violence was natural in the circumstances'. There was much victim-blaming in evidence, and additionally social workers were suspicious that women were not telling the truth or that they were invested in the violence. One case record stated:

> Mr Blank apparently likes to dominate his wife, probably to compensate for her inabilities, and in spite of her complaints this is probably what the wife responds to.

Mary Maynard concluded that various obvious preconceptions underlay the entries in the files. These, she suggested, formed systematic patterns governing how social workers reacted to clients, rather than being down to the views of individual workers. They included a tendency to regard housewifely deviation (from an unspecified norm) as evidence of a woman's 'inadequacy', to disbelieve what abused women say about their domestic situations, and tacitly to support the nuclear family structure and the inferior position of women within it. The major concern of social workers was often to restore a domestic equilibrium, even when quite severe violence was still occurring.

As we noted in Chapter 3, such ideas and assumptions are further complicated in social work by theories of 'cycles of violence' or 'inter-generational transmission of violence', which some academics and professionals use to claim a connection between the adult use of violence and childhood experiences of abuse or witnessing abuse. It seems clear that while this is sometimes true, it is often not. There are many examples of women and men who were abused or who witnessed abuse in childhood who do not enter abusive relationships as adults. There are also many examples of people who were not exposed to abuse in childhood who experience abuse either as the abuser or as the victim of abuse in adulthood. Nevertheless, the theory holds enormous sway.

Assumptions, preconceptions and theories of these various types still underlie much of social work today, despite the developments in good practice which we have discussed. Now, however, social workers have to deal with different legislation, although it appears that much of this legislation is founded on the same assumptions which Maynard and others identified.

The Children Act 1989

Social workers, voluntary sector workers and court welfare officers (who are trained probation officers) are all now involved in the operation of the Children Act 1989. The Act is a far-reaching piece of legislation which changes much of previous childcare law and brings new measures into effect. It assumes that children are best brought up in families involving both parents, and that statutory intervention should be kept to a minimum. The Act introduces a new concept of 'parental responsibility' which applies to mothers and to married couples. Fathers who are not married to their partners can now apply for parental responsibility, thus increasing their rights over the children. This can be further supported by 'contact orders' for fathers. For women fleeing domestic violence, these provisions can create additional problems and erode their ability to escape the violence to a new life.

Position papers and recommendations on the Act from WAFE explain that the Act makes no mention at all of domestic violence. It assumes that parents are reasonable and responsible, that fathers should be substantially involved in children's lives after divorce or separation, and that even after such a separation parents will be able to arrive at amicable childcare decisions through joint negotiation. For many women who have suffered violence, however, it is not safe to be in contact with their violent ex-partner. The Children Act has only been in force for a relatively short time, but already there are many examples of women suffering further abuse because their whereabouts were revealed to their ex-partners through contact orders for the fathers under the Act. In a few cases, actual addresses of refuges have been given out.

The Act includes a new provision for 'residence orders' which replaces the previous custody arrangements. There is a presumption in the legislation that, in granting such orders, the child should ideally not have to move home. This has already led to a few alarming cases of children being ordered to live in their previous home with their father while their mother was in a refuge. These decisions appear to have been made purely on housing grounds with little regard to the domestic violence issues. The fact that domestic violence is quite frequently linked with child abuse, and the doubtful wisdom of leaving children with a violent man while his partner is driven away by his violence, are issues which appear to have been overlooked in these cases.

In addition, court welfare officers have attempted automatically to involve both parties in joint discussion about the child's welfare even where domestic violence has occurred. While the officers concerned are attempting to act in the spirit of the legislation, such meetings can be a terrifying experience for the woman, and one in which she probably will be disadvantaged in terms of expressing her opinions and decisions in a powerful and equal way. In some cases, the practice has led to further threats of violence both inside and outside the meetings. The Act itself does not stipulate that such joint meetings should occur, and the Association of Chief Officers of Probation (ACOP) recommends that separate meetings should be held if requested. Many court welfare officers do not yet follow this guidance, however, and neglect to inform women that they have the right to be seen separately. There have been substantial numbers of reports from refuges of women being, or feeling, forced to attend joint meetings. Clearly the role of court welfare officers and the right of women not to attend joint meetings need to be clarified. In a recent WAFE survey, 50 per cent of the refuges surveyed had evidence that women had been further abused after contact with their ex-partners made necessary by the Act.

The recommendations of WAFE as regards the Children Act include the following:

Government guidance relating to the issues and good practice regarding domestic violence should be drawn up to accompany the Children Act, or to be incorporated into existing guidance, for use in all court proceedings under the Act. It will not always be known to the court that domestic violence is involved, and so any good practice guideline should apply to all cases.

All solicitors, child welfare officers, judges and magistrates working in family courts should have training on domestic violence awareness and the implications for children.

Good practice guidelines should be developed for each of the professional agencies involved or, where they exist (e.g. the ACOP position statement on domestic violence), they should be monitored and enforced.

Guidance should include the requirement to be mindful of the woman's safety when making orders for children who are in her care. There should also be clear guidance on how the child's wishes can be heard safely in court proceedings and Social Services investigations.

Under the Children Act, a social services department can fund services to meet both its 'children in need' and its housing requirements, but to date a mere handful of refuges have managed to secure new or increased funding for work with children through this route. Social services appear to be skirting the issue of funding at the moment, but are continuing to get a good children's service from refuges 'on the cheap'.

Social security and the Child Support Act 1991

Often one of the main contributions which social workers can make to improving life for women who have suffered domestic violence is to act as their advocates, especially when dealing with the Children Act and with the social security system. Achieving economic independence after leaving home due to violence is one of the most important issues for women. Various researchers have demonstrated that there is now overwhelming evidence that the most important factors in a woman's efforts to leave a violent relationship are her economic and employment positions. Abused women often have to depend on the social security system for financial support, especially if they have children. Women in this situation are eligible for income support payments from the Department of Social Security for themselves and their children, and can obtain crisis loans to enable them to deal with the immediate trauma of leaving home possibly with no money whatsoever. They are also eligible for housing benefit paid through local authority housing departments.

Many women who have left home due to violence have never claimed benefits before and may feel nervous about approaching such a formidable institution as the Department of Social Security. Refuge staff and social workers can offer valuable support and advocacy. They can also help to ensure that women and children get the money to which they are entitled. Having a social worker speaking on one's behalf can substantially influence what happens and improve the service available.

However, the level of social security benefits has been significantly eroded over the last few years. Massive changes in the availability of benefits were introduced in 1988 with the establishment of the Social Fund. This fund instigated loans rather than grants in many cases, and has resulted in a substantial reduction in available benefits. More changes involving cutbacks in benefits, not to mention the much-discussed 'workfare' schemes, may be on their way.

The Child Support Act 1991 is a new measure which attempts to make fathers responsible for maintenance of their children. Its aim is to cut the cost to the taxpayer of child support for the children of single parents. If the mother is on income support, she potentially faces a 20 per cent reduction in her benefit if she does not reveal the name of the father. The Act is administered through the special Child Support Agency, rather than through existing Department of Social Security offices. It has engendered considerable opposition, and a variety of campaigning actions against it have been held.

Like the Children Act, it paid scant regard in its original form to the existence of domestic violence. During the passage of the bill through Parliament, WAFE and other organizations tried very hard to ensure that issues about domestic violence were considered. As a result of this and other work, the Act now says that a woman will not be penalized for failing to give the name of the father of her children, if she has good reason to 'fear harm or distress' to herself or her children as a result of doing so. WAFE also lobbied to try to ensure that a woman's evidence as to the abuse which she might experience would be accepted, without the need for corroboration. In consequence, the Department of Social Security has issued guidelines saying that the caring parent has the right to be believed, and that the welfare of any children living with the parent must be considered.

WAFE is monitoring the implementation of the Act, and individual refuge groups advise women on its implications. It recommends that all training on the Child Support Act should contain considerations of its use in cases of domestic violence. As yet, it is unclear how much evidence of distress and harm the Child Support Agency is demanding, or exactly how the Act is working out in practice. There is some evidence that men who have previously had no involvement with their children and their ex-partner are starting to insist on contact if they are being forced to pay. The Act also has implications for the 'clean break' method of settling divorce cases, in which a woman voluntarily forgoes maintenance payments in exchange for the ownership of the house. These implications have yet to be resolved.

Doctors and medical services

Most people with physical injuries go to the doctor to get them treated: most people, that is, unless they are women who have suffered violence. In the Dobashes' original study, for example, only 3 per cent of all the beatings which the women received in the course of violent marriages were reported to a doctor. Sometimes women are too embarrassed to go to see their general practitioner (GP). Often they do not go because of fear. The Dobashes found that, where women did make visits to the doctor, these visits were usually in defiance of the husband's explicit prohibition, or were allowed by him only after the woman had given assurances that she would not tell how she came by the injuries.

We have personal contact with several women who experienced violence in the home for many years, but who rarely obtained medical help due to fear of repercussions. One woman who suffered very serious abuse over a long period told us:

> Some days I could not get up. Once I was in bed for seven days. I could not get up with the swelling. I didn't go to the doctor, I couldn't. Once I did call the emergency doctor when he was out at work, but then I was too scared in case he found out. He would have killed me if he'd found I'd been to the doctor. I cancelled it. Just one time I did see the doctor in secret and she said I must go at once to the hospital. But I said no. I was too scared to go to the hospital. I even threw away the pills that she said I must take to get better in case he found them. I threw them away. I cannot forget these things until my death.

The results of failing to get medical attention can be scarring and permanent damage, and the enduring of unnecessary and unrelieved pain. Each year, many thousands of abused women in Britain suffer substantial untreated injuries.

The medical profession, however, remains a principal port of call for women experiencing domestic violence, even though many avoid going to see their doctor whenever they can. Women who have suffered violence turn to their GPs for help with either physical or psychological problems resulting from the violence, or are taken to casualty departments with their injuries. In very many cases, though, women disguise the source of the injuries with the result that the incidence of domestic violence reported to doctors and to hospitals is always artificially low.

Doctors often know the family or woman in question quite well and, from this knowledge and their medical expertise, they may be well aware of how the injuries were caused. Many, however, are reluctant to say anything about it. Women who have suffered violence tell of how doctors appear to collude with them in a conspiracy of silence, perhaps because of a desire on the part of the GP to be even-handed, especially if the man is also their patient. Such a situation can make it very difficult for a woman to confide in or to trust her doctor, even when she is in desperate need of help. Sometimes the cause of the violence is left hidden because of reserve and embarrassment on the part of the doctor, or opinions that she or he may hold about the privacy of family relationships and about not intervening in people's intimate lives. Various research studies have pointed out how doctors are trained to deal principally with physical illness. They are not trained in coping with complicated emotional issues, and may therefore be insufficiently socially skilled to be able to engage in detailed discussions about intimate matters.

General practitioners are also very busy, and always have been. The cutbacks in the National Health Service, however, are now placing many of them under even greater pressure. Very many doctors have five-minute appointment times, so that there is no time to deal with anything except the first symptoms described. In consequence, the underlying reasons why a woman is in the doctor's surgery may well go by the board during the consultation. Where is the doctor to find the time to deal with such a distressing subject as domestic violence with all its layers of complexity and personal pain? Women may also get the unspoken message that the GP does not really have time to hear what they have to say. They may already feel apologetic about taking up the doctor's time, and this can amplify feelings of worthlessness which they may be experiencing.

There are few guidelines available for how doctors should respond to abused women. Usually it is up to the individual. The help a woman receives, apart from straightforward physical treatment, can be very much the luck of the draw, depending on which doctor she happens to go to. Conservative doctors of the 'old school' of medicine, for example, have always treated patients in a somewhat paternalistic way. Women who have suffered violence may find themselves patronized or disbelieved by such doctors. At the other extreme, feminist women doctors are often very supportive of abused women and children. They may provide counselling support, and both time and space for women to talk about their experiences, as well as up-to-date information and medical treatment. Some doctors go out of their way to assist abused women, and organizations of women in medicine exist which may have domestic violence as one of their areas of concern. However, there is little consistency in medical practice about domestic violence. Often, it is not seen by doctors as something which is part of their job. They may know little about it, and may not feel confident in dealing with it.

Differences in social class and power between doctor and patients are often an important factor in medical consultations, and may be compounded for women by gender differences if the doctor is a man. These differences frequently militate against women talking openly to doctors, especially about such personally embarrassing subjects as abuse. Studies have also shown that many doctors have quite rigid ideas about family life and about the role of women in the family as housewives and mothers. Such doctors may find it hard to take domestic violence seriously. This is particularly the case when, as often happens, women do not present spectacular or specific injuries, but rather describe a range of physical and mental conditions which doctors may be tempted to brush to one side or to regard as 'not proper medicine'. Many women describe how debilitating it is, not only to have suffered abuse, but then to be fobbed off by their doctors or to be clearly regarded as a bit of a nuisance.

If the physical injuries are severe enough that they need to be taken seriously on a medical level, however, many doctors take a different approach. As well as providing the required medical treatment, they may also give the woman some information, possibly including telling her about the local refuge. But it appears that very often the advice which they offer is rather limited and may consist simply of telling women that they should leave their violent partners. Doctors do not always appreciate how difficult such a decision may be. For an abused woman, it can mean breaking up the family, leaving the partner she may well love, taking children away from their father, losing the love and companionship of a partner (in the good times), admitting to the outside world that the relationship has failed, losing financial support and material possessions and facing potentially extreme poverty, possibly becoming homeless, trying to find somewhere to go on both a temporary and permanent basis, and facing life alone as a single parent. These are not easy things. One wonders how the doctor who tells the woman to leave, and cannot understand why she does not, would deal with such a life option.

We have known various women who have gone back several times to their doctor with injuries and have been told by him, or her, that they will not be seen again unless they leave their partner. Such threats can hardly be regarded as ethical. Other women who have felt unable to follow the doctor's advice to 'up and leave' may feel too guilty or embarrassed to seek medical help again if they receive fresh injuries. Popular opinion has it that it is feminists who try to break up the family and encourage women to leave their husbands or male partners. In fact, the converse is often true. Women's Aid and feminist GPs are frequently the ones who appreciate the complexity of the issue for women, who understand why they may not be able to leave, who believe in supporting the woman whatever her decision, and who do not give up on her if she keeps going back.

Whether or not women choose to leave their violent partners, it can certainly be helpful if doctors' surgeries prominently display up-to-date information about refuges and other services available, particularly telephone helplines. Doctors also need to ensure that information which they give to women during consultations is correct and not out-dated. GPs are often highly respected by their patients and the giving out of faulty information can have disastrous effects. Where several community languages are spoken, information needs to be provided in the languages concerned. However, various projects and groups concerned with the needs of black women and women from other minority ethnic communities in relation to domestic violence have noted that many GPs tend neither to bother with interpreters nor, when they are present, to listen to them carefully or to make good use of their services. Where complex and delicate issues of abuse are concerned, this can lead to an effective silencing of women whose first language is not English.

As for most professionals, the majority of doctors in Britain are white, despite the increasing entry into the profession of recruits from a variety of ethnic heritages. Indeed, a study in 1993, involving matched applications for hospital doctor jobs by a black and a white doctor, has revealed systematic discrimination in the way that doctors are selected and employed. Where a white doctor is treating a black woman who has experienced abuse, issues of power and control which exist between all doctors and their patients can be exacerbated by racism and by cultural differences. In her study, Mama highlighted such issues. She also pointed out that male doctors from minority ethnic communities may be less than helpful to women from their own community seeking assistance following violence. For example, some Asian women in her study found that their GPs, who might be respected community figures, sided with their husbands and stated that women should not try to leave violent marriages. Other women in the study were helpfully advised and assisted by their GPs, indicating that doctors can play a more positive role.

Doctors have a particularly key position in regard to providing services for older women and for women with disabilities or with mental health problems who are experiencing domestic violence. Their expertise in these areas can be of crucial importance, since they may have unique access to abused women facing these difficulties. However, many doctors may have a tendency to overlook domestic violence in these situations, since they may not be expecting it. Like social workers, doctors also need to be aware of domestic abuse in their involvement with various pieces of legislation, such as compulsory admissions to psychiatric hospital under the Mental Health Act.

Treatment

Prescribing patterns which doctors use with women who have suffered domestic violence show that the traditional way to treat an abused woman has been to tend to her injuries – and to prescribe tranquillizers or anti-depressants. In a study by Mervyn Murch and his team in Bristol back in 1975, sixteen out of seventeen women who had suffered violence approaching a GP were prescribed such drugs. Many similar studies have found the same thing, and refuge staff and women who have suffered violence confirm that such drugs are still regarded as an appropriate treatment. For example, a 1989 study of the experiences of abused women in medical settings in Nova Scotia, Canada, found that at least 60 per cent of the women had been prescribed tranquillizing drugs. Activists, researchers and providers of services in the domestic violence field have pointed out that the practice of prescribing such psychotropic drugs to women experiencing domestic violence can seem like treating a woman for her husband's behaviour. The result of male violence becomes that the man gets off more or less scot-free and the woman concerned ends up taking drugs.

Women may be resistant to taking tranquillizing drugs to start with. Alternatively, they may welcome the immediate relief which they bring. Drug therapy rapidly becomes a pattern, however. Very many abused women have ended up seriously addicted to tranquillizers because of the ease with which they were prescribed in the past. These days, doctors are far more careful about prescribing Valium and similar drugs, given the proven addictive qualities of these drugs. At the moment, however, anti-depressants which are meant to be non-addictive are freely prescribed. Very many women in refuges are taking them, and so are untold numbers of women still living at home with violent partners.

While the prescribing of tranquillizers, anti-depressants and sleeping pills can assist a woman to deal with the pain and anxiety in her life, many in the field believe that such drugs can limit a woman's ability to make clear life decisions at a time of crisis or, disturbingly, to escape physically from attack. Looked at from this angle, to drug a woman so that she may be more confused and lethargic than she would otherwise have been, and then to send her home to face potential assault, is to place her in increased danger. Such a course of action could be regarded both as immoral and as an alarming example of the unequal relations between men and women.

However, doctors often have few other treatment possibilities available. The Dobashes and others have argued that, given the lack of alternatives open to abused women and the lack of sanctions against abusive men, the paucity of services available, the social, economic and emotional pressures on women to stay in marriages, the lack of training for doctors in 'whole person' medicine and the low priority given in general to the medical treatment of the effects of male violence on women, sympathetic doctors often feel helpless and powerless to be of much assistance. Women approaching their GPs because of violence may be suicidal, anxious and frightened, or depressed, and may be experiencing a wide range of minor illnesses and types of malaise. What is the doctor to do? Drugs to treat such symptoms can play a vital part in a woman's recovery, providing the drug treatment does not become long-term. Some doctors attempt to empower the woman to make her own decisions about drug treatment by giving her as much information as possible, warning her about side effects, and working closely with her to monitor how the drug affects her. Such doctors would usually attempt to build a woman's trust and confidence in herself, and would encourage her to view the drug treatment as a tool to deal with a specific situation, rather than as a panacea.

The only available alternative or complement to drug therapy may be to refer the woman for psychiatric help. More than anything else, many women are grateful for the chance to talk about their feelings and experiences. Referrals to the psychiatric services or to counsellors may be welcomed by abused women seeking help, even though such a course of action can appear, like drug treatment, to be 'punishing' or pathologizing the woman for the violence which she has received from a man. Additionally, the psychiatric assistance offered is often imbued with traditional attitudes towards women's role in the family and blaming attitudes towards women in general, as we have previously noted. Many women, however, have constructive therapeutic relationships with psychiatrists and counsellors, and are assisted by them to grow stronger psychologically and to deal with the violence in their lives more effectively.

With so few treatment options available and so little concern about the issue in the medical profession, doctors and hospitals often simplify violence in the home and show an interest in it solely when it is the subject of a medical emergency in hospital accident and emergency departments. On a general level, there is no attempt to evolve a more comprehensive medical and social approach to the domestic abuse of women. A group of American researchers into health issues and domestic violence, including Evan Stark, Demie Kurz and Anne Flitcraft, talk about what they call 'the social construction of battering' by the American medical profession. These reseachers claim that the many complicated medical and psychological factors involved in domestic violence escape the medical gaze almost completely. Due, they suggest, to both gender and class biases within medicine, the profession does not take domestic violence seriously, fails to take on board the needs of abused women and the complex complaints which they may present, and 'labels' women who have suffered violence as problematic patients. In one American study of medical records, 20 per cent of 'battered' women but only 4 per cent of 'non-battered' women were labelled in some pejorative or punishing way in their records – for example, as a 'neurotic female' or an 'hysteric'. Looked at the other way around, 86 per cent of all the women who were labelled in this way had suffered violence and abuse. Stark and Flitcraft suggest that the medical profession tends to disbelieve and stigmatize abused women, and to use this stigmatization as a way to avoid acknowledging the inadequacies of the medical response to domestic violence. They have called this 'not-so-benign neglect'.

In recent years, since the renewed interest in domestic violence, there have been some improvements in this harsh picture and an increase in awareness about the inadequacies of current medical practice. In 1989 an article in the medical journal *Morbidity and Mortality Weekly Return* emphasized domestic violence as a major public health problem in the United States. The article also presented data from North American medical schools showing a lack of teaching on the subject, which meant that medical staff often failed to identify or to offer help to victims. Lorna Smith's Home Office study in 1989 showed that in Britain medical personnel are often the first people whom abused women approach, but that, as in North America, staff in accident and emergency departments very often fail to acknowledge the symptoms. The British Association of Emergency Medicine says, however, that 25 per cent of women attending casualty departments present a clinical picture consistent with abuse.

Training and guidelines

Medical training in Britain often includes nothing about domestic violence, or perhaps just one session which may not offer details of how to deal with patients clinically. While in-service training may be provided later for some medical and nursing staff in accident and emergency departments, there is often no protocol for dealing with domestic violence in hospitals. While appropriate medical treatment will be provided, there may be no consistent approach to offering other help and advice. Recommendations have been made that medical training should be improved as regards domestic violence, and regular in-service training should be held for accident and emergency staff, GPs and health visitors. Leaflets and information should also be provided for patient use, and medical staff should be trained to talk about domestic violence rather than ignoring the issue.

At best, the role of GPs can be a key one in dealing with domestic violence, since they provide an open access service which abused women can easily use. They are in a good position to talk through the issues, look at options and help women to make links and to obtain additional help. The evolution of guidelines for GPs on working with abused women and children could give scope for evolving a generally accepted understanding of what GPs are aiming for in their work with women who have suffered violence, and of how to go about achieving it. The Home Office review highlights the need for the medical profession as a whole to develop codes of good practice on domestic violence, and some health authorities are now doing so. Lorna Smith suggests that such codes of good practice could include guidelines for interviewing women whom medical or nursing staff suspect may have experienced domestic violence. She also recommends improved referral to and liaison with other agencies, the display of public information about refuges and services, and the use of better systems for recording data about domestic violence cases, especially details of injuries which might be needed in later court proceedings.

Good practice guidelines should emphasize the need for confidentiality, and the use of consultation methods which are respectful of a woman's privacy but also enable her to tell her own story and make it possible for her to reveal the source of her injuries. Such guidelines might also include recommendations that nursing or medical staff devise a safety plan with the patient. The British Association of Emergency Medicine is currently evolving guidelines for what it calls 'the management of victims of domestic violence' in casualty departments. While such guidelines may be couched in medical language which attempts to classify the symptoms of domestic violence rather like an illness which has to be 'managed' medically, they are a step in the right direction. Hopefully, hospitals, GPs and health authorities will continue to develop codes of good practice of this type.

The voluntary sector

Voluntary sector agencies may work together with doctors, social workers, housing departments and other service providers to assist abused women and their children. Women might be referred to these agencies by other organizations or might approach them directly themselves. They often find voluntary sector projects more friendly and welcoming than the statutory bodies. In addition to Women's Aid and other refuge groups, many voluntary sector and non-statutory agencies offer valuable support, and contribute to the support services needed to complement refuge provision.

Citizens' advice bureaux, advice agencies, community projects and even organizations such as mother and toddler groups, childminder groups and playgroups may provide assistance and advice to women suffering violence and their children. If they do not know the answers themselves, they usually know who does and can refer women on successfully. There are also many self-help groups in local communities, some of which focus specifically on violence in the home.

Children's projects can offer support and help to the children of abused women. Youth and children's workers in play-schemes and youth projects often demonstrate great empathy and sensitivity in dealing with the needs of children who have been abused themselves, or who have witnessed violence. Specialist groups and organizations for black women, for minority ethnic women, for lesbians, for older women, for young women, and for women with disabilities or special needs offer specific services which can be helpful to women and children fleeing violence. There are also voluntary sector women's projects which focus on mental health issues or on drug and alcohol dependency, all of which work as a matter of course with women who have suffered violence. The Samaritans, too, play a vital role in dealing with abused women who are suicidal.

Victim Support groups have been much encouraged by government to undertake larger amounts of work with women who have suffered violence, on the grounds that they are there to support victims of crime and that domestic violence is now regarded as a crime. However, Victim Support nationally does recognize that the lead agency in domestic violence work is Women's Aid. Local Victim Support groups may offer support to abused women and children, some of which can be good. Unlike Women's Aid, though, they are not specially equipped to do so, and may lack the required experience, training, expertise and understanding of the issue.

All of these agencies and groups are generally welcoming and sympathetic. While many could improve the information on violence which they provide or display, and could increase domestic violence training provision for staff, they are often better informed about the issue than some statutory agencies. Voluntary sector organizations frequently have strong policies on domestic violence and may operate equal opportunities policies which include commitments actively to oppose discrimination. The problem is that they are critically underfunded. If integrated and co-ordinated services are to develop, the underfunding of the voluntary sector will have to be addressed in the future.

At the moment, services come and go, although in current funding circumstances more probably go than come. Amina Mama found in her study, for example, that there was a long history of black women's autonomous organizing in Britain against domestic violence, but that such organizations and services, while deeply committed, were small, massively underresourced and understaffed. They existed on low and decreasing budgets, and frequently either went out of existence due to lack of funds or faced extreme difficulty in keeping going. However, many voluntary sector agencies which do exist are now joining with statutory bodies to develop good practice guidelines and inter-agency work on domestic violence. These developments, together with the need for a national strategy on domestic violence, are discussed in Chapter 8.

8
National policy and inter-agency co-operation

National policy – where is it?

Providing services for abused women and their children, and initiating or improving policy measures which deal with domestic violence, have always been difficult tasks. One of the problems is that domestic violence spans a whole variety of agencies and national and local government departments. It refuses to fit tidily into one slot. As a result, it can be difficult to get anybody to take it on.

Divided responsibility

There is no one clear funding source for refuges, and no funding source at all for many of the community support services that women who are experiencing violence and their children need. For many years, refuge finance has been caught in a cleft stick. Refuge groups have been able to get money for housing costs from one set of funders, who have not been interested in the 'social care' costs which refuges incur in providing staff and support services for residents; similarly, they have obtained money for social care costs from another set of funders, who have not been interested in housing costs. Refuge projects, of course, need both. Because there are no clearly identifiable financial policies as regards refuges and the situation varies widely from one area to another, refuge groups have ended up scrabbling around for bits of funding as best they can – and then trying to fit them together.

Building a coherent funding base for a project in this situation is particularly difficult. Some refuges are funded by housing associations and social services departments, by housing departments or Women's Equality Committees of local councils, or by one-off government funding programmes and a variety of specialized grants. For some of these grants, the application process is extraordinarily complex and difficult to understand. Trying to build a 'basket' of funding from a variety of complicated sources is even more difficult where one source of finance is dependent on another – which it often is. This can hardly be regarded as a satisfactory situation. Applying frequently for different types of funding and trying to stitch together an adequate funding strategy can be almost a full-time job. It is certainly a skilled one. Hard-pressed refuge staff and voluntary managers, already struggling to keep their service going in the face of seemingly bottomless need, may have neither the time nor the financial expertise to do it. The best-funded refuges now employ administrators or finance workers to carry out this work for them. But many refuge groups have next to no funding at all, or employ just one or two workers who are almost always overworked and overstretched. Volunteer workers and management committee members are also likely to be hard-pressed.

Abused women and their children need a variety of support services in the community linked to refuge provision and integrally part of the advocacy and support role of Women's Aid. These include projects and groups for children who have been abused themselves or who have witnessed abuse, outreach services for women suffering violence who do not wish to come into a refuge, specialist services for black women and women from ethnic minorities, and follow-up services for women establishing new lives after escaping domestic violence. Because domestic violence is a complex and widespread social problem, there is no one way of dealing with it. A range of co-ordinated services and options is required, working hand-in-hand with legal and policy measures. Legal remedies for domestic violence, for instance, can only work if they run alongside the provision of safe temporary and permanent housing, and vice versa. Police policies which encourage the arrest of violent men are only effective if backed up by adequate refuge provision and community support and services for the women partners.

Often, however, this local co-operation does not happen. Some councils, for example, refuse to rehouse women homeless because of violence, and insist instead that they seek legal advice with a view to returning home after taking out injunctions against the violent man, regardless of the woman's wishes or of how effective such injunctions might be. The end result of this type of approach is that the legal system and the housing agencies work against each other instead of in tandem. Another example is that a woman may be denied legal aid to pursue legal remedies if she is living temporarily in a refuge, or her social worker may stop coming to see her for the same reason. Shifting responsibility from one agency to another is easy. There is a lot of buck-passing.

It does not help that, because domestic violence affects all aspects of women's and children's lives, responsibility for providing services and support falls across a range of government departments. Some responsibility lies with the Department of the Environment; some with the Home Office; some with the Department of Health; some with the Department of Social Security; and some with the Department for Education. These various responsibilities have yet to be effectively co-ordinated across the departments involved. Up until now, there has been a tendency for government activity on domestic violence to fall between two stools – or three, or four. This problem extends to the funding for research into domestic violence as well as to service provision.

When responsibility is spread in this way, it seems that some government departments can manage to take none at all. In the past, no single department has taken an initiating role. As a result, government responses to domestic violence have been fragmented. It may come as no surprise to abused women, and to feminists and others representing them, that issues of violence against women are not very high up on government agendas. In crime prevention work, for example, crimes against property attract far more attention than crimes against women. Government remains a male-dominated affair, despite the efforts of many pioneering women politicians and civil servants to break in. Although they make up half the adult population, women have rarely been able to command government attention for very long in order to look specifically at problems which affect women. And particularly in times of financial cutback, services for women and concerns about women's issues are often the first to go.

Recent developments

As we have indicated, there is now some public and government interest in domestic violence, which has been demonstrated by the improved police response. As a consequence of this initiative on the police, the Home Office has tended to be regarded recently as the government department which will take the lead. From now on it will be co-ordinating interdepartmental activity. An interdepartmental committee has been established and a Ministerial Group on domestic violence may also be convened. However, domestic violence is an issue which stretches way beyond the law and crime, and we have yet to see how this new initiative by the Home Office will work out in practice.

Other departments have also taken up the issue to some extent. For example, domestic violence featured in the work of the recent working party on relationship breakdown convened by the Department of the Environment. But this interest may not always extend to opening the public purse-strings and spending money. As a result, all services for women who have experienced violence and their children are crucially and severely underfunded.

All the concerned bodies and organizations working in the field have recommended many times that central government should ensure that refuges and support services are adequately funded, at least to the level recommended by the 1975 Select Committee on Violence in Marriage. The Women's Aid federations, supported by the 1992 National Inter-Agency Working Party Report on domestic violence, have continually emphasized that government needs to develop a funding policy at a national level both for refuges and for linked support services for abused women and children. They recommend that such a national funding strategy should include funding for specialist refuges and outreach services for black women and women from other minority ethnic communities and their children, and for access to existing and new refuge services for women with disabilities and special needs.

In its submission to the Ministerial Group on Women's Issues in 1989, the Women's Aid Federation (England) recommended specific funding designated for refuges, together with the evolution of a finance strategy linking funds from central government to funding from local authorities. It has since proposed that such specific funding should be 'ring-fenced' by central government rather than coming out of general moneys for special needs funding. Both WAFE and Welsh Women's Aid have proposed that such 'ring-fenced' funding must be made available by central government for distribution locally according to population and other needs. A national funding strategy should also include funding for a properly resourced and publicized Women's Aid national 24-hour helpline. At the moment, the national helpline is staffed by twenty volunteers with two co-ordinators, but it cannot provide guaranteed 24-hour cover, a situation which is clearly untenable for a national service. In March 1993, the government Home Affairs Committee recommended the adoption of a central, co-ordinated policy for refuge provision, so change may be on its way. However, it remains to be seen whether the government will act on this advice.

The refuge network, with its national co-ordinating bodies which take up issues on a nationwide level, is the lifeblood of all services for women experiencing domestic violence. It occupies a unique position. Thus, there is no way that it can be regarded as just one service provider among several in the voluntary sector, although the contribution of other agencies must be recognized and respected. The Women's Aid refuges and federations, and the rest of the refuge movement, provide the only agencies which work solely on domestic violence issues – and have done for twenty years. They are in day-to-day contact with thousands of women fleeing domestic violence, and there is no question that they are rich in knowledge, experience and expertise. From humble beginnings in the early 1970s, Women's Aid is now widely accepted as the key agency dealing with domestic violence. It is therefore surprising that Victim Support is sometimes promoted by the government as the lead agency, although it has itself declined this role in favour of Women's Aid, and that the refuge movement is so severely under-funded and understaffed.

Moreover, this underfunding and understaffing is experienced not only at local but also at national level. The Women's Aid Federation (England) needs twice as many national workers as it has in order to fulfil its remit and to meet the many demands which it faces. It is illuminating in this respect to compare WAFE with Welsh Women's Aid. Welsh Women's Aid deals directly with the Welsh Office. Unlike WAFE, it does have input into a co-ordinating government body. Partly as a result of this situation, it currently has eight full-time and four part-time workers co-ordinating and servicing 35 refuges with several more projects in development. WAFE has the equivalent of six full-time workers and nearly 200 refuges. In England, co-ordination of the type possible in Wales is desperately needed between refuges, WAFE and government departments.

These problems of uneven or fragmented services and lack of systematic funding are characteristic of government approaches to domestic violence. There are no co-ordinated or concerted government policies or strategies. In fact there are very few government policies on domestic violence at all. It seems fairly clear that, despite some interest in recent years, the overall response of national government is inadequate. This can be demonstrated particularly starkly in the light of international commitments and initiatives on domestic violence.

In Australia, a National Committee on Violence Against Women was established in 1990. This committee is engaged in developing a national strategy on violence against women. The strategy is comprehensive and visionary – and way beyond anything dreamt of in Britain. It is built on the twin premises of empowering women and ending male violence. It holds that condoning and excusing male violence impedes social change and reinforces the oppression of women. In October 1992, it listed its objectives as follows:

> To ensure that all women escaping violence have immediate access to police intervention and legal protection which prioritize safety for the woman, safe shelter, confidential services and the longer-term resources needed to live independently and free from violence.

> To work towards a universal intolerance of the use of violence in Australian society in general and, in particular, to achieve full acknowledgment by all Australians that violence against women is a crime, regardless of the circumstances, the background or the culture of the violent person or the victim.

> To achieve more just and equitable responses by the criminal justice system, which highlight the seriousness of the offences, and to strengthen the authority of the law in its effective and important role of influencing community attitudes and supporting social change.

> To build on the significant reforms, policy and program work of all levels of government and the community, towards improving the status of women, including the elimination of violence against all women.

From Canada, the news is also good. In 1991 Health and Welfare Canada, the lead federal agency on family violence, established a four-year, $136-million Federal Initiative on Family Violence. The aims of the initiative are to involve all Canadians within it, to mobilize community action, to improve treatment and support services, to share information and solutions, and to co-ordinate federal action on domestic violence. This includes strengthening legal remedies, providing more housing for abused women and their children, and establishing services for Indian, Inuit and Métis communities. Committees involving representatives of many agencies work with the initiative at federal, provincial and local levels.

Cutbacks and ways forward

In contrast, the lack of a coherent British government domestic violence policy and programme speaks volumes about its commitment to the issue. The 1993 report of the House of Commons Home Affairs Committee Inquiry into Domestic Violence and the Home Office initiatives on the police response are steps in the right direction, but in general the current Conservative government has not translated the concern about domestic violence which it sometimes expresses into much action. As we saw in Chapter 7, the far-reaching Children Act 1989 more or less forgot the difficulties and dangers which women who have experienced violence would encounter in meeting its provisions. And some of these provisions unfortunately undermine the positive effects of advances in policing and in the civil and criminal law so that the overall effect is contradictory for abused women and their children. For example, proposals to improve the legislation on injunctions are to be welcomed, but these improvements may be undermined by severe reductions in the availability of legal aid. Public services which women and children use are disappearing. The cutbacks in social security benefits, in services run by local authorities, and crucially in the supply of council housing as a result of government policy have had devastating effects on women and children made homeless by violence.

Many agencies including Women's Aid have consistently drawn attention to these problems – but in vain. Politicians, academics, pressure groups and political activists have all highlighted and campaigned about the effects of the Conservative government's social policies on the least advantaged members of society, and on women and children in particular. Commentators and activists have pointed out that, despite its protestations in favour of ordinary people and despite the supposedly ordinary grammar school boy who heads it, the government appears to favour the rich at the expense of the poor.

As part of a gradual reduction in benefit levels over several years, this government's Conservative predecessor introduced shattering cutbacks, euphemistically named 'reforms', in the social security system in 1988. These were accompanied by a budget which gave unprecedented tax relief to the rich. The social security changes affected women fleeing violence particularly badly. Emergency and exceptional needs payments, which had been a lifeline for women homeless due to violence, were abolished to be replaced by the discretionary Social Fund from which women can often obtain only loans – or nothing at all. Board and lodging payments to refuges were also abolished, to be replaced by housing benefit, a change from which many refuges have yet to recover financially.

Despite all of this, the voluntary sector and the refuge movement have attempted to respond positively as well as critically. They have tried to develop forward-looking policy on domestic violence and to press the government to do the same. Now that the Home Office is being established as the lead governmental agency and inter-departmental work is beginning, it is important that the departments and interdepartmental initiatives involved are staffed at an adequate level to allow them to function effectively. They can then ensure that there is co-ordination between all the government departments involved, and can also help to encourage co-operation between responsible bodies in local areas.

The National Inter-Agency Working Party Report recommends that one of the first tasks of such a lead government department should be to facilitate and create a co-ordinated national policy on domestic violence. The possible future significance of this recommendation cannot be overemphasized. The report says:

> We know that the country cannot afford the waste of human resources or the public cost of domestic violence. No policy will work, unless it is subject to regular review and adequate resources are devoted to its implementation.

As a result, the recommendation is that resources should be immediately provided to draw up a national policy. The report suggests that a coherent policy cannot be constructed without the full involvement of the voluntary sector, within which it identifies Women's Aid as the key agency in the field. Adequate financial and other resources would then be required to put into practice a wide-ranging programme of timed implementation and review procedures for the new policy. It should be monitored by an independent research programme with an advisory group made up of relevant statutory and voluntary bodies, and there should be an emphasis on seeking the views of women who have suffered domestic violence.

This report builds on earlier recommendations put forward by the Women's Aid federations. It has since been followed in 1993 by WAFE's written evidence to the House of Commons Home Affairs Committee Inquiry into Domestic Violence, which puts forward similar proposals for a national strategy to be co-ordinated between the various government departments concerned, and argues for a range of measures to support abused women and children. It makes constructive proposals relating to the civil and criminal law, the police, housing, outreach services, children's needs, welfare benefits, and training and public awareness. Welsh Women's Aid also put forward similar recommendations. In March 1993, the government Home Affairs Committee Report endorsed many of these proposals, so the stage is now set for potentially wide-ranging improvements in services and measures against domestic violence. Following all of these recommendations would provide Britain with a comprehensive programme against domestic violence. To long-term activists, such a possibility might seem pie in the sky and almost too good to be true. But it has happened in other countries, and it may now happen in Britain.

Inter-agency work: way forward or smoke-screen?

What is needed is co-ordinated local action against domestic violence backed up by national policy and resources. Inter-agency co-ordination has come to be seen as an appropriate formal and officially sanctioned response to abuse of various types. Child abuse is the most obvious example, with inter-agency collaboration having an important role to play in the handling of individual cases. For domestic violence, however, the approach so far has been more informal and low key. It has not had the same emphasis on individual case work, and it would be inappropriate and unhelpful for it to do so. This is partly because there are statutory obligations to protect children but none to protect women: society on a general level does not take violence against women as seriously as violence against children. For inter-agency work, however, this has meant that there is more scope for innovation.

Multi-agency or inter-agency initiatives on domestic violence have grown in prominence in recent years. In her 1989 Home Office study, Lorna Smith highlighted the importance of co-operation between the diverse agencies involved in order to deal effectively with the host of interrelated problems which domestic violence engenders. Home Office circulars and other government documents clearly point out the relevance of inter-agency working. It was also recommended in 1985 by the Women's National Commission, in 1986 by the UN Expert Group on Violence in the Family, in 1987 by the Brussels Council of Europe Colloquy on Violence within the Family, and in 1992 by the UN *Manual for Practitioners on Domestic Violence.*

A multi-agency response to domestic violence is now being consciously pursued in many countries. In New South Wales, Australia, for example, the development of services and policy is overseen at state level by a committee consisting of representatives from many agencies. Local domestic violence committees have also been established on the initiative of local communities in different areas of New South Wales. Their job is to develop liaison, co-operation and consultation, to make policy recommendations to the New South Wales Domestic Violence Committee and to promote community education and the recognition that domestic violence is a crime. Some of the actions and campaigns of local domestic violence committees include the setting up of court support schemes, training and education workshops, domestic violence support groups, and domestic violence phone-ins. Directories of services and good practice guidelines have also been produced.

In Scotland at the end of 1990, the Convention of Scottish Local Authorities set up a Women and Violence Working Group at which representatives of Scottish Women's Aid met with elected members and officers representing Scottish authorities. The Working Group published a report at the end of 1991 which formally recognized the need for sufficient safe refuges run by women, and for high-quality information and support services which empower women to make decisions about their own futures. The Working Group recognized the importance of multi-agency work and, as a matter of urgency, recommended that the development of multi-agency co-operation be encouraged and facilitated.

Within Britain as a whole, Women's Aid groups have in the past often attempted to establish inter-agency co-operation, and some were successful in doing so. In this sense, it is not a new idea at all, but one which Women's Aid groups have always espoused. The difference is that in the past the relevant agencies showed little interest. Now the establishment of local inter-agency domestic violence forums has been strongly recommended by the government Home Affairs Committee and by the National Inter-Agency Working Party Report. The latter recommends the formation of local multi-agency domestic violence forums with clear aims, structures and policies, and adequate funding.

The report also suggests some provisos to assist agencies thinking about setting up an inter-agency domestic violence forum. For example, it points out that inter-agency initiatives must always be used to improve direct services for abused women. This may sound ridiculously elementary. However, there are many examples of statutory and voluntary agencies holding considerable numbers of joint meetings about a variety of issues and achieving no change whatsoever in the services provided. Also some agencies, such as men's projects, may be engaged in preventive work which, while very important, should not divert funds from front-line services for abused women (see Chapter 9).

The Working Party also suggests that inter-agency work should increase public awareness about domestic violence, should attempt to widen the choices and options available to women in both the short and the long term, and should provide a firm public message that domestic violence is unacceptable. Multi-agency initiatives need both clear aims and objectives and a clear structure so that they know where they are going and what they are trying to achieve. They also need a strong sense of purpose, but it can take a while to work this out, and there can be some false starts. In addition, projects need to re-assess as time goes on, and perhaps to change direction. The services available in local areas vary so much that each inter-agency initiative needs to be tailored specifically to the requirements of its locality. In other words, there is no single formula for a successful inter-agency initiative.

The National Association of Local Government Women's Committees discussed this diversity in a 1990 publication on local authority initiatives to counter violence against women. Their publication is appropriately entitled *Responding with Authority* to underline the weightiness of these matters and the seriousness with which local councils should take them. They point out that the aim of the inter-agency approach is to bring together different agencies and local authority departments in an area, specifically so that the work done against domestic violence is first consistent, second well-informed and third co-ordinated. Put like this, it sounds like straightforward common sense. The idea of multi-agency work is a remarkably simple one. It has become a fashionable response in all sorts of areas of crime prevention. Putting it into practice, however, is not a simple matter at all.

Nevertheless, the concept is catching on in domestic violence work. There are several formal multi-agency initiatives in existence and more in the pipeline. The first few of them were set up at the end of the 1980s.

For some Women's Aid groups, the establishment of inter-agency work was the culmination of repeated efforts to raise the profile of domestic violence issues in their locality. Constructive liaison with local councils became easier in the 1980s when some authorities set up council Women's Committees and/or established officer posts with special responsibility for women's issues in a variety of departments and units. As a result, some of these authorities hosted local conferences on violence against women which were widely attended, provided a space for the issues to be aired, and helped to build the impetus for improving local services. Inter-agency projects were set up in several cases as an outcome of the conferences.

Some women in Women's Aid, who had battled with local councils for many years to try to get them to improve their service provision, were almost taken aback by these developments. The very idea of councils taking such initiatives had been inconceivable a few years earlier. Then it suddenly seemed as though at least some local authorities could not wait to take on the issue of violence against women. It was the Women's Committees and Units which made it happen in the main, with the final Labour-led Greater London Council and a few pioneering London boroughs and urban district councils forging the way forward. A small number of committed feminists had entered the County Halls and Council Houses and had brought women's issues into, if not the heart, then at least the margins of municipal Britain.

The changes in the police response to domestic violence have also had an effect. Inter-agency working is recommended in the new guidelines, and local police forces in a few areas have developed their domestic violence practice to a greater extent than other agencies and have been instrumental in establishing multi-agency projects on domestic violence as a response to this advice and as part of crime prevention work. Now, however, the agency which takes the lead in initiating such projects, and in getting the whole thing started, seems to vary widely. In some areas, it is the local refuge group which does it, sometimes after years of pressurizing the council for such a development. Most often, it is still the local authority which is the initiator. It can happen as a result of initiatives by women officers in housing departments, in social services departments or in Women's Equality Units or Community Safety Units, if and where these exist. However, the financial stringency which central government has imposed on local authorities in the early 1990s has meant that such units and initiatives are under severe threat of being cut – or have been cut already.

Inter-agency work in practice

In a few areas of Britain, inter-agency domestic violence forums have now been established for several years. Leeds, Nottinghamshire, Wolverhampton and the borough of Hammersmith and Fulham in London are examples. In other areas, initiatives are only just beginning: inter-agency groups started up recently in Cleveland and in Bristol, for instance. A variety of projects now exist up and down the country.

The wide diversity of approaches is welcome in one sense, as agencies in different areas figure out what they need to do and set about doing it. But in another sense, it can be confusing and even immobilizing. New projects may feel overwhelmed by the volume of work that they could take on, and not know where to start. This is where established projects can step in to offer advice and help, and they are always willing to do so if they can. Often, though, there is no spare time or money for this sort of liaison and co-operation.

There have been some attempts to set up a national network of inter-agency projects, and to hold national networking meetings involving a variety of inter-agency workers, domestic violence activists and Women's Aid representatives. But, to date, these attempts are very much in their early stages. The issue of national co-ordination, and of the crucial involvement of Women's Aid and of refuges within this, remains under discussion. Women working in inter-agency projects in London have tried to overcome this problem by organizing joint meetings to exchange ideas and information, and there have been similar joint meetings in some other areas, such as West Yorkshire.

Keeping domestic violence forums going is often hard work. They stand the most chance of success if they are properly resourced and have some secretarial and administrative support. Meetings can then be relatively easily set up, minutes taken, and information circulated. Very few of the participating agencies will have the spare labour power to provide such services on a voluntary basis, even if the tasks involved are rotated between members. If there is funding available from the local authority or from elsewhere, paid workers may be able to take on the servicing and administration, and co-ordinate the project. Funding for inter-agency work can be obtained in some cases from special government grants: it was Safer Cities money from the Home Office which funded the project in Wolverhampton.

Domestic violence forums can become quite large if the majority of local statutory and voluntary agencies participate in them. All the members of a forum may meet together only once every three or six months, and may delegate work to be done in between. Often, therefore, the first task for a forum is to set up a steering group for itself, and to draw up aims and objectives. These may vary considerably. A good example is provided by the Nottinghamshire Domestic Violence Forum. Its 1992 Aims and Objectives include commitments to increase agencies' awareness of each other, to encourage each agency to develop policies and procedures for responding to domestic violence, to promote inter-agency training, to raise public awareness of the needs of abused women and children, to promote new services and preventive measures, and to examine the connection between domestic violence and the abuse of women and of children in society as a whole.

In most cases, the remit for action adopted by inter-agency projects and domestic violence forums consists of promoting changes within the local authority concerned and within other agencies, such as the police force and the health service. This often entails the development of good practice guidelines and explicit domestic violence policies within these agencies. Inter-agency projects also instigate training on domestic violence in both statutory and voluntary organizations. They can set up unusual, forward-looking projects: for example, the Keighley Domestic Violence Forum employs a youth education worker to raise awareness of the issue of domestic violence with young people, youth workers and teachers. Domestic violence forums very often initiate public information campaigns – they might assist member agencies to produce leaflets, booklets, information packs and posters on domestic violence, or produce these themselves. Since the new Home Office guidelines, the police in particular have taken on the task of producing leaflets and booklets in local areas, with participation and help from inter-agency forums. These useful publications usually talk about domestic violence, explain what the police can do and list local services.

Local authorities may also produce publicity and information material about domestic violence. The leaflets, posters and booklets which they produce are often attractive and glossy, and are widely distributed in council offices and elsewhere in the area concerned. Until recently, the only available leaflets have been produced by the Women's Aid federations and by local groups. This Women's Aid material gives information on the rights of abused women and children which, even now, most other leaflets omit. However, the new leaflets, handbooks and posters provide much-needed information and are to be welcomed – especially in the light of the dearth of public information campaigns against domestic violence in Britain compared with other countries. Glossy leaflets and posters are of limited value, however, without the services to match them.

At best, local authorities will expand their approach to domestic violence to make it a 'corporate' one. This means that awareness of domestic violence and the provision of training and services to combat it will span the whole of the authority's work, and will be taken on as a general, council-wide commitment. This often includes provisions for women employees of the council itself who are experiencing domestic violence. Most of the local authorities who do this are in the cities and the majority are Labour-led. In developing a corporate response to domestic violence, councils are usually encouraged and assisted by local inter-agency initiatives and refuge groups – and, of course, by their own women's equality and community safety officers where they have them.

Dedicated work of this nature has taken place over several years in the London Borough of Hammersmith and Fulham within its Community Safety Unit, and the housing and other departments, in liaison with the voluntary sector. The borough has initiated a co-ordinated response including training for local authority officers, and it has produced a variety of information packs, good practice guidelines and publicity literature. A large-scale training programme for workers throughout the area is now being developed by the domestic violence forum. The borough has also helped to initiate the Hammersmith Domestic Violence Intervention Project. In 1991 it hosted a landmark national conference on preventing crime against women, which prominently featured domestic violence. A few other national conferences have been held in various places, bringing together statutory and voluntary sector officers and workers from widely different backgrounds, agencies and localities.

The inter-agency forums in Hammersmith and Fulham, in Nottinghamshire and elsewhere have all given rise to a number of small inter-agency sub-groups in their areas, which include representatives from the statutory agencies, the refuge movement and the voluntary sector. In Nottinghamshire, for example, a unique domestic violence group involving members of all the local health authorities was set up in 1992 to arrange training days and to work on a code of good practice.

The initiatives which the Nottinghamshire forum has facilitated are diverse. They include a 'Support to Court' project to provide support for abused women entering the criminal justice process and a project to produce a touring exhibition on domestic violence. Domestic violence awareness-raising sessions have been offered throughout the authority to a variety of organizations, both statutory and voluntary, and about three hundred professionals have attended the sessions.

The pioneering inter-agency projects in Nottinghamshire and in Hammersmith and Fulham are just two examples among several. Workers in the projects emphasize the positive effects of this work. Sometimes the networking which goes on can be as important as the more formal initiatives. People from different agencies who have previously worked quite separately get together and exchange information and ideas. This can break down hostilities and misunderstandings between agencies, and can lead to both informal and formal co-operation. As a result of a domestic violence forum, workers in different agencies may phone each other up informally and arrange pieces of joint work. Inter-agency workers point out, however, that it is important to avoid the 'lowest common denominator' effect, in which activity is limited by the views of the agencies who know the least and have the least commitment to domestic violence work.

In fact, a major problem in setting up multi-agency groups can be a conflict of interests and approaches between member agencies. It can be better to acknowledge these differences and allow them to stand rather than to muddy the waters by pretending to agree or by negotiating a false or fudged compromise. The involvement of the police in inter-agency work has proved particularly difficult from this point of view in some areas, although constructive dialogue and joint work can take place. The problem of liaison with the police is discussed further at the end of this chapter.

Perhaps one of the most important parts of inter-agency work is the developing of good policy and practice guidelines, including training initiatives, in agencies which work with women survivors of domestic violence. Women's Aid refuges have generally developed positive ways of working with women and children. These are now in the process of being written down into good practice documents. Housing departments, social services, health authorities and the police have all developed quite extensive practice guidelines in some areas. Financial cutbacks in local authorities and the health service, however, tend to pull in the opposite direction. Domestic violence policies can be obvious targets for the axe. The experience of Hammersmith and Fulham has been particularly salutary in this respect. As we saw in Chapter 6, the progressive and generous domestic violence housing policy adopted by the authority in 1990 was rescinded mainly for financial reasons after less than a year. In the 1990s, the availability of resources dominates everything. The innovations that inter-agency work can engender are severely limited as a result.

Probably the most innovative and extensive inter-agency project, and one of the few which has managed to attract much in the way of resources, is in Leeds. The inter-agency project there started off through the establishment of a local domestic violence forum which then initiated organized inter-agency work. The project was based from the beginning in the Leeds Women's Aid Outreach Office, and it has always had strong connections with Women's Aid and with black women's projects and organizations in the city, from which it has learned a great deal. The basic premise of the project is that abusers seek to exert power and control over women in various ways. Its commitment, therefore, is to the empowerment of women to take back control over their lives, and it attempts to achieve this using a variety of types of approach. In this, it is perhaps one of the projects in Britain most similar to the comprehensive, community-wide Duluth model, discussed in Chapter 9. It does not run programmes for violent men, but it will work with and advise any agency which does so.

The Leeds inter-agency forum has two tiers. The first is the whole forum of 60 agencies which meets quarterly for information-sharing and networking. The second is the management group which steers the project and includes representatives of all the local agencies, including refuges and the Black Women's Forum. The project has drawn up a resource information pack for women and has been involved in developing both publicity material and comprehensive policy and practice guidelines for local agencies. As we have seen, the police are particularly active in combatting domestic violence in West Yorkshire, and the inter-agency project has liaised extensively with them, doing educational work and assisting in evolving good practice. It also provides outreach work with African-Caribbean and Asian women.

Perhaps the most innovatory part of the work in Leeds is the comprehensive domestic violence training scheme which it has pioneered, and the Good Practice Pilot Project which has been successfully launched in one area of the city. In an ambitious initiative, all relevant workers in all the agencies in the area have been trained in domestic violence awareness and good work practice. This has been achieved through a rigorous 'training the trainers' scheme in which people from different agencies are trained in order to be able then to train their colleagues in multi-agency groups.

The Good Practice Pilot Project contains a variety of other innovations. Educational programmes about domestic violence and about non-violent resolution of conflict are being developed in two schools, and support services are being provided for abused women in two GP surgeries. A court-based advocacy service is being established, together with domestic violence training for all court-based professionals. In addition, the needs of black women who have suffered violence are being identified through outreach work. The whole project is being fully monitored and evaluated to test its potential as a more general model of domestic violence work.

The Leeds model has been lucky to attract a basket of funding which is unlikely to be available in many other places, especially those where refuge provision itself is less established and therefore more in need of financial support. Recognizing this difficulty, the Leeds project is committed to ensuring proper funding for local refuges and support services, and for specialist projects for black women.

The Leeds project and the other leading inter-agency projects have taken a strong line against racism, heterosexism and all other sorts of discrimination. For multi-agency approaches to be effective, it is vital that they represent the needs of groups who have previously been disadvantaged or neglected in terms of the provision of services. If black women and women from ethnic minorities are not represented or are underrepresented, it is likely – if past experience is anything to go by – that their needs will be overlooked in any initiatives taken. It has been the experience of some black women's groups dealing with violence that they have been marginalized in domestic violence forums. This can be especially so where forums are dominated by white professionals, as is still too often the case. Inter-agency initiatives need to take on the issue of combatting racism on all its many levels if they are serious about improving services for women who have experienced violence in multi-racial communities.

The needs of women with disabilities who have suffered violence can also be neglected in inter-agency work. It is sobering – and, for people with disabilities, distressing and infuriating – how often gatherings of workers from different agencies suddenly place disability on their agendas as soon as a disabled person attends. Analysis of past minutes often reveals that the subject has been comprehensively absent from previous discussions. Lesbians too find that their interests and needs are often overlooked – in fact totally ignored – in the work of such bodies as domestic violence forums. They may find that they have been rendered totally invisible. As a result, few inter-agency forums have seriously considered services for lesbians who have suffered violence.

As regards finance, most projects – even the relatively well-resourced ones such as the Leeds initiative – have funding in the short to medium term only. Other inter-agency groups have extremely insecure funding and may have quite a limited survival time. Few projects have paid workers in post. It could be that, in general, multi-agency work on domestic violence will have a short life. Nevertheless, it does seem that the British government currently favours inter-agency approaches in line with other countries, and that it may continue to encourage their formation. Some domestic violence activists have suggested that this is because they do not cost much money, but make it look as though both central and local government are doing something. According to this argument, adequate government funding for refuges and other services for abused women and children might be a better way forward.

How effective is inter-agency work?

No one is yet very sure whether multi-agency work makes things any better for women and children who have suffered violence. If workers are given training in domestic violence awareness and operate codes of good practice, does anything change? Do women survivors of violence notice a difference? Workers in the field think and hope that the answer is yes, if the development is viewed from an overall perspective. In some local areas, refuge staff and women escaping domestic violence have reported improvements in services and in the responses which they get from other agencies. Women who have suffered violence may initially notice little change, though, and may be unaware that an inter-agency initiative is going on in their area. The point is gradually to improve provision through the adoption of good practice guidelines, to co-ordinate local responses better and to provide a more comprehensive and sensitive service. Thus, there is a need for an independent and comprehensive evaluation of the effectiveness of the inter-agency approach, regarding both its direct impact upon the lives of women who have experienced domestic violence and its indirect effect through better co-ordinated provision.

One of the most obvious dangers is that it can become a talking shop. Attending a domestic violence forum can be a time for professionals who are deeply involved in domestic violence work to get together, have lunch perhaps and chat to their friends. What they talk about will almost always be related to improving agency practice and may well result in the provision of enhanced services and in the undertaking of fresh innovations. However, an abused woman who is on the streets and trying to find her way to a run-down, underfunded refuge which is already full to overflowing may have little patience with this approach.

In times of financial insecurity and competition, there is a danger that funding will be diverted away from essential refuge provision and emergency services towards the cheaper but perhaps more fashionable option of inter-agency work. The presence of multi-agency domestic violence forums can permit funders, local and central government agencies and the public to delude themselves that all is well on the domestic violence front. In reality, all that might be happening is that the chronic lack of grass-roots services is being disguised. Most inter-agency workers are well aware of these problems. They attempt to ensure that any funding which they receive is not at the expense of local refuges, and they publicize wherever they can the lack of basic grass-roots provision. Often, though, these matters are beyond their control.

The relationship between inter-agency work and the refuge network is a complex and sometimes contradictory one. What underlies it is the overall relationship between the refuge network on the one hand and both local and central government on the other. The setting up of Women's Equality Committees and Units, and the development of pro-women policies and practices, in some local authorities has meant that refuges now work more closely with such authorities than they ever thought they would. Feminists working in local authorities, attempting to challenge male-dominated councils and bureaucratic systems and to push for women-centred policies, may even become the local flag-bearers on behalf of abused women, replacing the autonomous refuge network. Many local authority women officers engaged on women's work are aware of this difficulty, but it sometimes happens that refuges, and the movement of which they are a part, lose the initiative.

Inter-agency workers and refuge staff point out that there can be a real problem when councils start to feel that they have the expertise and commitment to promote and control innovatory change, and to 'front' local initiatives. Some authorities, for example, have wanted to set up and run refuges themselves, ignoring the expertise and experience of Women's Aid. Others have begun, it seems, to regard Women's Aid as just one of several voluntary sector agencies involved. The important thing is that there are independent services which meet the needs of women who have suffered violence and their children, and Women's Aid continues to be the key agency in this respect. It is also important that inter-agency initiatives remember that much of their expertise comes from the experiences, views and knowledge of women active at the grass-roots level who do not always themselves have the opportunity to express this knowledge and experience publicly. Multi-agency work owes a debt to all these 'invisible' women.

Women's Aid and the refuge network as a whole have welcomed inter-agency work and applaud its intentions and the improved services which it can engender. But there are reservations. Traditionally, there has been some hostility between the statutory sector and the voluntary sector, including refuges, in most local authorities. Additionally, as a feminist organization, Women's Aid has always stood apart from local government, however forward-looking. Multi-agency co-operation can help to ease this animosity, but the tension often remains. For example, local authorities may not appreciate the dynamic working processes which are necessary in refuges to meet the needs of women and children, and refuge groups involved with never-ending crisis work may not have had the time to develop very effective management systems. The introduction of the currently fashionable service contracts for voluntary sector staff and of increased monitoring and surveillance by local authorities of the services provided, while often leading to more efficient practices, can also appear to threaten the independence of the refuge network.

Within inter-agency projects themselves, refuges and women who have experienced domestic violence may find themselves marginalized. There are examples of refuge staff being overlooked in the development and management of new initiatives. Workers in refuges may themselves have little time to participate in local domestic violence initiatives or to make sure that their views are heard. The unpredictable, emergency nature of their work and the understaffing which plagues most refuges mean that they may have to miss crucial meetings and may appear to lack commitment to the issues under consideration. At worst, this can mean that multi-agency initiatives become almost divorced from what is going on locally for women fleeing domestic violence. Refuges and projects for black women, which are often even more severely underfunded and overworked, can be similarly cut off. But if refuges are not properly represented in and consulted about inter-agency work, the two can go their own separate ways with disastrous consequences.

Various strategies can be adopted to ensure that this does not happen. For example, refuge groups can have built-in, guaranteed positions on the steering groups of inter-agency projects, and can be automatically offered the chance to comment on all draft policies and documents. It is vital that Women's Aid, the refuge network and women who have suffered violence have a key role in the further development of inter-agency work, and are included in all planning and implementation procedures – or at the very least are fully consulted. Without the contribution of this network and movement over the last twenty years, inter-agency initiatives would not exist. The initiatives are valuable in themselves, and they may lead to vastly improved service provision in the future. But they are only part of the picture. The social movement of women against violence, however diverse, must be at its foundation.

Domestic violence training

The Women's Aid federations, the National Inter-Agency Working Party Report and a variety of other agencies point out that domestic violence training is of key importance in identifying good practice in service provision. It is now becoming widely accepted that officers in the police force, in local authorities and in the voluntary sector need to be trained in how to work with women who have experienced domestic violence. This realization has been a long time coming. In general, domestic violence training has been absent in the past from the agendas of statutory and voluntary agencies. Women's Aid groups throughout the country have been initiating and running occasional training sessions on an ad hoc basis for years, but there was never much of an interest in them until recently. Now training seems to be the order of the day. Once again, some workers in the domestic violence field have expressed a degree of scepticism. It is perfectly possible, they suggest, for officers to go on training courses but then to continue their work exactly as they did before.

Inter-agency projects have been at the forefront of instigating the new training schemes, and generally make it a priority to provide training for workers in member agencies. Codes of good practice for statutory and voluntary organizations almost always contain commitments to provide domestic violence training. The provision of training for all statutory and voluntary sector officers has been recommended by all the relevant professional bodies and research studies, including the *Domestic Violence and Housing* report prepared by our own domestic violence research group and published jointly by WAFE and the University of Bristol in 1993.

This rather sudden interest in domestic violence training must be understood in the context of the explosion in short-term training of all sorts in the late 1980s and early 1990s. Training has become something of a watchword in the caring professions, and elsewhere. Training initiatives and agencies – and, indeed, actual training needs – have all grown substantially in number. As far as training goes, everyone seems to be doing it.

Within this context, however, domestic violence training is certainly an advance. It is now becoming more generally available, mainly due to the pioneering efforts of a handful of women who have devised courses. Training of this sort generally includes domestic violence awareness with or without an additional consideration of any policies and procedures used by the agency in question. The awareness aspect is usually facilitated through a series of exercises, role plays and case studies. Workers are given the opportunity to consider their own attitudes to domestic violence and other people's too, and can learn more about the reality of the experience. Usually there is an attempt by the facilitators to provide an environment which is both supportive and challenging, so that participants feel able to explore their feelings and beliefs honestly rather than hiding behind a veneer of 'political correctness'. All trainers say that they often have to deal with prejudiced or stereotyped opinions about domestic violence, and they try to do so in a positive way. The most effective training covers wider issues about policy and about how services are delivered within the framework of domestic violence work in general.

It is important that an awareness of class and race issues runs through domestic violence training as an integral part of it, rather than being tacked on almost as an afterthought – as happens far too often in the provision of general training services. In domestic violence training, for example, there can be a tendency for black women to be 'added on' to an analysis of violence in the home which is purely based on white women's experience. Integrating an analysis of discrimination and disadvantage into the very fabric of the course structure and design leads to a richer type of training which is more real and truthful. Offering this sort of training means being committed to combatting oppression not just of women (as manifested by the violence) but wherever it occurs. The grounds for oppression, as we have discussed before, are many – class, race, age, sexuality, disability, culture, religion. The Hammersmith and Fulham/University of North London study, *What Support?*, and other research studies recommend that, in addition to addressing racism, issues about lesbians, older women, young women and women with disabilities who have suffered violence are included in all training programmes. Information on domestic violence training is available from the Women's Aid federations which maintain an overview of the issue. They can advise on what is available and they also produce relevant publications and leaflets. Scottish Women's Aid has produced a useful training pack called *Women Counselling Women*. An excellent training and resource pack, *Challenging Domestic Violence*, is also available from the London Borough of Hammersmith and Fulham, which is a development of an original 'training for trainers' course evolved some years ago by Andrea Tara-Chand, now co-ordinator of the Leeds inter-agency project, and by Liz Kelly.

As we have discussed, 'training for trainers' is now being used by the Leeds inter-agency project scheme, and is being developed elsewhere. The Leeds training draws on the experience of the Duluth project (see Chapter 9), and includes material on the use of psychological and emotional violence by abusers within a web of controlling behaviour. The good practice element of the training involves an in-depth explanation of practical ways to do inter-agency work. Training workers to train others means that training can be provided systematically and economically.

The Leeds experience, and that of other projects and Women's Aid, is that to be successful training needs to be offered to all front-line workers as a mandatory part of working conditions, rather than something which a few people with a special interest in the subject attend. To date, it has perhaps been offered most often to police officers and to housing officers, frequently to the latter as part of the implementation of domestic violence and homelessness policy and practice guidelines. The London Borough of Newham, for example, provided in 1991 a particularly comprehensive training programme throughout its housing department, run through a local housing advice service. In areas with well-developed inter-agency projects, training may be offered in cross-agency groups as originally pioneered by the Nottinghamshire domestic violence forum, and as now being developed by 'training for trainers' initiatives.

In other areas, however, some agencies seem to think that they should just put on one short domestic violence training course, pat themselves on the back, and then leave it at that. But it will not work that way: training needs to be provided on a rolling programme, perhaps on an annual basis with follow-up sessions. A systematic commitment is required from the management of the agency involved.

The next stumbling block can be that, once the management has taken this lesson to heart, it may be tempted to regard training as a panacea – and to implement training initiatives without accompanying policy and practice developments. Without the services, however, even the best training programme in the world will have little effect. At best, it may result in service providers saying 'no' in a more respectful and humane way. Women survivors of violence are likely to appreciate this courtesy – being treated with dignity can be empowering in itself. But more should not be claimed on behalf of training than it can deliver. The provision of concrete resources and services must always be primary.

In 1992 and 1993, there has been a growth in the number of domestic violence training options. Sometimes training is provided by Women's Aid staff, both locally and nationally, with proper payment and support for their services. Often, though, it is provided by freelance trainers or training consultants who frequently have a background in the refuge movement or in local authority domestic violence work. As and if the demand for training continues to expand, there will be a need for more and more trainers throughout the country. As a result, there may be a problem about co-ordination and course content. There have been some moves by Women's Aid and others to set up a co-ordinating group, but this has yet to happen. At the moment there are no controls or guidelines about who teaches what, and anyone can set themselves up as a domestic violence trainer.

One of the problems with this somewhat piecemeal approach is that training enterprises can become cut off from the Women's Aid network and from the direct, everyday experience of women advocates in refuges and of women who have suffered violence. It is essential that this does not happen. Number one in the 'Golden guidelines for training' in the Hammersmith training and resource pack is to involve local refuges and Women's Aid groups, wherever possible, in the planning and delivery of training courses. Some trainers have run joint training sessions with Women's Aid. At the very least, Women's Aid and other local refuge groups – including, crucially, specialist services for black, ethnic minority and other women fleeing violence – should be consulted about training provision and involved in an adviser capacity. As for inter-agency work as a whole, it would be a tragedy if domestic violence training became detached from Women's Aid and from local specialist provision for black, ethnic minority and other women.

One final point should be noted. There have been differing views within and between refuge groups both about providing training for the police and about engaging in inter-agency co-operation with them. The role of the police as social controllers of political protest and the public exposure of oppressive policing in black and Irish communities have led on occasion to calls by black groups, the left and others for non-co-operation with the police. The resultant dilemma for some members of refuge groups has different outcomes at different times and in different places. The police role in combatting domestic violence is one of the most essential, and their handling of violence cases is of key significance to women because of the traumatic and crucial point at which they are asked to intervene on women's behalf. In addition, the police have not been previously noted for pro-women sympathies, so the new police policies are demanding changes in long-established police practices and attitudes. For all these reasons, domestic violence training and inter-agency co-operation can be even more vital for the police than for other agencies. In addition, a constitutional objective of the Women's Aid federations is to educate other bodies, which of course includes the police. Some local Women's Aid groups have been delivering training to local police forces since the 1970s. After a joint conference between Welsh Women's Aid and the police in the 1980s, Welsh Women's Aid pioneered nationally based police training, and for the last two years WAFE has had input into national training at the National Police Training School in England.

9
Men's programmes, public education and campaigning

Programmes for violent men

Political campaigns against domestic violence and for the empowerment of women have a vital role to play in transforming both individual
men's attitudes and behaviour, and society in general. As we have
emphasized throughout this book, it is only because of the political
movement of women against violence that domestic violence is such a
public issue today. Women working for and with women have
revolutionized the way in which we think about violence in the home
and the services available for women survivors. But what about the
men?

Activists and domestic violence workers giving publicity talks are
asked this question so often it can become tiresome. 'What are you
doing to stop the men being violent?' 'Can't you work with the men as
well?' 'Nothing will change unless you do something about the men, will
it?' Public concerns like these are understandable, and locate the
problem accurately. It is indeed the men who have to stop being violent.
But refuge workers can find these questions frustrating, especially in
situations of financial insecurity when even basic provision for women
is inadequate. The refuge movement believes that its responsibility is
to work with women, to represent women, to empower women, to take
women's side. It is hard-pressed enough to do this with the diminishing
resources available; to expect it to take on the men as well is perhaps
too much.

Domestic violence activists suggest that the responsibility for dealing
with men's violence lies, not with the women's movement, but with
society in general and men in particular. Women campaigners have

worked hard to strengthen the law against domestic violence and the penalties available. They have watched and even participated in the setting up of some of the new programmes for violent men. But in the end, it is men themselves who need to take responsibility for male violence and do something about it. It is they who must provide the services. The suggestion usually is that this is best done in liaison with – and, loosely speaking, with leadership from – the campaigns and services for abused women. This means that women can influence and advise the men's services but that they do not have to undertake too much of the work themselves (although a few projects for violent men do employ women workers).

Despite adhering to this broad position, however, there is a lot of doubt and scepticism in the refuge movement as to whether men's programmes, especially the more therapeutic ones, can work. When we discussed the issue with a friend who has established a new life after fleeing domestic violence, she said after a long and serious pause:

> I'm sorry but I don't think it can work. I wish it could but I don't think it will, ever. Once a batterer, always a batterer. You're not going to get them to change just like that. Maybe a few of them, but not many. They don't really want to change, do they?

In our many years working in refuges, you could probably count on two hands the number of male partners of women living there who would have entered a programme for violent men willingly, or at least with an open mind. Most of them would have regarded such a programme with derision.

Although individual men, and some groups of men, may be lacking in personal power and self-esteem, the phenomenon of male violence as a whole is about men exerting power and control over women. And male power and control over women, even in 1990s Britain, is still institutionalized in various forms throughout society. A quick look at who controls what throughout the institutions of society can demonstrate it with ease, although men's power over women is cut across by social class and other factors. The weight of centuries of male-dominated society remains behind men. To try to challenge by a few small programmes this great mass of tradition, history, economics, culture and social organization, which backs up and bolsters aggressive or violent male behaviour, can seem a hopeless task.

From this point of view, structural change in society is what we need, brought about through political, economic and social movements for change. Many women who have suffered violence, or who are activists in the field, neither believe men's programmes can work without larger changes in society, nor trust men to carry them out effectively. Women's fingers have been burnt too many times. They may point out that, for any other crime of violence, men are put into prison, not sent on a therapy programme and allowed to go on living with the very person whom they attacked.

Others argue that it is nevertheless worth a try. Men's programmes, they say, seem to be here to stay, and domestic violence activists are better off exerting some influence over them than being excluded and possibly regretting it later. There is now quite a variety of programmes available for violent men. In North America, in particular, these programmes have thrived, but they are being set up in other countries throughout the world. In Britain, there are a small number of projects at the moment, with more planned. We will undoubtedly hear and see more of them in the future.

Rebecca and Russell Dobash devote a whole section of their book *Women, Violence and Social Change* to what they call the 'therapeutic society', particularly in North America. They explain how the North American approach tends to regard most social and economic problems as faulty traits in people's personalities which require therapy to be put right – after which everything will be fine. The burgeoning psychological and therapeutic professions in the States, treating ever-increasing numbers of people, have become a significant part of the American economy. New York City now has more psychoanalysts than any single European country. The Dobashes describe how these professions feed into American culture and history, which encourages a grasping individualism and which discourages social movements.

The new men's programmes must be understood in this context. David Adams, an expert on American men's programmes and a co-founder of one of the most progressive – and pro-feminist – ones, EMERGE, in Boston, has provided a useful analysis of the five major models of treatment programmes for men. His analysis is contained in an article in the American book *Feminist Perspectives on Wife Abuse*, edited by Kersti Yllo and Michelle Bograd, and in various other places. The five models which he suggests have been quite widely used and adapted – for example, by the Domestic Violence Strategic Plan on programmes for violent perpetrators in New South Wales, Australia.

Adams and others highlight a major problem with many of the therapeutic programmes, which is that, in such programmes, the battering, violent behaviour is usually not identified as a main treatment issue, but rather as a symptom of some other underlying problem. Men in the programmes can then get the message that non-violence is negotiable – in other words, that until and unless they make the larger underlying changes, the violence is understandable, although of course undesirable. Some approaches may actually collude with the violent man in avoiding the issue of his violence. The programmes which Adams discusses use group and individual therapy. They are far more firmly established in the United States and Canada, but they are beginning to be established in Britain as well – albeit in less high-powered therapeutic packages.

Men's programmes in North America

The first type of North American programme is the 'insight model', a traditional approach to understanding violence. The idea is that the man is violent because he is frustrated or depressed, has poor impulse control or some other psychological problem. If he could become more aware of how he has been affected by past experience, more insightful into his own problems, then he could learn to respond less violently to his current situation. Part and parcel of this approach is the idea that men who are violent have a very fragile sense of self, that they are trying to live up to an impossible, 'macho', masculine ideal, and that they take it out on their wives when they cannot do so. Feminist criticisms of these programmes do not dispute the value of insight therapy as a tool for personal change. Many women and men have used similar therapeutic or counselling approaches to understand their lives and their behaviour. But critics are extremely doubtful about the fact that challenging the abuse is not a central part of the programme – and in fact may still be going on while the man is attending the sessions.

Feminists are also critical of the use of a purely psychological explanation of abuse which ignores the wider social and political factors. For example, the insight model usually overlooks the way that violence is instrumental to men in terms of wielding power and control over women. The model of treatment makes out that it is a matter of individual failure for the man concerned and his impaired intra-psychic processes. In 1985 a national survey was conducted in the United States by two researchers, M. Pirog-Good and J. Stets-Keeley. They looked at 59 'battering prevention programs' and found that 'increasing self-esteem' was a primary treatment goal for 90 per cent of them. 'Having the abuser take responsibility for his violence' was regarded as an important goal in only 14 per cent. The insight model can also lead to situations in which men may in fact learn to identify their use of violence as part of a power dynamic, but continue to use it anyway, or learn to use other means to the same end. Gaining insight does not necessarily mean making changes. Feminists additionally criticize the model for the way in which clients are therapeutically bolstered up and validated at all times due to their supposedly fragile sense of themselves. The approach is as unthreatening and non-challenging as possible.

The second model is the 'ventilation model'. It is about people's need to 'get rid of' their anger rather than suppressing it. This idea can be detected in a lot of new counselling methods which have developed since the 1960s. It refers to the concept of ventilating one's angry feelings in a safe, non-physical way. Feminists would not dispute that bottling up anger is bad for people. But there tends to be, in this model, a belief that showing anger verbally will make physical violence less likely. Research tends to show just the opposite – that domestic violence often escalates from the solely verbal to the physical. Verbal violence and aggression can in itself be extremely distressing and part of a pattern of abuse.

The third model is the 'interaction model', in which couples are seen together and joint therapy takes place. This model derives from the family systems school of thought in social work and family therapy which we mentioned in Chapter 7. Its problem is that it tends to equalize responsibility for the violence between the woman and the man, so that both are held to be to blame for the interactive cycle which leads to abuse. The differences in power between them are often not acknowledged, and women may be frightened and disadvantaged in joint negotiating and therapy sessions. The best therapists recognize these problems and try to build up the woman's strength and ability to challenge her partner safely. However, a problem with this model of intervention is the identification of who is to be held responsible if difficulties are encountered or if it goes wrong. Women can end up being further penalized, or held responsible, for their own abuse.

Some women, of course, may wish to engage in 'conjoint' therapy of this type. And there can be value in it – which of us could not do with a bit of counselling help with our intimate relationships? But it is vital for women to be aware of the dangers. One of the most pernicious aspects of the interactive approach is that the man's violence may be regarded as a highly regrettable but understandable response to provocative or difficult behaviour by the woman. Adams points out that the issue of who is responsible for the violence is clouded. And the therapy itself can be dangerous for women partners. Women may expose themselves to further violence by expressing previously disguised dissatisfactions during family therapy sessions. Many women who have previously suffered violence apparently report further violent incidents in the aftermath of such sessions.

The fourth type of model which Adams identifies is rather grandiosely and mystifyingly called the 'cognitive behavioural and psycho-educational' model. This approach does make the violence the prime focus of counselling. The men participate in groups. The idea is that violence is learned behaviour, and can therefore be unlearned. Skills of stress reduction, relaxation and non-aggressive assertion are taught. And men are encouraged to observe and learn about their behaviour so that they can find out what their triggers are – what sets them off and when the point of no return is passed. They are encouraged to learn to take 'time out' to interrupt the build-up of potentially violent anger by literally walking out of the situation temporarily. Members of the group learn about each other's rigid anger responses and can challenge each other and work out alternative ways of responding.

Basically, the men learn useful anger management techniques. They learn how to control their anger, how to communicate and generally how to cope with life better so that they do not get angry in the first place. However, an American monitoring programme of apparently reformed violent men found they merely switched, after the programme, from anger to other psychological means to control their wives. In addition, anger control can let the community off the hook yet again by making out that domestic violence is an individual problem of men who cannot cope adequately with life and with angering situations.

Edward Gondolf and David Russell dissected these problems in a 1986 article entitled, 'The case against anger control treatment programs for batterers'. They pointed out that anger control may imply that the victim provoked the anger and so precipitated the abuse, and that it can be seen as a 'quick fix' which might actually endanger women in the long run. In other words, the man has anger control treatment and then everyone thinks things are OK, but in reality nothing has changed.

While all this is often true, the best of the programmes using anger management approaches do address controlling behaviour by men and include an analysis of power between men and women. Without this analysis, it is difficult for anger control programmes to explain why so many men who cannot cope with anger, and need to develop new skills to do so, attack only their wives and not other people. At their best, assertion practice, anger control techniques and other education programmes are linked to a call for stronger legal remedies against domestic violence and for a society-wide condemnation of it.

Even such a schematic and inevitably somewhat caricatured account as this shows that there is some useful material in each of these four models of therapeutic intervention. They are often used in combination. Men's programmes may take some bits from one approach and some from another. What they all clearly need, from a feminist point of view, is an analysis of the violence which takes gender politics into account.

The fifth type of programme does just this. In North America, it is often called the pro-feminist approach and consists of men's programmes which work closely alongside, and in support of, the women's movement against male violence. These programmes understand violence against women as one form of controlling behaviour which helps to maintain the imbalance of power and dominance by men over women. They recognize the need for participants to learn how to take care of others, to be educated in non-violence and to develop communication and assertion skills. But they hang these methods on a core structure of principles and politics which is committed to challenging male controlling behaviour and ending male dominance and violence.

These mainly North American programmes have become more skilled over time. While each one varies in its approach, they have developed some common features which are a standard part of their philosophy and practice. They tend, for example, to use group methods of counselling. And their first priority is always the safety of women partners. Men participants are expected to make 'safety plans' to minimize the possibility of continued violence. The safety plans must be strictly adhered to and are usually monitored. Separate contact with the woman is often made through the shelter movement or through an autonomous but connected sister project.

Throughout the programme, the man's violence is centre-stage. Other underlying or contributing problems which he might have will be addressed, but will not be allowed to dislodge his violent and controlling behaviour from its position as the primary focus of attention. Most pro-feminist programmes confront as a priority two important and very common defences consciously or subconsciously used by violent men. The first is denial, either of the violence or of responsibility for it – the 'it wasn't my fault' approach. The second is minimizing the extent of the violence or its impact on women recipients. Thus one of the primary identified tasks of the programme is to get participants to take full responsibility for their own behaviour. And this means doing so in a real and deep way, rather than making excuses, refusing to face it, or blaming someone else (usually their women partners) as men often do. The taking of personal responsibility by men for their own actions is of key importance in the programme. It includes not only the violence but also all the other forms of controlling behaviour which men might later substitute for it, but which they may be reluctant to acknowledge or recognize.

Men are often expected to keep anger diaries and 'control logs' in which they must detail their controlling and angry behaviour for consideration by the group. They may also keep a written checklist of their violent and controlling behaviour traits, and learn how each of these may be damaging to their partners. This can be achieved through the use of videos, role play, and group and individual exercises. Later in the programme, attitudes, expectations and feelings are also examined, especially in the light of the way men often devalue or undervalue their women partners and women in general. Issues of power and control between men and women are continually confronted. Pro-feminist programmes see violence, much as the feminist women's services do, as one part of a long continuum of male controlling behaviour.

One of the first of the American pro-feminist men's programmes was EMERGE, mentioned earlier. Formed in Boston in 1977 at the request of the local shelter movement, EMERGE was then and has remained a model of good practice for men's programmes. It has always regarded it as a priority to campaign for funding for the women's movement and for shelters, and to ensure that resources are not diverted from women's projects. EMERGE recognizes that men's projects can create a lot of publicity and can attract money relatively easily, while shelters often remain starved of funding. Feminist guidelines for funding were developed jointly between EMERGE and local women's organizations and were adopted in 1980. They state that:

No program for men who batter should be funded without the existence of shelters or safe home projects for battered women in the immediate community ... (The availability of refuge for battered women when the abuser is in treatment is critical for reasons of safety of the women and children and of the efficacy of treatment for the abuser.)

Treatment programs for men who abuse must work cooperatively with shelters or safe home projects in their area. Programs for abusers must share the same philosophical understandings of the reasons for violence against women and must work in concert with the shelter movement to end violence against women.

Where the amount of funding in a community, foundation, or corporation is limited and insufficient to sustain both the shelter and abusers program, the financial resources should be directed to shelter programs until they achieve financial stability.

EMERGE has always had a political approach. All of its work revolves around issues of power and control, both between men and women, and between men. As a result it has no hierarchy itself, but organizes collectively and uses consensus decision-making. It campaigns for legal and economic changes in the position of women and actively supports women's movement initiatives. EMERGE was formed as a result of initiatives by committedly anti-sexist men who had been influenced by the Women's Liberation movement, and who often had a history as political organizers in the vibrant and extraordinarily widespread movements of the 1960s in North America. These gave rise to women's

and gay liberation, and later to something which is sometimes called the men's movement. This 'men's movement' started out with a commitment to anti-sexist organizing and struggle. One end of it gradually developed towards New Age philosophy and eventually gave rise to the non-political American men's groups that we know today, such as the 'movement' run by Robert Bly which has attracted so much publicity. The other end of the men's group spectrum stayed more political and connected to women's struggles. EMERGE and most of the other pro-feminist American programmes for violent men fit into the latter category. There has been some conflict in North America between the two ends of the spectrum and some attempts to harness both together, which can make the scenario a confusing one to an outside observer.

The more political men's organizations have been involved in national organizing work in the United States to end violence against women. National and local conferences have been held on men and masculinity for many years. Men's groups have launched various national and local initiatives, including the *Brother* national newsletters. A national networking organization, now called the National Organization for Men Against Sexism, has been in existence since 1982. It has developed task groups to focus on specific issues – for example, ending male violence, child custody, fathering, gay rights, homophobia, male/female relationships and so on. In 1985 the 'ending male violence' task group of this national organization launched Brother Peace, an annual international day of action to end male violence.

In Canada also, men's groups dedicated to opposing violence exist in every city. In many, they have established men's forums to work on violence issues in a more co-ordinated way. Some of these North American groups and organizations have been facilitated by academic studies of masculinity and the beginning of men's studies as an academic discipline. They take a wide political view and may campaign actively for greater legal protection and service provision for abused women.

A notable example of a men's project which takes this view is Man Alive, the men's programme affiliated to the Marin Abused Women's Service in Marin County, California, and initiated by them as part of their community response to domestic violence. Another example is the long-established RAVEN (Rape And Violence End Now), set up in St Louis in 1977 and providing counselling in mixed groups of court-mandated and self-referred men. All of these projects are dynamically linked to the women's movement and to shelter and advocacy services.

Pro-feminist projects usually believe that a public examination of and awareness about male violence can help to prevent it. And so they attempt to promote a principled stance against male violence at all times. Projects like EMERGE and Man Alive, for example, try to forge community links and to publicize their work and their anti-sexist politics as widely as they can. So they frequently give talks to schools, to male professional groups and to community organizations. They may set up conferences and educational initiatives, and some produce manuals and guidebooks. They also publicize the reasons why they disagree with the traditional, therapeutic programmes and attempt to engage in public debate about the issue.

How effective are they?

The effectiveness of even the best programmes has yet to be demonstrated, although the Dobashes have suggested that the limited amount of research which has been done shows some success in reducing violence. They point out that what we do not yet know is whether men's programmes result in sustained and permanent patterns of non-violent behaviour, and whether they make meaningful contributions to wider social change.

One of the most recent considerations of these North American programmes is presented by a Canadian therapist, Ron Thorne-Finch, in a wide-ranging book, *Ending the Silence: The Origins and Treatment of Male Violence Against Women*, published in 1992. He points out that there are growing numbers of men criticizing male violence and working towards sweeping changes in our ideas about masculinity and about what being a man means. An Ottawa-based group, Partners in Change, calls it negotiating the transition for men from 'power-over' to 'power-with'. However, as Thorne-Finch suggests, the overall percentage of men involved in these activities is very small, and they are split in their approaches to male violence, in the school of feminist thought which they follow, and in their relationship to wider political struggles about issues of class, wealth, race and so on. The potential for great things is there, but will it be realized?

Many women in the shelter movement say 'no'. The Pennsylvania Coalition Against Domestic Violence undertook the ambitious task of studying pro-feminist services for batterers and published their findings in a 1988 publication, *Safety for Women: Monitoring Batterers' Programs*, by Barbara Hart. Hart suggests that most activists believe counselling and education for violent men work in the short term only, and that what is needed is a strong and consistent community intolerance of domestic violence. She contends that

> Programs for men could be no more than a dangerous charade which holds out false hope to battered women. Many activists have concluded that work with batterers is an inappropriate diversion from the more critical tasks of enabling battered women and children to escape violence and establish safe lives.

As a result of the study, the following guidelines (which further expand the previous guidelines developed with EMERGE) have been evolved. The first is that services for women must have primacy. No programme for men should be initiated unless the women's programme is successfully funded. Second, women advocates for women who have suffered violence should participate in the design and implementation of the programme. Third, the primary goal should be to end violence against women and to focus on confronting male violence. It is vital that men make a formal contract to be non-violent as part of the programme, and that there are adverse consequences for non-compliance. Fourth, all programmes must be evaluated.

Barbara Hart points out that the initial belief was that men should participate in the programmes voluntarily so that they would be motivated to change. However, many women and men activists have come round to the position that programmes should have the force of law and of community intolerance of violence behind them. Programmes should not be seen as an easy way out – a soft alternative. Rather they should be established as one part of a strong legal and community response. Under the influence of women's movement services, this viewpoint has grown in prominence and has led to a growth of court-ordered programmes in which violent men must participate as mandated by the courts. EMERGE, RAVEN and Man Alive all run programmes for offenders. But court-ordered programmes in Duluth and Minneapolis, together with others in San Francisco, Atlanta, Denver and Seattle, have taken the lead in pioneering this approach and in initiating pro-arrest policies in the criminal justice system.

Perhaps the best known, and certainly one of the most highly thought of in feminist circles, is the comprehensive and highly developed Domestic Abuse Intervention Project (DAIP) in Duluth, Minnesota. Ellen Pence, who has written widely about the project, very often preludes any discussion by emphasizing the favourable political climate which has nurtured it, due to the long tradition of socially responsive government and grass-roots activism in Minnesota.

The Duluth project has always sought to influence the criminal justice system and the social services involved with domestic violence. It incorporates men's programmes into a wide-ranging community-based strategy which also involves women's services and policy and practice initiatives throughout the locality. Originally, local agencies came together under the banner of the DAIP and adopted written guidelines, policies and procedures governing their responses to domestic abuse cases. In consequence, the police adopted strong pro-arrest policies which were co-ordinated with the response of the courts. The DAIP now monitors and co-ordinates the intervention of law enforcement, criminal justice, human services and battered women's shelter and advocacy programmes. Policy changes have been implemented throughout the caring services and the justice system as a result. The monitoring role of the DAIP is to prevent community collusion with abusers, and Ellen Pence has written a helpful 1988 paper about the project, *Batterers' Programs: Shifting from Community Collusion to Community Confrontation.*

In implementing the programme, workers attempt to put feminist ideas into action. At each step practice is matched against theory, and input is obtained from women who have suffered domestic violence themselves. The grass-roots approach is one of empowerment of women, and this strategy is then expected, indeed made, to pervade all the services and programmes provided. The involvement of women survivors of violence and of the shelter movement is seen to be vital. Women are nurtured, supported and encouraged throughout their use of the courts, and advocacy work with women is also undertaken, whether or not they are using shelters. Women advocates establish empowering educational groups for women which meet in various neighbourhoods to discuss in a secure and non-threatening environment such topics as 'the dynamics of battering'. They are linked to other projects for developing awareness in local communities that domestic violence is unacceptable. Support for women, both through the programme and in the community, is seen to be an essential part of the project. Without it, the pro-arrest policies and men's programmes cannot work effectively and women may be placed in even more danger.

The courts require that abusers participate in a 26-week counselling and educational programme co-ordinated by the DAIP. For twelve weeks the groups focus on stopping the violence, with an emphasis on anger management training and on confronting men's minimizing and denying behaviour towards their violent acts. The men then enter a second phase of the programme run by community activists trained by the DAIP. They are encouraged to stay in the programme after the court mandate is completed.

The assumptions of the programme are that men who batter use a range of abusive tactics. Violence is rarely used to the exclusion of other methods. The DAIP has developed a chart showing how the different types of abuse relate to each other. It was elaborated in extensive consultation with women survivors of violence and takes the form of a wheel known as the 'power and control wheel'. It is widely used by the project itself and by others in several countries. A second wheel diagram, the 'equality wheel', is used towards the end of the men's programme to assist them in developing more equal, honest and non-controlling ways of relating.

The Duluth project has been replicated in over twenty other Minnesota communities, although the organizers are well aware that each community is different and needs to develop its own approach. The Duluth model, however, has acted as a source of inspiration and of good working ideas for many agencies and for women's movement services in various countries. A closely connected project is the Domestic Abuse Project established in Minneapolis in 1979 and providing a similar multi-systems intervention project.

Men's projects in Britain

In Britain, men's projects are in their infancy compared with the situation in the United States. While they will undoubtedly develop further in coming years, it is doubtful that the most traditional, therapeutic American programmes will take root, since British society is so much less 'therapized'. However, many of the other debates and approaches used in the States are beginning to crop up in Britain. One such is the debate between projects which believe in voluntary self-referral by men and those which believe in court-ordered programmes. Men attending voluntary programmes might be more motivated to learn and change, whereas men who are court-mandated often have such a long history of violence behind them, before they reach the stage of being ordered by the court to attend a programme, that they may be hardened in their ways. However, court-ordered programmes give domestic violence greater weight and seriousness as a criminal and legal issue. In Britain, a few projects of both types exist. The self-referral ones are often one-off projects run by committed men. The court-mandated ones tend to be part of a broader approach to domestic violence, and are often connected into a more multi-layered community response.

An example of the former type is the Everyman Centre in Brixton, London, which provides help for men who want to stop being violent. Voluntary individual counselling is offered for twelve weeks followed by six to nine months in a group. There is also a confidential phone line. The Everyman Centre, like many other men's projects, encourages men to use the 'time out' approach – to take time away from their partners when an argument threatens to escalate. The partners get together again later to discuss the argument. A second technique used is to teach the man to make the conscious decision to keep a distance of 6 feet away from his partner.

Other examples of such groups are the well-thought-of Men's Centre in London, and also Men Overcoming Violence (MOVE). There have been various MOVE groups over the years which have come and gone, often due to lack of funding, and men usually offer counselling skills on a voluntary basis in addition to their paid jobs, which can be stressful. Some of the counsellors are connected to the co-counselling movement. There are currently MOVE groups in a few cities in the UK with the most well known being the group in Bolton. MOVE groups do not offer support to the women partners of violent men, and on occasion their activities have been a source of anxiety for Women's Aid groups due to their lack of consultation with Women's Aid. While MOVE groups emphasize the way that men are negatively socialized into violent behaviour, some Women's Aid groups claim that they lack an analysis of the power dynamic between men and women, and that they overlook the importance of sexual, emotional and financial violence. Bolton MOVE have produced a self-help manual on combatting domestic violence which contains practical advice and suggestions.

A second debate among men's projects is about diversion schemes. A few programmes have developed as an alternative to custodial action: in other words, men are 'diverted' either from imprisonment, or from prosecution in the first place. Several men's projects, however, following the Duluth approach, uphold the idea that programmes must be part of a strong legal and criminal justice approach, and that they should themselves campaign for a strengthening of the law. Years of experience of diversion programmes in North America, often through the American family court system, have shown that they do not work well in cases of domestic violence. This is not to say, however, that exposure to a tough and degrading prison regime is any more successful.

In Britain, diversion schemes have been mainly used in Scotland, where various diversion schemes are in operation for different types of offence. Scottish Women's Aid, however, has objected strongly, and to some effect, to the use of such schemes in cases of domestic violence, and they have not in any case been much used in this context. In Lothian, domestic violence perpetrators were specifically excluded from diversion schemes in 1987. Other regional councils, such as Fife and Grampian, have also followed this course of action. Rebecca and Russell Dobash have detailed the objections to the use of diversion schemes in domestic violence cases in various recent publications.

Lothian Regional Council Social Services Department has implemented an innovative alternative to diversion schemes which seeks to re-educate violent men without allowing them to bypass the criminal justice system. Thus, the men come through the justice system rather than being diverted away from it. They are placed on probation and ordered by the court to participate actively in the programme. In this way, treatment is offered but domestic violence is not de-criminalized. Schemes of this sort are sometimes called post-court diversion schemes in that the man goes through the court process but is diverted away from a custodial sentence. In addition, there are now several programmes for violent men in England in which men who are on probation attend a group. However, most of them are not mandated by the courts to do so.

The main argument against diversion schemes of all types is that men should face the legal consequences of their actions rather than being given a 'soft' option. They should learn that the law will not allow them to get away with domestic violence, that society will not stand for it. Even at their worst, however, the present legal penalties are fairly mild. It is rare either for men to be sent to prison for domestic violence or for any prison sentence imposed to be longer than a few days or weeks. Even probation is a more serious sentence than men often get. It is not usually the case that attending a men's programme while on probation allows the man to escape a more severe penalty. Some women argue, however, that the existence of men's programmes will militate against legal changes which could result in violent men being dealt with more seriously in the future.

Abused women want the violence to stop; however, they may not want their partner to go to prison. The possibility that this could happen may deter a woman from reporting the violence at all. She may fear that, if her partner does serve a sentence, she will experience violent repercussions when he comes out. She may also wish to avoid a harshly punitive response, and may prefer the possibility of a community-based option. Such considerations can be particularly relevant for black women. A woman whose partner or ex-partner is African-Caribbean, for example, may be very wary of exposing him to possible prison sentences due to the unfair and racist treatment which he might receive at the hands of the criminal justice and prison system.

The CHANGE project in Central Region, Scotland, and the Domestic Violence Intervention Project in Hammersmith, London, are the two British projects which currently most resemble the American projects like Man Alive, EMERGE and the Duluth programme. They take a firm line against domestic violence and in favour of a stronger criminal justice response, and they also have links with domestic violence services and networks for women.

The CHANGE project was set up before the Lothian project and works with men on probation who are directed to attend the project by order of the court. The men's programme began in 1990. It offers a group approach designed to ensure that the offender takes full responsibility for his own actions. During the programme, the man should learn about power and control issues in relationships between men and women, and about how to change his own controlling, dominating actions. The project focuses clearly at all times on stopping the violence, and on attempting to change men's attitudes to the abuse of their partner. It attempts to demystify and expose the ways in which men often blame their partner, or deny or minimize their own violent actions. One of its prime aims is to protect the safety of women and children associated with men on the programme, although its staff and others point out that there can clearly be no guarantee about this. The CHANGE project also has a wider remit which includes liaison, training, education and stimulating a broad debate about the issue of violence to women. It has, for example, devised a training package used as in-service training for social workers.

CHANGE has hosted two international conferences which were addressed by representatives from the Marin Abused Women's Service, Man Alive, the Duluth Abuse Intervention Project, Scottish Women's Aid and others. In January 1992 it held a further national conference. Rebecca and Russell Dobash, who were involved in the initial impetus to establish the project, are conducting an extensive comparative evaluation of the two Scottish projects. Many women's group are suspicious of CHANGE, however, and wish to wait for the results of the evaluation before making a judgement about it. It has the cautious support of WAFE and, most importantly, of Scottish Women's Aid which contributes to its management.

Scottish Women's Aid has evolved various conditions which regulate its support of men's programmes. These include the provision of support and safety for the women and children involved, the understanding that violence in the home is a result of the relative positions of men and women in society, an emphasis on men taking full and unequivocal responsibility for their violence, the use of court mandates, equal funding for Women's Aid and support for increased provision of refuges and other options for women and children, the recognition of Women's Aid's expertise, and the importance of effective monitoring, evaluation and research. These conditions have been further discussed by Scottish Women's Aid and CHANGE, and resulted in a joint policy statement agreed in August 1991.

A new project which has recently been piloted in London may offer an alternative way forward in dealing with the difficulties of providing adequate support for the women partners or ex-partners. The Hammersmith Domestic Violence Intervention Project is the first programme in England to accept referrals through the courts. It accepts both court-mandated and voluntarily referred violent men, although most of the men currently do not come through the courts. An important innovation is that, like some of the North American programmes, the men's programme of counselling is accompanied by a separate sister project providing support and assistance for the women. The women's project runs from different premises so that the women partners and ex-partners can feel secure attending, and enjoys the support of local Women's Aid groups.

The Hammersmith project is currently in danger of closing due to lack of funding, and most of the other men's projects are financed on a short-term basis only. How effective they are at preventing violence remains to be seen. It seems clear that they can have short-term beneficial effects on men's behaviour, but whether these changes will be maintained permanently is not known. In the next few years, as programmes are evaluated in the medium to long term, we might find out.

Schools, community education and publicity campaigns

We live in a society in which cultural representations of violence are commonplace. For pleasure people often choose to to sit passively watching episodes of repeated and sometimes extreme violence, perhaps in violent sport or on television. Violent books are massively popular, and violent crime is on the increase. But the violence is not randomly distributed. Generally speaking, violent behaviour is associated with men, not women. Society and culture in western societies are full of images of men being aggressive, angry and violent, and of women being passive and often scantily clad. To confirm this view it is enough to glance at any edition of the *Sun*, to trawl through the TV channels on a Saturday night, to go into a video shop, or to look at the films of the moment which are the biggest box office successes – *Terminator* perhaps, or *Robocop*. Often these films consist principally of violent episodes strung together one after the other. They are seen by millions, and particularly by teenagers. Even in the case of comedies and romances, it is hard to find a super-popular film which does not include at least one scene in which the principal male characters are engaging in quite severe violence. It is also rare to find such a film in which the relationships between men and women are truly equal, and in which women characters are not dominated or devalued in some way by the men.

Even though many men are not themselves violent, popular culture encourages us all to see aggression and violence as appropriate male behaviour. Men in the media who are emotional, gentle and reluctant to engage in violence are frequently presented as figures of derision, contempt and ridicule. Toyshops are rigidly segregated by gender, and the boys' section looks like a war and weapons storehouse. It is chilling to see a two-year-old boy running around with a plastic machine gun pretending to murder everybody; or to see larger boys huddled together over computer screens for hours, zapping and destroying enemies.

People trying to bring up boys in this culture in an anti-sexist, non-violent way face a tough job. They have to pit themselves against the might of television, against the enormous advertising industry aimed at children, and against playground pressure from young peers. As a consequence of all this, they tend to be subjected to unremitting demands from their offspring to provide toys and games which glorify male violence. Very often the best that they can achieve is a damage limitation exercise. It becomes a question of strategic giving-in – on violent cartoons for pre-schoolers, on forts and soldiers, on computer games, on aggressive sports, on bombers and guns.

In other households, boys are allowed to engage in fantasy violence and to play with war toys. Many people claim that such fantasy play releases aggression rather than adding to it, and that, in any case, fantasy does not usually lead to the real thing. Others still encourage boys to be 'macho' and aggressive as a matter of course. Fathers and sons may conspire in violent play and in activities which repress emotions of tenderness and softness. Playground games and organized activities for boys are frequently rough and unforgiving. Boys are often brought up to be tough, to hide and repress their feelings, and only in the most traumatic circumstances to display vulnerability or fear or, worst of all, to cry.

If bringing up boys to be non-violent and to be able to express their feelings is a monumental task, so too is the project of bringing up boys to respect women and to learn how to engage in equal, mutually supportive adult relationships. Much work in education and psychology has shown at what a young age boys learn to devalue their mothers and other women and girls, and to believe that girls are less important, less instrumental in the world, than boys. It operates in reverse for girls. Everything from My Little Pony to teen romance to clothes and make-up teaches them to be compliant, emotionally nurturing and expressive, non-violent and sexually alluring to men.

It is beyond the scope of this book to investigate these vast subjects. This brief anecdotal account can only indicate what a huge task it is to attempt to change popular culture. None of us can escape it. In our lives, it is both a mirror and a cause of why we behave as we do, although it is not without contradictions. This applies as much to male violence as to anything else. There are sanctions against it and public outcry about its prevalence. Veiled, however, behind popular culture about male violence lies the reality of unequal economic and social relations between men and women, within an economic system which values qualities of toughness and competition and downgrades values of collectivity, sharing and tenderness.

If domestic violence is finally to end, the vast project of transforming these social and economic relations and of challenging male domination throughout society and culture must be embraced. Raising boys to be non-violent is one small part of it. And of course in some places efforts are being made to do just that. Most playgroups, nursery schools and primary schools operate policies of non-violence and of teaching children to relate to each other in equal, respectful ways. Secondary schools also condemn violence. Some run sessions on domestic violence and courses on how to develop caring adult relationships. Genuine discussions about sexual feelings, responses and ways of engaging in equal, mutually satisfying sexual relationships are apparently seen as controversial, however, and are rarely held in schools.

Some children's TV programmes are consciously pro-women and anti-violence, and there are plenty of children's books and games easily available now which combat violence and present men as being capable of being gentle and retiring, and women as being strong and powerful. Some organizations specialize in selling anti-sexist and anti-racist books which try to break down cultural stereotyping of male and female roles, and notions of power and control by men over women. Such books also attempt to counter racism and other sorts of discrimination. There are guidebooks for parents on anti-sexist child-rearing, and both formalized and informal attempts to limit children's exposure to violence on TV and film.

Feminists have long argued for the development of education, of community services and of parenting patterns which work against the stereotyping of gender roles between women and men, and which attempt to minimize dominating and violent behaviour in boys and submissive behaviour in girls. To this end, refuge staff give talks in schools and colleges, and work closely when they can with teachers and educators. The inter-agency projects discussed in Chapter 8 have also instigated education initiatives in schools and among youth workers, such as those in the Leeds Pilot Project and in Keighley, West Yorkshire. Attempts are increasingly being made to mount small interventions in school curricula so that domestic violence makes it into the standard classroom, rather than being an optional extra dealt with occasionally by progressive or feminist teachers, or touched on in passing during A-level social science courses but in no others.

The Leeds inter-agency project and others are attempting to develop programmes in schools which deal with the creative and non-violent resolution of conflict. Developments in other countries can be helpful here. The field of conflict resolution originated in the business world, but has now filtered through to schools in some places. In the United States, for example, progressive programmes on limiting boys' violence and on conflict resolution are currently being practised in a number of schools.

New York City is arguably one of the most violent cities in the world. Though the vast majority of New Yorkers are as law-abiding and non-violent as anyone else, nevertheless, poverty, deprivation and a viciously racist social system have taken their toll. Sections of some neighbourhoods are unsafe, parts of the city look like a war-zone, and some statistics estimate as many as one in four young black men dies a violent death. In the teeth of all this, hundreds of grade school teachers from 50 New York City schools were trained in the late 1980s in ways of resolving conflict non-violently. Myriam Miedzian, in *Boys Will Be Boys: Breaking the Links Between Masculinity and Violence*, explains how teachers and students learned that

> 'handling conflict well is a skill like riding a bike or using a computer'. Such an explanation is necessary because the ability to resolve conflicts in a mutually supportive and non-violent way has never been thought of as something one learns in schools. Until recently it was not thought of as something one learns at all.

The New York project is called the Resolving Conflict Creatively Program. Classes are both consciousness-raising for children in terms of their understanding of non-violence and also affirming. The latter part of the programme rests on the belief that people who have a strong sense of self-worth are more likely to value others – even those whom they are in conflict with. Through drama and discussion, the children learn that being non-violent is not passive or sissy. They are taught specific techniques for resolving arguments and conflicts without resorting to fighting.

Schools in a variety of parts of Canada and the United States teach anti-violence programmes, often centring on the destructiveness of war and the preponderance of genocide in human history. Veterans of the Vietnam War have been particularly active in some of these programmes. Some schools in Britain run similar programme, but few of the programmes involved cover male violence in the home.

The Women's Aid federations and the National Inter-Agency Working Party Report on domestic violence have called for a programme of public education to raise awareness about domestic violence. This should involve specific work with schools, and also a wider community training initiative. The Working Party Report recommends that existing voluntary organizations, in particular Women's Aid, be called in to help in the preparation of such a programme.

The theory is that community education would lead to a greater public intolerance of domestic violence. What is visualized is something similar to the part of the Duluth programme which concentrates on community involvement and which aims to convert acceptance or apathy regarding domestic violence to a public attitude of abhorrence and confrontation of abusers. Widespread public education campaigns have been held in many countries, but not so far in Britain.

In Canada, for example, a campaign of public information and awareness has been going on for seven years now. In most Canadian provinces, graphic television advertising abhorring domestic violence is accompanied by large billboard advertisements, posters and radio announcements, and the provision of a free public helpline for women to use. All this is financed through the various levels of government and is accompanied by 'government health warnings' that the federal and provincial governments will not tolerate domestic violence and find it unacceptable. As part of the current Family Violence Initiative, the federal government is now attempting to spread awareness of the problem further and to promote individual and community action against it. This includes creating resources for public education, instigating community projects, and updating and expanding public education material.

Recently, the second international 'Sixteen Days of Activism against Gender Violence' was held in Zimbabwe. With the slogan, 'It's your mother, your daughter, your sister', women produced plays, demonstrations, television and radio programmes, and a variety of public and community events which drew connections between gender violence and current political issues in the country. The sixteen days were a success leading to unprecedented public discussion about the issue.

One of the major focuses of the work of the Australian National Committee on Violence Against Women is on public and community awareness. The Committee holds that violence will stop only when men stop being violent and when the community as a whole stops condoning it. In consequence, it states that 'everyone, everywhere must become intolerant of violence against women and uphold the belief that no woman deserves violence and that the use of violence is a crime'. The work of the Committee is geared towards protection and community safety for women, and towards the development of collective community responsibility for elevating the status of women and building a society in which violence against women is not tolerated.

Such inspiring commitments sound a long way away from 1990s Britain, which faces new and massive cuts in public expenditure on top of previous reductions. The National Inter-Agency Working Party recommends, however, that a national publicity campaign on domestic violence should be launched, funded by central government. It recommends a preventive programme of action coupled with a publicity drive which emphasizes women's rights to protection, support and access to readily available services. The 1993 all-party Home Affairs Committee Report also recommends that a public awareness campaign should be held, funded by central government.

In January 1993, the Radio 4 programme *Woman's Hour* interviewed a Women's Unit officer from Lothian in Scotland who described an innovative poster campaign which was going on in Edinburgh. The posters showed scenes of domestic violence, and interviewers had gone out into the streets to see if men were taking any notice. Most of them were not, because it was all too small-scale. But the outcome of the programme was general agreement that national publicity on TV and radio and with posters would be a success, and that perhaps the Edinburgh campaign could be the 'spark to ignite the national flame'. The programme asked if we are all prepared to live in a society which accepts and tolerates domestic violence, and suggested that a national publicity campaign should be taking the message throughout the land that domestic violence is unacceptable.

Campaigning and lobbying

Community education and national publicity campaigns are a far cry from the situation back in the early 1970s, when none of these things had even been mooted. Sometimes we forget all that has happened in between. We continually need to remind ourselves and each other that the current response to domestic violence, both nationally and internationally, is a product of the social movement of women for liberation from degradation and violation by men. These days, though, such memories can get lost in the daily struggle of trying to keep services open or to initiate new ones.

Throughout this book, we have emphasized the role and importance of Women's Aid and the rest of the refuge network. We have also noted the contradictions which the movement has had to face in its dealings with the local and national state. Political activity against male violence and the establishment of widespread feminist services for women survivors in the last twenty years were something new. In some ways, the refuge movement was able to learn from other experiences and social movements. Largely, however, it found itself having to make up the rules itself, having to create something out of nothing with very few guidelines or models around of how to go about it. As the Dobashes have pointed out in *Women, Violence and Social Change*,

> being 'new' within one's own historical period may mean a freedom to work out how to reconstruct social life in an alternative fashion, but it also means that activists have to continue to work to develop the model while at the same time finding little or no support, and possibly a great deal of external opposition.

Keeping a hold on the long-term aim can be hard when the external opposition seems to be gaining the upper hand.

An example is the way that the pioneering commitment of the refuge network to empowerment and collectivity is continually subjected to outside forces pulling it the other way. Women's Aid and other refuge workers live under these conflicting forces all the time. They often feel as though they are being wrenched first one way and then the other by their own determination to work in a new and experimental way, and by the demands of funders and other agencies. Trying to work collectively is constantly undermined by pervasive notions of authority and hierarchy. Add to this the problems of underfunding, overwork, exhaustion and lack of support, and then the painful nature of work with women who have been abused by men, of endless exposure to the effects of male violence and brutality towards women, and it is hardly surprising that refuge staff sometimes feel overwhelmed and that the burn-out rate is high.

One of the dilemmas of the refuge network has always been between, on the one hand, staying true to its ideals and, on the other, trying to provide the best possible services for women and children – and facing possible co-optation in the search for funding to provide these services. Co-optation means giving up on the 'new' and being sucked back into traditional ways of doing things. It means being forced to compromise strongly held beliefs and visions of how things could be different. Back in the 1980s, the American activist Susan Schechter wrote an inspirational book, *Women and Male Violence: The Visions and Struggles of the Battered Women's Movement*. She detailed the dangers of co-optation in the American movement and made an impassioned case for retaining the political vision of liberation and social transformation. In Britain, the movement has retained a substantial degree of independence and political autonomy. But the increasing number of professionals in the domestic violence field and its possible incorporation into the mainstream are clear concerns for activists looking towards the future. Financial cutbacks have aggravated this situation. If services are to survive, raising funds is the priority. Survival is the order of the day.

Nevertheless, the refuge network keeps on going. Although under siege in some areas due to lack of finance, it maintains its zeal and its commitment to feminist ways of organizing and to improving services for abused women and their children. The national Women's Aid federations continue their vital role in monitoring legislation and policy, and in lobbying and putting pressure on government. They also participate in, and on occasion initiate, direct campaigning work on behalf of women who have suffered violence and their children.

Over the years, there have been a variety of campaigns about domestic violence. Southall Black Sisters (SBS), the dedicated and long-serving campaigning group based in the Asian community in Southall, London, have always been committed to working against male violence towards women. Founded in 1979, they have campaigned both against racism and on behalf of women and girls ever since. In recent years they have taken an important role in the Women Against Fundamentalism movement, which received considerably publicity due to its active opposition to the orthodox Muslim position on the death sentence imposed on the author Salman Rushdie. Southall Black Sisters have been deeply involved in political work about domestic violence on many levels, from one-off actions publicizing individual cases to national campaigns about policy issues.

Women Against Violence Against Women (WAVAW) was a political organization working against male violence from the late 1970s through to the mid-1980s. It organized political actions, meetings and conferences, and had local groups in towns and cities all over the country. Actions and campaigns have also been organized by women's groups running services for rape and incest survivors. The Wages for Housework organization has been associated for many years with the anti-rape campaigning group, Women Against Rape. All of these groups have organized actions about male violence but have concentrated mainly on rape and pornography issues, and rarely specifically on domestic violence.

What campaigns there have been have often been small and localized. Many Women's Aid groups, for example, have mounted local actions on behalf of women murdered by their husbands. Due to their position as both a local and a national political organization, some of the most publicized of these campaigns have been conducted by Southall Black Sisters in conjunction with Brent Asian Women's Refuge. In 1985, for example, a national series of actions and demonstrations was held after the tragic murder of Balwant Kaur inside refuge premises. These widespread actions involved many Women's Aid groups. There have been other similar although smaller campaigns on behalf of individual women in a variety of towns and cities, involving a range of political actions.

Many national demonstrations against violence against women have been held over the years, and local vigils, lobbies and demonstrations have been organized in different parts of the country. In recent years, these have often been directed against local authorities because of cutbacks in the funding of women's services. Political actions and demonstrations have also been held in response to specific pieces of legislation, such as the Child Support Act 1991.

In the last three or four years, Southall Black Sisters and other organizations have been involved in campaigns against the victimization of women who have suffered domestic violence. In 1991 Justice for Women, a feminist organization set up to campaign against discrimination within the legal system towards women subjected to male violence, was established. Justice for Women is a small group which is not linked to service provision. It specifically campaigns against the life sentences imposed on abused women who kill their husbands after enduring domestic violence, perhaps for many years. The campaign has pointed out how men who kill their wives quite frequently receive lighter sentences than women who kill their husbands. In 1991, for example, Joseph McGrail received a suspended sentence after a manslaughter conviction for killing his common-law wife. The judge in the case commented that 'this lady would have tried the patience of a saint'. In 1992 Singh Bisla also walked free with a suspended sentence after strangling his wife. Thomas Corlette was convicted of manslaughter after killing his wife in 1987, and received a three-year sentence. Women who kill their husbands are very often convicted of murder rather than manslaughter, and murder carries a mandatory life sentence. It seems that the British courts frequently regard nagging by a woman as a more extenuating circumstance than prolonged and often severe domestic violence by a man.

Action on behalf of abused women who kill was spearheaded by the Kiranjit Ahluwalia campaign primarily co-ordinated by Southall Black Sisters, initially with the involvement of Crawley Women's Aid, and supported by Justice for Women and many Women's Aid groups. Kiranjit Ahluwalia killed her husband after enduring ten years of beatings, rapes and burnings. When she was imprisoned for life in 1989, her case attracted widespread press and public interest. Women campaigned on her behalf up and down the country, and a large number of campaigning groups became involved. Kiranjit Ahluwalia was finally released amid jubilation in the summer of 1992 when her case came to appeal, a triumph for the many organizations involved.

Justice for Women, Southall Black Sisters and other organizations have also supported active local campaigns on behalf of many other women, and they continue to do so. These women include Amelia Rossiter, Janet Gardner, Sara Thornton, Carol Peters, Elizabeth Line, June Scotland and Pamela Sainsbury. In many of these cases the campaigns have been successful and women have been released on appeal or, as in the case of Elizabeth Line, have received suspended sentences. The campaign on behalf of Sara Thornton has elicited support from a variety of political parties and organizations. Local and national demonstrations, petitions, pickets, vigils outside prisons and the Home Office, representations and lobbies have been organized. At the time of writing, however, Sara Thornton remains in prison.

Women's Aid, Justice for Women and Southall Black Sisters continue the fight. The successes of campaigns on behalf of some women have run alongside other cases in which women have continued to receive punitive convictions and sentences. As yet, the law shows little consistency. Together with Rights of Women and other organizations, Justice for Women is now calling for a reform of the law. They claim that the defence of provocation which can reduce a charge from murder to manslaughter works unfairly against women. In fact, it has been called a male privilege. Provocation can only be claimed if the killing happens immediately and the person is provoked into a sudden loss of self-control. If any time elapses between the provocation and the killing, it is regarded as a cooling-off period and the defence is usually disallowed. Women, however, are much less likely to kill men on a sudden loss of self-control than men are to kill women, because of their lesser physical strength.

Some feminists have claimed that the cooling-off period can in fact be a boiling-over period, and that the rules regarding provocation should be changed to remove the requirement for the loss of self-control to be sudden. A private member's bill put forward by Jack Ashley to amend the law on provocation failed to get through Parliament before the 1992 general election. Some feminist legal experts and activists believe, however, that a relaxation of the rules on provocation might work against women. They argue that it is already such an easy defence for men to use to justify killing women that it might be dangerous to make it any easier. Rights of Women recommends that, instead, a new partial defence of 'self-preservation' on the grounds of prolonged abuse and intimidation should be introduced.

Whether or not these initiatives to change the law will be successful remains to be seen. However, the successes of the individual campaigns to reduce harsh sentences imposed on abused women who kill have been moving for women who have suffered domestic violence, and for activists in the movement. They are a tribute to the power of campaigning, although we have yet to see whether they will lead to permanent changes.

Women involved in domestic violence work and feminist activists have been arguing for many years that we need a major political campaign against domestic violence, but the effort to provide services has tended to push campaigning on to the back burner. Now that political action against domestic violence is on the agenda, however, it is disturbing to find that there is not one campaign grouping, but two. The Campaign Against Domestic Violence (CADV) was established in 1991. The CADV is a mixed organization and has a loose connection with the Militant tendency, the left-wing group which was formerly part of the Labour Party, although very many CADV activists are not in Militant. In March 1992 it held a national conference against domestic violence for both women and men which was well attended. Unfortunately, it has antagonized various women's organizations, and it has not established links with SBS or Justice for Women. The CADV puts forward a class analysis of domestic violence. While it acknowledges the contribution of Women's Aid as a service to women and children, it has not recognized the role of autonomous women's groups in campaigning work, nor has it contributed to other campaigns. It has established various local campaigning groups of its own which initiate or participate in autonomous local actions, and it has gained support from a number of trade unions, some of which have a history of work against domestic violence.

In the last few years, successful actions against domestic violence organized by all the different groups have been held around Britain. It is heartening to see the issue on the political and public agenda. Now, in the 1990s, there is political campaigning work going on. There are national demonstrations. There are lobbies and vigils. And there are new and innovative services, domestic violence good practice guidelines, inter-agency initiatives, men's programmes against violence, and international agreements and actions. Current activity against domestic violence is powerful and creative, and is linked in various obvious and not so obvious ways into the international movement of women against inequality and injustice. Worldwide, there is a vast network of refuges, services, activities, policies and legislation on behalf of abused women. Twenty years ago, there was nothing.

It is a considerable achievement. Throughout this book, we have continually reiterated the importance of acknowledging and recognizing that achievement. The most important time to remember it can be when the going gets tough, when mistakes are made, when everyone involved is tired, and when the whole enterprise feels like banging your head persistently against a brick wall. Despite the recent favourable government recommendations, with funding still deeply inadequate, insecure or disappearing, there is no room for complacency. The vital recognition of all that has been achieved, of how fundamental and comprehensive the changes are, must be balanced against an awareness of how much more there is to be done. There is a need for more funding, more community services for abused women and their children, more refuges, including specialist refuges for specific groups of women, better remedies in both criminal and civil law, improved policing, better housing provision, more inter-agency co-ordination, more political campaigns.

It is of crucial importance that, in all future developments, the Women's Aid network and the rest of the movement against domestic violence stays centre-stage and does not become marginalized if, or as, violence in the home becomes more unacceptable to society, and opposition to it continues to edge towards the mainstream. Most important of all is to preserve, to hang on to, and to be guided by the enduring vision among domestic violence activists of a world where women can live abuse-free lives and where male violence against women is finally a thing of the past.

Further information and useful addresses

Women experiencing domestic violence and their children can obtain advice, support and help from their local Women's Aid group, which usually has a public telephone number in the telephone directory. If the group does not have sufficient resources to operate both a public and a confidential number, it can usually be contacted through a variety of referral points, using paging systems or other agencies which may be able to contact a Women's Aid group member direct. Refuges outside Women's Aid may be listed by name in the Phone Book, or can sometimes be found under 'Social services' in the Yellow Pages.

Doctors' surgeries, council offices and community centres often display information about local refuges and available services, and in some local authorities helpful leaflets and booklets containing information on where to go for help are freely available. Women can also get help from the local police station, social services office, citizens' advice bureau, Samaritans, housing department office and other agencies. In some areas, specialist projects for women suffering domestic violence are available: for example, for black, immigrant or ethnic minority women, lesbians, very young women, and women who have suffered sexual abuse or have special needs. Some police stations now have Domestic Violence Units which can be particularly helpful to women at risk of or experiencing violence, if they wish to consider taking action against the abusive man.

In an emergency, the police or the social services (including the emergency social services team out of office hours) should enable a woman to get to a place of safety. The Women's Aid Federation (England) runs a national helpline (with a minicom system) for women threatened by or experiencing violence, and refuges work together to refer women and children to a safe location. In London, referrals to refuges are co-ordinated by London Women's Aid. All the Women's Aid federations can also offer assistance. The addresses and contact numbers are as follows:

Women's Aid National Helpline. Tel. 0272 633542 (with minicom for the hearing-impaired).

Women's Aid Federation (England), PO Box 391, Bristol BS99 7WS (Tel. 0272 633494).

Scottish Women's Aid, 13–19 North Bank Street, Edinburgh EH1 2LP (Tel. 031-225 8011/3321).

Welsh Women's Aid, 38–48 Crwys Road, Cardiff CF2 4NN (Tel. 0222 390874).

Northern Ireland Women's Aid, 129 University Street, Belfast BT7 1HP (Tel. 0232 249041/249358).

Information on local policies on domestic violence, on inter-agency work and on services available can be obtained from local Women's Aid groups and other refuges, and, where these exist, from local authority Women's Equality Committees and Units, from police Domestic Violence and Family Protection Units, from inter-agency projects on domestic violence and from specialist projects and organizations, such as for black women and women from different ethnic heritages.

References and further reading

Adams, D. (1988), 'Treatment models of men who batter: a pro-feminist analysis', in K. Yllo and M. Bograd (eds), *Feminist Perspective on Wife Abuse*, Sage.

Ahmed, S., Cheetham, J., and Small, J. (1988) *Social Work with Black Children and Their Families*, Batsford.

Association of Chief Officers of Probation (1992) *Position Statement on Domestic Violence*, ACOP.

Atkins, S., and Hoggett, B. (1984) *Women and the Law*, Basil Blackwell.

Barron, J. (1990) *Not Worth the Paper?: The Effectiveness of Legal Protection for Women and Children Experiencing Domestic Violence*, WAFE.

Binney, V., Harkell, G., and Nixon, J. (1981) *Leaving Violent Men*, WAFE.

Binney, V., Harkell, G., and Nixon, J. (1985) 'Refuges and housing for battered women', in J. Pahl (ed.), *Private Violence and Public Policy*, Routledge.

Birch, H. (ed.) (1993) *Moving Targets: Women, Murder and Representation*, Virago.

Borkowski, M., Murch, M., and Walker, V. (1983) *Marital Violence: The Community Response*, Tavistock.

Bourlet, A. (1990) *Police Intervention in Marital Violence*, Open University Press.

Bowker, L. (1982) *Beating Wife-Beating*, D. C. Heath.

Bowker, L., Arbitell, M., and McFerron, R. (1988), 'On the relationship between wife beating and child abuse', in K. Yllo and M. Bograd (eds), *Feminist Perspectives on Wife Abuse*, Sage.

Brailey, M. (1985) 'Making the break', in N. Johnson (ed.), *Marital Violence*, Routledge.

Breines, W., and Gordon, L. (1984) 'The new scholarship on family violence', *Signs*, 8, pp. 490–531.

Browne, A. (1987) *When Battered Women Kill*, Free Press.

Carew-Jones, M., and Watson, H. (1985) *Making the Break*, Pelican.

Cavanagh, K. (1978) 'Battered women and social control: a study of the help-seeking behaviour of battered women and the help-giving behaviour of those from whom they seek help', unpublished thesis, University of Stirling.

Cobbe, F. P. (1878) 'Wife torture in England', *Contemporary Review*, April, pp. 55–87.

Convention of Scottish Local Authorities (1991) *Women and Violence*, Convention of Scottish Local Authorities.

Davis, A., and MacNevin, A. (1989) 'Battered wives and medical service', *Atlantis*, 15, 1, pp. 123–35.

Department of the Environment (1991) *Homelessness: Code of Guidance for Local Authorities*, HMSO.

Dobash, R. E., and Dobash, R. (1980) *Violence Against Wives*, Open Books.

Dobash, R. E., and Dobash, R. (1992) *Women, Violence and Social Change*, Routledge.

Dobash, R. E., Dobash, R., and Cavanagh, K. (1985) 'The contact between battered women and social and medical agencies', in J. Pahl (ed.), *Private Violence and Public Policy*, Routledge.

Dunhill, C. (ed.) (1989) *The Boys in Blue*, Virago.

Edwards, S. (1986) 'The real risks of violence behind closed doors', *New Law Journal*, 136/628, pp. 1191–3.

Edwards, S. (1989) *Policing Domestic Violence*, Sage.

Eekelaar, J. M., and Katz, S. N. (1978) *Family Violence: An International, Interdisciplinary Study*, Butterworths.

Ellis, R. (1983) 'Family pastoral, family violence: battered women in rural areas', paper presented at BSA Conference, Cardiff, April.

Elston, E., Fuller, J., and Murch, M. (1976) *Battered Wives: The Problems of Violence in Marriage as Experienced by a Group of Petitioners in Undefended Divorce Cases*, Department of Social Work, University of Bristol.

Evason, E. (1982), *Hidden Violence: A Study of Battered Women in Northern Ireland*, Farset Press, Belfast.

Family Service Units (1988) *Domestic Violence: A Step-by-Step Guide for Social Workers and Others*, Family Service Units.

Faragher, T. (1985) 'The police response to violence against women in the home', in J. Pahl (ed.), *Private Violence and Public Policy*, Routledge.

Farmer, E., and Owen, M. (1993) *Decision Making, Intervention and Outcome in Child Protection Work*, report to the Department of Health.

Feminist Review (1988) 'Family Secrets: child sexual abuse', 28, spring.

Finkelhor, D., *et al.* (eds) (1983) *The Dark Side of Families: Current Family Violence Research*, Sage.

Freeman, M. (1987) *Dealing with Domestic Violence*, CCH Editions, Oxford.

Gayford, J. J. (1976) 'Ten types of battered wives', *Welfare Officer*, 1, 5, p. 9.

Gordon, L. (1988) *Heroes of Their Own Lives*, Viking.

Graham, D., Rawlings, E., and Rimini, N. (1988) 'Survivors of terror: battered women, hostages and the Stockholm syndrome', in K. Yllo and M. Bograd (eds), *Feminist Perspectives on Wife Abuse*, Sage.

Guru, S. (1986) 'An Asian women's refuge', in S. Ahmed, J. Cheetham and J. Small (eds), *Social Work with Black Children and Their Families*, Batsford.

Hague, G., Harwin, N., *et al.* (1989) 'Policing male violence in the home', in C. Dunhill (ed.), *The Boys in Blue*, Virago.

Hanmer, J., and Maynard, M. (eds) (1987) *Women, Violence and Social Control*, Macmillan.

Hanmer, J., and Saunders, S. (1984) *Well-Founded Fear: A Community Study of Violence to Women*, Hutchinson.

Hanmer, J., Radford, J., and Stanko, E. (1989) *Women, Policing and Male Violence*, Routledge.

Hart, B. (1988) *Safety for Women: Monitoring Batterers' Programs*, Pennsylvania Coalition Against Domestic Violence.

Hendessi, M. (1992) *Four in Ten: Report on Young Women who Become Homeless as a Result of Sexual Abuse*, CHAR.

Hoff, L. (1990) *Battered Women as Survivors*, Routledge.

Home Office (1990) Circular 60/90, HMSO.

Homer, M., Leonard, A., and Taylor, P. (1984) *Public Violence, Private Shame*, Cleveland Refuge and Aid for Women and Children.

Horley, S. (1988) *Love and Pain: A Survival Handbook for Women*, Bedford Square Press.

House of Commons Home Affairs Committee (1993) *Inquiry into Domestic Violence*, HMSO.

Jaffe, P., Wolfe, D., and Kaye, S. (1990) *Children of Battered Women*, Sage.

Johnson, N. (ed.) (1985) *Marital Violence*, Routledge.

Kelly, L. (1988) *Surviving Sexual Violence*, Polity Press.

Kelly, L., and Radford, J. (1990–1) 'Nothing really happened: the invalidation of women's experiences of sexual violence', *Critical Social Policy*, winter, pp. 39–53.

Kennedy, H. (1992) *Eve was Framed: Women and British Justice*, Chatto and Windus.

Kurz, D., and Stark, E. (1988) 'Not-so-benign neglect: the medical response to battering', in K. Yllo and M. Bograd (eds), *Feminist Perspectives on Wife Abuse*, Sage.

Law Commission (1988/9) *Draft Criminal Code for England and Wales*, Law Commission.

Law Commission (1992) *Family Law: Domestic Violence and Occupation of the Family Home*, Report No. 207, HMSO.

London Borough of Hammersmith and Fulham Community Safety Unit (1991) *Challenging Domestic Violence: A Training and Resource Pack*, London Borough of Hammersmith and Fulham.

London Borough of Islington Women's Equality Unit (1992) *A Good Practice Guide: Working with Those who have Experienced Domestic Violence*, London Borough of Islington.

London Housing Unit (1991) *Cutting it Out: Sexual Harassment – A Guide for Housing Organizations*, London Housing Unit.

London Strategic Policy Unit (1988) *Police Responses to Domestic Violence*, Police Monitoring and Research Group Briefing No. 1, LSPU.

McGibbon, A., Cooper, L., and Kelly, L. (1989) *What Support?*, Hammersmith and Fulham Council/Polytechnic of North London.

McGregor, H., and Hopkins, A. (1992) *Working for Change: The Movement Against Domestic Violence*, Allen and Unwin.

Maidment, S. (1983) 'Civil v. criminal: the use of civil remedies in responses to domestic violence in England and Wales', *Victimology*, 8, pp. 172–87.

Malos, E., and Hague, G. (1993) *Domestic Violence and Housing*, WAFE and University of Bristol.

Mama, A. (1989a) *The Hidden Struggle: Statutory and Voluntary Sector Responses to Violence Against Black Women in the Home*, London Race and Housing Research Unit.

Mama, A. (1989b) 'Black women and domestic violence: race, gender and state responses', *Feminist Review*, 32.

Martin, D. (1976) *Battered Wives*, Glide, San Francisco.

Martin, J. P. (ed.) (1978) *Violence in the Family*, Wiley.

Maynard, M. (1985) 'The response of social workers to domestic violence', in J. Pahl (ed.), *Private Violence and Public Policy*, Routledge.

Metropolitan Police (1987) *Force Orders*.

Miedzian, M. (1992) *Boys Will Be Boys: Breaking the Links Between Masculinity and Violence*, Virago.

Miller, K. (1993) 'The let down', *Roof*, March/April, pp. 20–1.

Morgan, E. (1972) *The Descent of Woman*, Bantam.

Morley, R. and Mullender, A. (forthcoming) *Preventing Domestic Violence to Women*, HMSO.

Muir, J., and Ross, M. (1993) *Housing the Poorer Sex*, London Housing Unit.

Mullender, A. (forthcoming) *Part of the Problem*, Routledge.

National Association of Local Government Women's Committees (1990) *Responding with Authority: Local Authority Initiatives to Counter Violence Against Women*, NALGWC.

National Committee on Violence Against Women (1992) *Discussion and Resource Kit for Use in Rural and Isolated Communities*, National Domestic Violence Education Program, Australia.

National Inter-Agency Working Party Report (1992) *Domestic Violence*, Victim Support.

New South Wales Women's Co-ordination Unit (1991) *Programs for Perpetrators of Domestic Violence*, New South Wales, Australia.

NiCarthy, G. (1990) *Getting Free: A Handbook for Women in Abusive Situations*, Journeyman (available from Welsh Women's Aid, Scottish Women's Aid and WAFE).

Nottinghamshire County Council (1989), *Putting a Stop to Domestic Violence: A Practical Guide for Advisers*, Nottinghamshire County Council Social Services Department.

O'Hara, M. (1992) 'Domestic violence and child abuse: making the links', *Childright*, 88, p. 4.

Osborne, J. (1990) *Domestic Violence Fact Pack*, Home Office.

Pagelow, M. D. (1981) *Women-Battering*, Sage.

Pagelow, M. D. (1984) *Family Violence*, Praeger.

Pagelow, M. D. (1985) 'The battered husband syndrome: a social problem or much ado about nothing?', in N. Johnson (ed.), *Marital Violence*, Routledge.

Pahl, J. (1978) *A Refuge for Battered Women*, HMSO.

Pahl, J. (1985) *Private Violence and Public Policy*, Routledge.

Pahl, J. (1989) *Money and Marriage*, Macmillan.

Parker, S. (1985) 'The legal background', in J. Pahl (ed.), *Private Violence and Public Policy*, Routledge.

Parliamentary Select Committee on Violence in Marriage (1975) *Report from the Select Committee on Violence in Marriage*, HMSO.

Pence, E. (1988) *Batterers' Programs: Shifting from Community Collusion to Community Confrontation*, Domestic Abuse Intervention Project, Duluth.

Pence, E., and Paymar, M. (1990) *Power and Control: Tactics of Men who*

Batter – An Educational Curriculum, Domestic Abuse Intervention Project, Duluth.

Pirog-Good, M., and Stets-Kealey, J. (1985) 'Male batterers and battering prevention programs: a national survey', *Response*, 8, pp. 8-12.

Pizzey, E. (1979) *Scream Quietly or the Neighbours Will Hear*, Penguin.

Pizzey, E., and Shapiro, J. (1982) *Prone to Violence*, Hamlyn.

Pleck, E. (1987) *Domestic Tyranny: The Making of Social Policy Against Family Violence from Colonial Times to the Present*, Oxford University Press.

Radford, J. (1987) 'Policing male violence – policing women', in J. Hanmer and M. Maynard (eds) *Women, Violence and Social Control*, Macmillan.

Radford, L. (1993) 'Pleading for time: justice for battered women who kill', in Helen Birch (ed.), *Moving Targets: Women, Murder and Representation*, Virago.

Russell, D. (1982) *Rape and Marriage*, Macmillan.

Russell, M. (1989) *Taking Stock: Survey into Refuge Provision in London*, Southwark Borough Council and LSPU.

Saunders, D. (1988) 'Wife abuse, husband abuse or mutual combat', in K. Yllo and M. Bograd (eds), *Feminist Perspectives on Wife Abuse*, Sage.

Schechter, S. (1982) *Women and Male Violence: The Visions and Struggles of the Battered Women's Movement*, Pluto.

Schechter, S. (1988) 'Building bridges between activists, professionals and researchers', in K. Yllo and M. Bograd (eds), *Feminist Perspectives on Wife Abuse*, Sage.

Scottish Women's Aid (1990) *Abused Women and Homelessness: A Report to the Women's National Commission*, Scottish Women's Aid.

Scottish Women's Aid (1991) *Women Talking to Women: A Counselling Training Pack*, 2nd edn, Scottish Women's Aid.

Scottish Women's Aid (1992) *Your Rights: A Legal Information Pack*, Scottish Women's Aid.

Shelter (1991) *Urgent Need for Homes*, Shelter.

Sherman, L., and Berk, R. (1984) 'The specific deterrent effects of arrest for domestic violence', *American Sociological Review*, 49, 2, pp. 261–72.

Smith, L. (1989) *Domestic Violence: An Overview of the Literature*, Home Office Research Studies, No. 107, HMSO.

Southall Black Sisters (1989) *Against the Grain: A Celebration of Survival and Struggle*, SBS.

Stanko, E. (1985) *Intimate Intrusions: Women's Experience of Male Violence*, Routledge.

Stark, E., Flitcraft, A., and Frazier, W. (1979) 'Medicine and patriarchal violence: the social construction of a "private" event', *International Journal of Health Studies*, 9, pp. 461–93.

Steinmetz, S. (1977) *The Cycle of Violence*, Praeger.

Steinmetz, S. (1978) 'The battered husband syndrome', *Victimology*, 2, pp. 499–509.

Straus, M. (1990a) 'Injury and frequency of assault and the "representative sample fallacy" in measuring wife beating and child abuse', in M. Straus and R. Gelles (eds), *Physical Violence in American Families*, Transaction.

Straus, M. (1990b) 'The Conflict Tactics Scale', in M. Straus and R. Gelles (eds), *Physical Violence in American Families*, Transaction.

Straus, M. and Gelles, R. (1990) *Physical Violence in American Families*, Transaction.

Straus, M., Gelles, R., and Steinmetz, S. (1980) *Behind Closed Doors: Violence in the American Family*, Anchor.

Thorne-Finch, R. (1992) *Ending the Silence: The Origins and Treatment of Male Violence Against Women*, University of Toronto Press.

Trivedi, P. (1984) 'To deny our fullness: Asian women in the making of history', in 'Many voices, one chant', *Feminist Review*, 17.

United Nations (1986) *Report of the Expert Group Meeting on Violence in the Family*, United Nations.

Walker, L. (1984) *The Battered Woman Syndrome*, Springer.

Ward, D., and Mullender, A. (1991) 'Empowerment and oppression: an indissoluble pairing for contemporary social work', *Critical Social Policy*, 32, autumn, pp. 21–30.

Warrior, B. (ed.) (1981) *Working on Wife Abuse*, Cambridge, Mass.

Wasoff, F. (1982) 'Legal protection from wife beating', *International Journal of the Sociology of Law*, 10, 2, pp. 187–204.

Welsh Women's Aid (1986) *The Answer is Maybe – and That's Final*, Welsh Women's Aid.

Welsh Women's Aid (1988) *Report of the International Women's Aid Conference*, Welsh Women's Aid.

Welsh Women's Aid (1989a) *Health and Safety in Women's Aid Refuges in Wales*, Welsh Women's Aid.

Welsh Women's Aid (1989b) *Homes fit for Heroines*, Welsh Women's Aid.

Wilson, E. (1983) *What's to be Done about Violence Against Women?*, Penguin.

Women's Aid Federation (England) (1987) *You Can't Beat a Woman: Women and Children in Refuges*, WAFE.

Women's Aid Federation (England) (1988) *Breaking Through: Women Surviving Male Violence*, WAFE.

Women's Aid Federation (England) (1989) *Women's Aid Housing Resource Pack*, WAFE, Welsh Women's Aid and Shelter.

Women's Aid Federation (England) (1992a) *A Woman's Aid Approach to Working with Children: An Information Pack for Women Working with Children in Refuges*, WAFE.

Women's Aid Federation (England) (1992b) *Written Evidence to the House of Commons Home Affairs Committee Inquiry into Domestic Violence*, WAFE.

Women's National Commission (1985) *Violence Against Women: Report of an ad hoc Working Group*, Cabinet Office, London.

Yllo, K., and Bograd, M. (eds) (1988) *Feminist Perspectives on Wife Abuse*, Sage.

Index